AAI-6125

24 95
GOB

P9-DYY-523

WITHDRAWN

Please remember that this is a library book,
and that it belongs only temporarily to each
person who uses it. Be considerate. Do
not write in this, or any, library book.

The World We Created at Hamilton High

The W·O·R·L·D
We Created at
HAMILTON
HIGH

GERALD GRANT

WITHDRAWN

Harvard University Press · Cambridge, Massachusetts · London, England   1988

Copyright © 1988 by the President and Fellows of Harvard College
All rights reserved
Printed in the United States of America
10 9 8 7 6 5 4 3 2 1

This book is printed on acid-free paper, and its binding materials
have been chosen for strength and durability.

Library of Congress Cataloging-in-Publication Data

Grant, Gerald.
    The world we created at Hamilton High.

Includes index.
    1. High schools—United States—Case studies.
2. Education, Urban—United States—Case studies.
3. Educational sociology—United States. I. Title.
LA222.G69   1988   373.73   87-26067
ISBN 0-674-96200-1 (alk. paper)

To the memory of my mother and father,
Ruth Almira Smith and G. Edward Grant,
and to Katharine, Sarah, and Robert

Contents

The World We Created at Hamilton High

Introduction

There is a profound confusion in America today about the school's role in shaping character. A corrosive individualism eats away at the heart of the enterprise. Teachers are doubtful about the grounds of their moral authority, parents organize themselves into special-interest groups, students are trained to become skillful consumers and clever advocates. We are uncertain how to give form to what Michael Walzer has called our program for social survival: "Education expresses what is, perhaps, our deepest wish: to continue, to go on, to persist in the face of time."[1]

This book attempts to provide a new cultural definition of our situation, to explain how our program for survival went askew, and to show how we may be able to go on. It aims to renew the ancient dialogue about the connection between the head and the heart without implying that there is any univocal solution. It seeks to avoid both the extreme pessimism of many voices on the left and the brittle moral formulas often advanced by those on the right.

A school is a community that cannot disavow responsibility for either intellectual or moral virtue. The adults epitomize some version of character to pupils—by ignoring or responding to incidents of racism in the classroom and hallway, by the manner in which they answer a child's earnest inquiry, by the respect they show for qualities of intellect, by the agreements they make about what behavior will not be tolerated as well as what actions will be honored. Schools are institutions that educate the emotions, indelibly affecting both heart and mind.[2]

The challenge we face is neither unique nor unprecedented, however. The problem was perhaps best stated by Aristotle in language that seems contemporary:

> In modern times there are opposing views about the practice of education. There is no general agreement about what the young should learn either in relation to virtue or in relation to the best in life; nor is it clear whether their education ought to be directed more towards the intellect than towards the character of the soul. The problem has been complicated by what we see happening before our eyes, and it is not certain whether training should be directed at things useful in life, or at those conducive to virtue, or at nonessentials. (All these answers have been given.) And there is no agreement as to what in fact does tend towards virtue. Men do not all prize most highly the same virtue, so naturally they differ also about the proper training for it.[3]

Aristotle had well-formulated responses to his own rhetorical questions; but every age must work out its own answers to the problem of what constitutes the proper mix of intellectual and moral virtue in a school. Parents and citizens today are no less concerned than they were in Aristotle's day about issues of social character and schooling. Educational research has often made things too simple by equating goodness with what can be measured by student scores on standardized tests. In recent years the nation has been virtually obsessed by the decline in test scores. Let us imagine for a moment that the Educational Testing Service discovered its computers had gone awry and that a reanalysis showed there had been *no* declines in scores over the past twenty years. Would the public be reassured about its schools? Gallup polls revealed consistent concern about the character of schooling long before steep test-score declines were reported. The polls going back to the 1968–69 school year show that anxiety about discipline was cited by the public more than any other issue. And "discipline" did not involve just law and order but lack of respect for teachers, flouting of rules and regulations, improper behavior in the classroom, and general disregard for authority.[4] I believe that parents interpreted test-score declines as confirming their fears rather than creating them. The public sensed not only that there was a connection between behavior and scores (that is, between establishing the conditions under which learning may take place and whether it does take place), but also that the way we establish those conditions affects the quality of life—the climate or the ethos—within the schools. It is the aim of this book to show how those connections may be made by developing a genuine sense of community and a strong positive ethos in modern public schools.

This book grew out of a study initiated by the National Institute of Education to answer the question, What makes a good school? It was an appealing question, because it reintroduced classical perspectives that have been deflected in technically oriented research. While the aim was to show how moral worlds are created, my five research assistants and I also wanted to ground our work in the realities of contemporary schools. The problem was to do so without adopting simplistic models of change that would fail to capture the complexity of life there.

In subsequent visits to schools, our approach was to illuminate the dynamics involved in creating a particular climate or ethos. We identified goals that adults in a particular school were attempting to achieve or programs they were attemping to create. In each of our visits we tried to understand the nature of the struggle toward those goals, within the network of relationships in which the adults acted.

In the spring of 1979 we traveled to thirty-three public and private schools in the northeastern United States, spending a day or two in each of them. On the basis of those visits we chose five schools for further study because they exhibited a markedly different ethos or because the adult leaders were consciously trying to change the climate. We also chose schools that represented both the public and private realm, and that varied in their social composition. The following academic year we carried out an extensive program of observations and interviews in these five schools, visiting each an average of one day a week throughout the school year. We asked certain teachers and students to keep journals for us, and we went to faculty meetings, parent meetings, and student social events. We wanted to be able to compare a wide range of practices within the school that affect both its intellectual and its moral climate.

The results of our research were published in two reports and a series of essays.[5] I gave a number of talks, the most memorable of which was a 1982 address to a group of school superintendents. I described what is here called Hamilton High as a place that had become more democratic but also more bureaucratic, more adversarial, and officially value neutral. It was not the best environment for adolescents. One of the superintendents, who said he was in sympathy with much of the portrait I had drawn, rose to ask, "What would you do if you were principal of such a school?" His was a provocative question. Almost to my own surprise, I answered: "I would try to hire the best anthropologist I could find who could pass for a teenager. I would turn him or her loose in the school for several months with the aim of writing a portrait of the moral life of the community. Then I would use that report to initiate a dialogue with all the members of the polity—students, parents, teachers, and staff. I would ask them, Is this portrait true? Is this the best we can do? If we repeated this experiment five or ten years from now, what kind of school would you hope to see reflected in it?"

The plain truth is, such matters are seldom discussed. There is no forum for such a dialogue, and nobody is asking these questions in a sustained way. Perhaps parents and teachers fear they no longer have the language to address them. One of the ironies of our present predicament may be that only the private school has a public—that is, in order to survive and to draw in tuition, it must be in dialogue with its public about the nature of both the moral and the intellectual life of the school.

In the ensuing months the colloquy with the superintendent kept coming to mind. But what principal could afford to hire an anthropologist, even if one could be found to meet my specifications? Then the thought came to me, Why not teach the students to be anthropologists? That is, teach them how to observe, to take notes, to interview, to analyze data—and then guide them in analyzing life in their own tribe, so to speak. Their findings could be used to raise critical questions about how to improve the quality of life in the school. It was never my idea that the students should do our philosophizing for us, but they could both learn some skills and open the dialogue in a compelling way.

I was able to gain the cooperation of the city school superintendent and the principal of Hamilton High. I was less successful in my pleas for financial support. But I did find a wonderful social studies teacher and a colleague in sociology who wanted to join in, and we three went ahead in the spring of 1984 and taught the urban anthropology course anyway.[6] In the second year we received support from an anonymous donor who liked what we were doing. We drew a mix of students—rich and poor, black and white, top students and C students. They did some stunning projects. In the first year two of the students wrote historical papers—one on the evolution of the curriculum over the last two decades, another an oral history of three teachers' experiences in the school. I was deeply influenced by the work of these students. Although I did not make a conscious connection at the time, I threw away the outline for a book I had been working on for two years and started over. I decided that far too many educational reports lacked historical perspective. Discovering what really happened in such a school in the postwar era was the key to understanding the complex causes of our educational dilemmas.

I turned my efforts to writing a sociologically informed history of Hamilton High—not a very long history, inasmuch as the school was built in 1953, but long enough to provide a critical perspective on some of the proposals for reform we have heard so much about lately. I interviewed many members of the faculty, some now retired, including a few who had taught during the first year. In addition to the usual historical sources—yearbooks, newspapers, pupil records, and school board minutes—I discovered a dissertation by Peter Clark, based on his year-long immersion in the school in 1971, when it had just undergone the huge transformation brought about by desegregation.[7] Thus, by the time I came to write this book, I had the benefit of four intensive examinations of life in the school over a seventeen-year period: the study by Clark, observations by Urmila Acharya and myself during the years 1979 to 1981, student research and my own participant observation as a teacher in the school in 1984 and 1985, and subsequent work with teachers and staff in examining the implications of that research in 1986–87.

One of the reasons Hamilton High interested me was that it represents not a "typical" school, but the kind of school that social policy in this country intended to produce: a racially, ethnically, and economically integrated public school that also serves a sizable number of disabled youngsters in regular classroom settings—in current parlance, a mainstreamed school. It is America in microcosm. Hamilton

High experienced all the overlapping social revolutions that fell, in a particularly powerful way, on schools in this society in the last thirty years. Schools were the major channel the nation chose to bring about a more equal society. And Hamilton High deserves close examination because these social revolutions have come to maturity there. Unlike many schools, Hamilton High has had a diverse population for fifteen years. We can say "Here is the future" and ask "Does it work?"

The first four chapters of this book examine that future as it happened. They trace events from the opening of the school in the buoyant and self-confident fifties, through a period of violence and radical deconstruction in the late sixties. They chart the rise of student power in the seventies, followed by new transformations of the school in the last decade occasioned in part by the arrival of disabled students and Asian immigrants. These chapters attempt to tell the story from the inside out, to convey how students and teachers felt as these social revolutions swept through the school.

It is a dramatic story, filled with anguish and hope. Things got very bad before they got better, but they did get better. The school went from white power to black power to genuine racial equality. Average test scores declined and then improved. Although test-score means did not return to their former levels, the gap in achievement between social classes decreased. Violence was replaced by a sense of safety and security. Measured by an ideal (our version of a strong positive ethos is delineated in Chapter 7), Hamilton High falls short. Tardiness and absenteeism are too common; high expectations and high ideals are too rare. Cheating is widespread. It is an individualistic, bureaucratic world, where altruism makes only an occasional visit. Like many schools in America, it is plagued by a sense of unease about the role of moral education. Despite specialists who minister to many different needs—more of them social than intellectual—students wonder whether faculty really care, and if so, about what. Yet there is more justice, more equality, fairer treatment for the disabled, and more protection of faculty rights than was the case when Hamilton High opened.

This book shows the way in which moral and intellectual worlds were made, then fell apart, then were reconstructed. The unique worlds of adolescents in America are shaped in significant ways by the kinds of schools they attend. In Part One, our biography of Hamilton High, we can see radical differences over time in these worlds, differences that affected the lives of all within the school, and we can see differences also among the various subcultures or subworlds within the school.

In Part Two we begin to contrast the world of Hamilton High with other possible worlds. The "we" of the book's title is intended to incorporate all members of the society, because all participate to some degree in shaping the worlds our children inherit. Chapter 5 is an explanation of how schools differ and what shapes the climate or ethos within them. It makes explicit the conceptual frame of our study. It attempts to show how every school can be seen as a network of authority relations shaped by cultural influences, an external policy matrix, family and social-class factors, and the moral and intellectual authority of faculty and staff. Chapter 6 utilizes this framework to examine the contemporary teacher's predicament as one in which external demands have increased while sources of authority have eroded. Chapter 7 contrasts the world of Hamilton High with three schools (one public and two private) that exhibit a strong positive ethos. It looks at the way the moral and intellectual worlds have been shattered in many contemporary public schools and asks whether they can be put back together again. It argues that even in the face of deep divisions on many moral questions there is a way to reconstruct the foundations of the moral world within public schools without falling into indoctrination. It recognizes at the same time that both teachers and students need to have some choice among schools, and that the quality of the moral life within the school depends critically on the state of the moral development of the faculty. Chapter 8 envisions two essential educational reforms—increasing the power of individual schools to make a world, and putting teachers in charge of their practice. A brief history of the changes in twentieth-century schools shows us that what happened at Hamilton High after the war was not unique. But the contemporary reform movement is often merely an echo of the 1950s in its failure to take account of what actually transpired there.

In the Epilogue I give the conclusions reached by the teachers of Hamilton High who have read this biography of their school. For the most part they affirm the account that has been given here. Their story is inspiring, but they leave us with some sober last words about the difficulties of improving either ourselves or our schools.

PART ONE

Biography of a School

CHAPTER ONE

An Elite Public School
1953–1965

We can hardly believe our good fortune.
—*Hamilton High yearbook, 1954*

In the fall of 1953 the city of Median opened a new high school on the east side of town. With a population of 220,000, Median was like a smaller Pittsburgh—a northeastern city whose expanding economy was a diversified mixture of old and new industries. Steel plants belched on the west side of town, and the northern suburbs were spotted with industrial parks for electronic and scientific equipment. It was a city in which ethnic and parish identity were apt to be the most prominent descriptors of social position. In the most heavily ethnic neighborhoods, housing seldom came on the open market but was sold by Italians, Poles, Irish, or Germans at the Turnverein or at a bingo game in the Church of the Assumption parish hall. More than a third of the city's children were enrolled in neighborhood parochial schools which, like most of the public schools, had a distinct ethnic and social composition.

The new school, Hamilton High, had been built in the hills of the newly developed upper-middle-class east side. Hamilton's students were primarily the children of managers, professionals, and faculty at the local university. The district also encompassed a middle-class Jewish neighborhood and drew a number of upwardly mobile ethnics, who had sacrificed life in their old neighborhoods to ascend the corporate ladder. Although suburban growth was beginning to escalate, the city's best academic high schools were still regarded as far superior to the small, noncentralized high schools in the surrounding towns. Some corporate executives left the countryside when their children entered high school, so that their sons and daughters could learn Latin, Greek, German, or Russian and choose sequences of advanced mathematics at Hamilton or old Central High. Salary scales for city teachers exceeded those in the suburbs, with the Central and Hamilton faculties being considered the elite of the teaching corps.

Later, after Sputnik, conservative critics would escalate their attacks on the schools; but in these early Eisenhower years, only an occasional cranky letter to the *Median Herald* was critical of the city's school system. There were no nationally administered tests, no published comparisons of school performance, no tax revolts. The schools were growing, and each decade produced a higher percentage of the age cohort completing high school. Median ran ahead of the national average, with two-thirds of the cohort completing high school in 1950. The local college and university doubled in size, encouraged by the GI Bill and the growing national faith in education as an avenue of upward mobility. Graduates of the city's schools found jobs in a booming economy or admission to an expanding system of higher education.

Opening day at Hamilton High was a festive occasion. The mayor spoke at the ribbon-cutting ceremony as proud parents stood by. Some of the fathers had recently turned out to mix cement and pour new sidewalks so that the school could open with something better than muddy paths (construction overruns had forced cancellation of this kind of finishing work). In the first year the parents raised $2,500 for the Hamilton High Athletic Association. Fifteen years later, Hamilton's parents, angered at the chaos and fearful for their children, would chain the doors and attempt to shut the school. But on this day in 1953, they admired the new audio labs, the acoustically designed auditorium, and the bold enameled lockers in twenty-seven different colors. Some joked that it was the Howard Johnson's of high schools. Its low-slung yellow brick and glass architecture set on a thirty-acre campus on the boundary between city and suburbs led to its also being called the Country Club. Hamilton presented a sharp contrast to the grimy brick and neoclassical style of the earlier city high schools. The other school teams took buses to practice in nearby city parks, whereas Hamilton High had its own tennis courts and playing fields. Hamilton's twelve hundred students were virtually all white, although an occasional black from the inner-city boundary of the Hamilton district would be admitted. Blacks were concentrated in the old fifteenth ward downtown, served by Central High. White children growing up in Median commonly referred to the fifteenth ward as "colored town" or "nigger town," just as they referred to the old area of Jewish bakeries and kosher meat shops as "Jew town." The Irish, on Emerald Hill, kept shooting out the red traffic light until police put the green on top, and their speech was sprinkled with frequent references to "wops" and "polacks." In later years, when a large wing housing vocational training programs was added, Central became Central Tech. Then an optional zone was created between Central Tech and Hamilton, and blacks were often advised to attend Tech because "they have the programs for you down there." But in the early 1950s the black school population was less than two thousand citywide and there were no perceptible tensions. The large gap between black and white graduation rates at Central Tech went for the most part unnoticed.

In candid photos, the students in Hamilton's first class are neatly groomed and clean-cut. Carefully coiffed girls in sweaters, skirts, and often pearls smile at boys in crew cuts and baggy khakis. The foreword to the 1954 yearbook sums up the spirit of pride and boosterism that characterized the school: "This first year has been spent in a school so different, so impressive in its usefulness and beauty, that we can hardly believe our good fortune. We do realize what a privilege it was for us to have been the first graduating class." The book was divided by headings such as "We Were Eager to Learn" and, referring to the teachers, "They Led Us to Achievement." High school students were still referred to as "boys" and "girls" and treated as minors—unless they left school to work or marry, which was expected for the girl who "got pregnant." The teenage years were a moratorium between childhood and adult status. Teens often had loose reins and light chaperonage, but recognized that the reins could be pulled tightly if bounds were overstepped. In a few decades students would demand adult rights, but now they were content to play symbolic leadership roles in the student status system. A student reporter for the school newspaper, the *Record*, wrote of the new student council president: "As one of his first duties as head of the Student Council, Peter will have to appoint a 'Lost and Found' committee to carry on this important duty. The student body can help this committee by placing found articles in the large green box outside the vice principal's office."[1] Earnest editorials in *The Record,* unselfconscious about male pronouns, urged students to strengthen school spirit:

> By participating in activities such as newspaper, sports, choir, Girls' League, one can develop an interest for himself. If homework is done when assigned, subjects and classrooms will be more inspiring. The pupil must be receptive to interests, activities, and classwork by cultivating the right attitudes.[2]

Students also criticized cheating in a school they granted was highly competitive, warning the transgressors: "Sooner or later you will be found out to be a phony and will feel like a worthless heel."[3] Pride in the school, its facilities, and its upkeep was a constant concern, with one editorial even scolding students for spilling their chicken soup and "gorging those hoagies as if their life depended on it." Another said "the pretty formica tops on the cafeteria tables should inspire students to be neat at lunch. Custom and good breeding require pupils to use proper receptacles for trash, bottles should be returned as directed, anything spilled should be mopped up."[4]

God and country were prominent themes in the school. All of Hamilton's students regularly donated blood during the Red Cross drives. President Eisenhower's proclamation changing the pledge of allegiance to read "one nation under God" was noted on the front page of the school paper, and a student poll in 1954 showed that 71 percent of the boys favored universal military service, as the draft was then called (78 percent of the boys and 96 percent of the girls also said girls should prepare for careers other than marriage, reflecting the white-collar and liberal cast of the school community). A school assembly was held that year to acknowledge the receipt of "twenty-eight authentic reproductions of the priceless documents of America's freedom," which had been part of the Freedom Train exhibit that passed through town. The president of the local patriotic group that presented the gift assured the students that "no boy or girl who knows and reveres these documents will ever become a Communist."[5]

The adolescent status hierarchies at Hamilton were similar to those delineated by James Coleman in his study of American high schools in the late 1950s.[6] There was a strong emphasis on being popular, being "good looking," and wearing stylish clothes. The most highly esteemed males were the athlete-scholars, while the warmest admiration was given to the girls who were most popular with boys and in the "leading crowd." Even though the girls learned to appear not to pursue academic success, they respected scholarly girls. Each issue of the student paper profiled an admired student. A typical male entry highlights active leadership on and off the field:

> Actions speak louder than words, and Bill H. is the personification of this adage. Football, track, sophomore and A Cappella choirs, plus majors in Latin, Math, and Science keep Bill constantly on the move. Hard work has its rewards. Not only was he Hamilton's delegate to Boys' State . . . this summer, but he was also the recipient of the Harvard Book Award in 1955.

The girl's profile in the same issue subordinates her academic record to her friendliness and style-consciousness:

> Every Tuesday afternoon after school the voice of a tall blonde with a friendly smile can be heard saying, "The meeting will now come to order." That girl is Karen W., president of the Girls' League. Karen, one of the most active members of the senior class, has participated in many school sports and is now a traffic guide. An alumna of Johnson's Fashion Board, she modeled this summer at the State Fair . . . Karen maintains an A average and hopes to take Liberal Arts at Smith, Vassar, or Wellesley. We feel that she will continue her excellent scholastic and social standing wherever she goes.[7]

Karen and Bill were members of the leading crowd who set the norms of the peer culture and, as in Coleman's study, accentuated the most prominent characteristics of the social class of the school. "A boy or girl in such a system," he wrote, "finds it governed by an elite whose backgrounds exemplify, in the extreme, those of the dominant population group. Hence a working class boy or girl will be most left out in an upper middle class school."[8] This certainly characterized Hamilton High of the 1950s, when fewer than 15 percent of its students would have been classified as working class, and only a handful as poor enough to need to apply to the school's loan fund to rent textbooks that had been purchased by other students. For the most part these students either dropped out of school when at age sixteen they were permitted to do so, or they attempted to emulate the leaders in a bid for social mobility.

The eight Greek-letter societies played a key role in assigning student status. The most cherished success was to win acceptance into a fraternity or a sorority. One fraternity and two sororities were reserved for Jews, and the best sorority had at one time admitted only two Catholics each year. These policies resembled those of the parents' country clubs, although some liberal and intellectual parents frowned on the fraternity culture. While not officially recognized, the Greek societies established the school's real social calendar, with hayrides and elaborate rushing parties in the fall and dances in the spring. A former sorority president recalled how the school's vice principal discreetly inquired about the sorority's schedule before fixing dates for official school activities. Hazing practices, such as requiring initiates to wear bizarre clothing to school, were never questioned at a time when the school had stiff dress codes. The fraternities used a blackball system, passing around a little box with white and black marbles when it came time to vote. A female former student said, "I guess it wasn't fair. Well, I mean my friends got in and our relatives got in. But there were plenty of girls who just weren't popular enough or attractive enough, or clever enough and the same thing applied to boys, and yet they might have been wonderful people."

Although it was painful to be rejected, the values underlying the marketing of personality were widely accepted. Teachers controlled the academic awards, but students allocated esteem in the peer culture. At Hamilton most students worked hard both at their books and at being accepted. The rules of the game were taken for granted. Some students might be afflicted by doubts about the rightness of their world, as indicated by an editorial asking "Are We Snobs?"[9] but doubts were the exception, self-confidence the rule. Privilege was balanced by an emphasis on volunteer service and good works. Hamilton thought itself liberal and proudly sponsored early foreign-student exchanges arranged by the American Field Service. In the 1950s most students saw no conflict between accepting fraternities segregated by race and religion, and writing editorials condemning the practice of segregation in the South. Commenting on the Supreme Court school desegregation decision, a student wrote: "We have found, to our great surprise, that our country is not so perfect . . . We have found that in the southern part of the United States discrimination beyond belief has been practiced—right under our own noses"[10] Northern de facto segregation was still unnoticed, but in two decades it would affect the life of virtually every student in the city.

By 1960 Hamilton was regarded as the leading high school in the area. When more than a score of county high schools competed for sixty scholarships awarded by state examination, Hamilton students won twenty-three of them.[11] A team of twenty-six evaluators headed by a professor from Temple University visited the school in the 1959–60 academic year as part of the Middle States accreditation process. It was the first time any city school had undergone such a process, and the *Median Herald* bannered the result: "Hamilton High Named Top-Ranking Institution." The evaluators found that over 85 percent of Hamilton graduates went on to some form of postsecondary education. Teachers and administrators were cited for "maintaining superior discipline, high morale, willingness to take on extra school responsibility, and high professional training and background." While the school was commended for "its excellent academic program for college-bound students," the report concluded that the "business education training" for those seeking employment after graduation was only "adequate." "A strong, almost pathological resistance to taking non-college preparation courses exists in this school community," the evaluators noted, adding that the staff "blames this almost exclusively upon parents and students . . . we wonder, however, how much of this feeling is due, at least in part, to the strong emphasis, and just pride, of the staff and its program for the majority."[12]

The competition for grades was keen, and teachers recall that students could be fiercely persistent in arguing for half a point on an exam. The Hamilton *Record* offered articles on how to study for tests and ran a regular feature, "College Corner," profiling colleges to which students might apply.[13] Following a tradition more common to preparatory schools than to public high schools, at the end of each year the *Record* ran a list of the colleges to which seniors had been admitted, a list that always included a number of the most selective liberal arts colleges in the East. The anxiety about getting into the right college is reflected in this essay in the 1960 Hamilton yearbook:

> We worked especially hard this year because we knew that this was our last chance to raise those marks for college entrance, but sometimes it was hard to buckle down with so many things to do—work on scholarship examinations, and of course fill out those endless college appli-

cations. It was certainly hard for some to choose a college with the names of so many fine schools buzzing in our heads, but we fought to meet the deadlines, and then all we could do was buckle down and wait.

The level of achievement in the school was undoubtedly related to the high expectations of parents, teachers, and students. Although only sixteen units were required for graduation—including one year of math and science and no foreign language—most college-bound students took two or three years of these subjects. The school day was short, beginning at 9:00 A.M. and ending at 2:30 P.M., with an hour and a half off for three lunch periods. Students spent less than four hours a day in academic classes, but homework usually required two hours or more a night.

Staff appointment to Hamilton was regarded as a plum, and faculty who came in those years recall that it was an ideal place to teach. The school was orderly; hallways glistened and lateness to class was a rarity. Students showed deference to teachers and seldom needed more than a stern glance to correct misbehavior. In fact, students vied to serve teachers, releasing them from onerous policing tasks. Honor-roll students were selected to oversee the cafeteria during lunch hours and to check passes and regulate hallway traffic. One could readily distinguish the students from the teachers—male teachers wore jackets and ties, female teachers wore dresses or skirts. A teacher would never be hugged in the hallway. The dress code reflected social distance and respect for authority.

There was also hierarchy among the staff. Young teachers did not make waves or challenge the senior staff. Department heads enjoyed reduced teaching loads, and some had little "offices" with private telephones in the corner of their classrooms. Innovations were adopted slowly and differences in teaching philosophy were muted. A teacher appointed in 1962 who spent the first semester as a "floater" with no permanent room of her own remembers the reprimand she received for pushing another teacher's desk aside to suit her informal lecturing style. At lunch on her first day in 1955 a young teacher was told by an older teacher, "You took my parking space this morning."

Harry Payne, a former coach and chemistry teacher, came to Hamilton High as principal in 1953. He remained in the post until his retirement in 1968, although he was not widely admired. The best teachers found him loud and insensitive, but he ruled with unquestioned authority. Like the students and a number of the teachers, he lived in the neighborhood. It was, as a student of the fifties described it, "a homogeneous social structure that's so tight, where everybody knows everybody and has gone over to everybody's house and you've called people up all the time." Payne had few doubts about what most parents expected of him: that he would enforce middle-class standards of courtesy and respect, emphasize a college preparatory curriculum, and put winning teams on the Hamilton field—especially the football field. Few rules and regulations needed to be written down; they were assumed to be understood and shared by all. Parents and teachers might occasionally disagree with Payne's interpretation. He had a "Queeg-like streak," one teacher said, referring to the obsessive fictional character, and once called an assembly to lecture students for letting their shirt tails hang out. He was a large man—6 feet 4 inches, and physically intimidating. On rare occasions when a boy "got out of line," Payne might shove him against his office door for an eyeball-to-eyeball talk.

Once appointed, principals were rarely removed and they expected to run their schools with a free hand. The district had few guidelines and interference was minimal, as long as a school was orderly. Payne enjoyed wide discretion in interpreting and enforcing the rules, hiring or removing teachers, suspending or expelling students. He was known to play favorites among teachers and students, but he was seldom challenged—appealing a principal's decision was virtually unheard of.

Although he visited the classes of new teachers and would seek to transfer those not up to Hamilton's standards, Payne was not seen as a curriculum or instruction leader. He was credited with running a tight ship and was popular in the community because his teams were generally winners—he had formerly raised money to take a championship football team to Florida. The school earned a strong academic reputation because it drew highly motivated college-bound students whom the best teachers wanted to teach, especially in such a pleasant campus setting. The success of the school, however, had little to do with the principal-as-leader theories that became popular several decades later. The school enjoyed high community esteem built on a strong parental consensus about the aim of education: to get their children into "good" colleges.

By 1960 there were two blacks among the three hundred fifty stu-

dents who graduated from Hamilton High. Suburban growth quick-
ened and the 1960 census showed a population decline in the city.
The loss was slight, about 2 percent, although it indicated a pattern
of whites leaving as the black population in the inner city more than
doubled in the 1950s, from five thousand to twelve thousand. Four-
fifths of the black population lived in the center of the city in eight
of Median's sixty-one census tracts. When civil rights organizations
began to press the issue of racial imbalance in the early 1960s, the
school board of Median denied that desegregation was its proper concern. Most black children attended two elementary schools in the
central city. To relieve overcrowding there, in 1962 the board attempted to redraw attendance zones in a way that would have created
a third predominantly black school. The Congress for Racial Equality
(CORE) opposed the boundary changes and demanded that the board
examine the patterns of segregation citywide in order to reduce racial
imbalance in the schools. The president of the board rejected the
request: "I don't accept that racial imbalance creates any kind of missed
opportunity. I don't think the schools accept responsibility for solving
what is basically a housing problem."[14]

So CORE picketed the Board of Education headquarters and organized a successful boycott at a virtually all-black elementary school,
thereby bringing black demands for quality desegregated education to
the attention of the wider community. Several months later, in August
1962, the mayor responded to CORE's request by establishing an
Education Study Committee under the aegis of the state's Commission
for Human Rights. This brought civil rights activists, school staff, and
school board members into regular communication. A year later the
state commissioner of education required all state school districts to
report the extent of racial imbalance and propose plans to eliminate
it. The mayor's education committee reported to the Board of Education a month later, declaring that "there does exist a pattern of
racial imbalance in our public schools [that] . . . is inconsistent with
basic principles of education in a free democratic society."[15] It urged
the board to formulate proposals for redistricting the schools with the
aim of achieving racial balance a primary consideration.

In the fall of 1963 a new school superintendent was appointed and
the school board adopted a policy statement that partially accepted
the stance recommended by the mayor's education committee. It said,

"Racial balance is an additional factor to be considered in boundary revisions," but in a manner consistent with providing "the best possible education for all pupils . . . in the neighborhood schools."[16] In the next two years the school board did close some elementary schools and changed boundaries to create more racial balance at the grade-school level.

Previously the board's primary response to civil rights protests had been compensatory education to upgrade and enrich the education offered in the predominantly black schools. This effort was known as the Jefferson Area Project, after the junior high school in the fifteenth ward. Supported by Ford Foundation and state education department grants, the project reduced class sizes to a 15:1 student-teacher ratio in the predominantly black schools. It also provided special instruction in reading and mathematics, team teaching, cultural enrichment, and summer school programs. When the project was evaluated in 1965, the progress of black students at Jefferson was compared with that of some of their classmates who had been transferred to Eastern, the junior high that Hamilton students attended.

The evaluation showed that the compensatory education programs had had a positive effect on attendance at Jefferson and had increased community concern for education, but there was no significant improvement in academic achievement at Jefferson. There had been a substantial improvement, however, in achievement on the part of the black students who had been transferred to Eastern without the benefit of any special compensatory programs.

The results impressed the school board, and in particular the president who had earlier denied that the board should take responsibility for remedying neighborhood segregation. Not just the improved scores impressed him, but the realization that Jefferson and Eastern had distinctly different climates for achievement. He said he learned that Jefferson students felt that "if you cooperated with your teacher and did your homework, you were a 'kook.' At Eastern Junior High School, if you don't cooperate with the teacher and don't do your homework, you were a 'kook.' " Testifying later at a hearing conducted by the U.S. Civil Rights Commission, he said, "This is what persuaded me . . . and this evidence was good enough so that it was reasonably persuasive to anybody who wanted to be open-minded about it."[17]

Simultaneously, an urban renewal project in the Jefferson area demolished hundreds of homes occupied by poor blacks in order to clear land for new highways, a medical center, and middle-income and university student housing. Renewal officials told the school board that the schools must be upgraded to attract whites to the new middle-income housing. Public housing for blacks and low-income families was also being constructed in outlying areas, some of it within the Hamilton district. The first major federal aid program for elementary and secondary education had passed in 1965, and unless de facto as well as de jure segregated schooling was abolished, federal aid would be withheld.

All of these influences helped create a watershed in school policy. The school administration developed a comprehensive desegregation plan to begin in the 1965–66 school year. It involved closing one of the segregated elementary schools as well as Jefferson Junior High, and busing nine hundred black students to nineteen predominantly white schools throughout the city. Notably, no white students would be bused.

Hamilton High had been little affected by the earlier, broader changes in the city. The few black families who had moved into the Hamilton district during the early 1960s were those of ministers and middle-class professionals. In yearbook pictures the sons emulated Sidney Poitier and the daughters wore their hair like Jacqueline Kennedy. Whites did not think of these families as tokenism; most were proud that Hamilton High was an integrated school. Liberal Hamilton parents and their children participated in the March on Washington in 1963. Social studies teachers recall the fervor with which students discussed Martin Luther King's now-famous address. Like the student who had written the editorial in 1956 applauding the Supreme Court school desegregation decision, a majority viewed racism as primarily a southern problem.

While the letters to the Hamilton *Record* continued to debate issues such as school spirit and whether girls should be permitted to wear miniskirts to school, students who had participated in the civil rights demonstration began to voice other protests. A student who won a writing award, described in the *Record* as "active in the peace movement" and a participant in "teach-ins and demonstrations," used the occasion to criticize the bureaucracy at Hamilton. "The purpose of education is to disseminate knowledge, not to enforce conformity."[18]

The fraternity and sorority system was also criticized. After agreeing that members of these organizations do some charitable work, one student wrote:

> Don't these societies instill a false sense of values in their members? . . . Emphasis on admittance into groups like these may permanently mar both those who are and those who are not accepted. For some students rejection may mean resentment, feelings of inferiority and lasting hatred of the upper classes of our society. Unfortunately, the toll taken on the vast number who belong is even worse. Prejudice and conformity of some sort are ingrained in their souls.[19]

The letter brought spirited rebuttals by defenders of the fraternity-sorority system, which continued into the 1970s at Hamilton. An insult at a fraternity party was alleged to be the cause of the first major riot at Hamilton in 1968. By that time, the younger siblings of those who had marched to Washington were accusing the blacks who came to Hamilton in greater numbers of "ruining our school."

CHAPTER TWO

Deconstruction of the Old World 1966–1971

[Harry] Payne couldn't cope [with the change brought about by desegregation], and he wouldn't face it. He went to Miltown [the tranquilizer] if you want to know the truth.

—*A retired Hamilton teacher*

In those days, there were no rules . . .

—*William Massucco, who in 1968 succeeded Payne*
   as principal of Hamilton

I do recall mornings . . . when I felt I was driving to a combat zone. I'd say, God what's the matter? This is not what I went to graduate school for, to fight wars.

—*Paul Cunneen, who in 1970 succeeded Massucco*
   as principal of Hamilton

When the first black faculty member—a chemistry teacher—came to Hamilton in 1966, she found a school that was orderly and perceived by most whites as a model of integration. New housing patterns and revised school boundaries had caused black enrollment to creep up to 90 out of a total of 1,105 students. When President Lyndon B. Johnson came to Median that year to speak at the university, the First Lady visited Hamilton to spotlight the peaceful integration the President hoped to bring to the North as well as the South. Federal courts endorsed Johnson's aggressive civil rights posture, which required school districts to take affirmative action to overcome a history of unequal educational opportunity. Plans that gave black students "freedom of choice" to attend previously all-white schools were no longer adequate if they did not result in actual desegregation. Although these federal guidelines, which established target percentages of black enrollment in previously all-white schools, were aimed primarily at the legally enforced segregation in the deep South, they would also have an impact on the North, pressing school boards there to move more aggressively to overcome de facto or neighborhood segregation. And in a number of states, including the state in which Median was located, progressive legislatures adopted racial balance laws. In Median this would eventually mean that a school's minority population could not deviate by more than 15 percent from that minority's representation in the public school system as a whole.

In the 1960s the black population of Median nearly doubled again. There were 5,000 blacks in 1950, 12,000 in 1960, and 21,000 in the 1970 census. Meanwhile, the city's white population fell by nearly 30,000 as suburban growth rose sharply. In 1960, the public school system had been 15 percent black, and most blacks were enrolled in predominantly black schools in the fifteenth ward. In 1970, as a result of desegregation plans, blacks were distributed more widely and the system was a quarter black.

The major desegregation program, launched in the school year 1965–66 with the closing of the Jefferson area junior high and the predominantly black elementary school, was initially opposed by black as well as white parents. Even though civil rights organizations had pushed for the plan, blacks resented that only their children were bused, and some, like whites, wanted a good education provided for their children in neighborhood schools. White parents in one of the newly integrated elementary schools formed the Council for Better Education to preserve neighborhood schools. They argued that busing would downgrade the schools and lead middle-income families to move to the suburbs in greater numbers.[1] They criticized the school board for closing the Jefferson area schools and called for a referendum on the board's desegregation plan. With strong support from Median's daily newspapers, the Mayor's Commission on Human Rights, and the Median Committee for Integrated Education, however, the movement for a referendum was tabled. The plan, which initially affected only elementary and junior high schools, was adopted.

A field study by the U.S. Civil Rights Commission found that few teachers were prepared for desegregation. Most had no experience in interracial classrooms nor in teaching black students typically two years behind their white classmates. Standards of discipline differed markedly from the predominantly black schools in the inner city to the mostly middle-class schools who received the black pupils. A principal at one of the receiving white schools, who had taught at a black school prior to its closing, noted improvement in the black children's academic performance. Asked what accounted for the change, he replied: "At Washington there was constant chaos . . . no learning could take place. Here there is an atmosphere more conducive to learning."[2]

In classrooms, many children were fearful of associating with peers of another race. Interviews revealed that "teachers, mostly white, were frequently unprepared, indeed reluctant, to deal with racial problems . . . Many staff members were unable to cope with situations in desegregated classrooms . . . Some Negro children found the predominantly white environment somewhat hostile." A white fifth-grade student explained what desegregation meant to her: "Most of them were friends and they didn't know anybody, and we didn't know any of them. We just did not want to play with any of them because we thought they would want to start fights." A black boy explained that he was not eager to associate with whites: "When we go outside, the white kids . . . don't want to play with us; they call us all kind of names. They call us ugly and tell us we came from Africa."

According to the commission's investigation, students felt uncomfortable when race or color was mentioned in class. Black students reported that when references to blacks or Negroes were made, white students would stare at them, and teachers would not correct whites for behavior blacks considered offensive. One black pupil explained: "In social studies class the teacher will say something about Negro kids and everybody will look at you . . . When we talk about white students, we don't look at them."

Teachers and some principals complained that black children "exhibited rough manners, were impudent, and were involved in frequent fights." White teachers worried about a "lack of respect for authority." One commented: "Some of the children I have had . . . have joined the other group without any problem at all. Then there are others with a spirit of belligerency, defiance—I just don't know how to cope with it. It is difficult to discipline the Negro children. They are resentful and defiant of discipline."

The Civil Rights Commission concluded that the behavior of such children "appeared to stem from their hostility toward both white and Negro authority figures and from their feelings of persecution and discrimination in the desegregated school." One black boy, reporting that a bus driver had called students "niggers," said "I'm going to hit him back. I ain't gonna let no white person hit me." Blacks also complained of different treatment: "Sometimes when the white kids bother us we go tell the teacher and she doesn't do anything about it. When we hit the white kids, she wants to fuss at us and holler." Another girl felt her white principal took sides against blacks: "The principal at our school will just ignore you. She's on the white people's side. They won't do anything for you." And a black boy expected that a black principal should choose sides: "He should try to be on his own side. If they get a whole bunch of Negroes on the white people's side and we have . . . a war . . . we're just going to be dead."

The commission's analysis captured the teachers' fears and resentments, at the same time stressing their failure to understand the causes of black children's hurts. One teacher spoke of a black child as "sullen," which she described as "very characteristic of these youngsters . . . And then if you say anything, they will make a face, as much as to say, 'How dare you.' White children don't pout." Another teacher felt "the desire of Negro children to retaliate is what makes it so difficult. The desire to get even with teachers and students." She interpreted incidents of vandalism after school as acts of retaliation. Some teachers were frank about their confusion: "I was never sure how to handle the Negro situation if it came up in the classroom." Others denied that it did come up. A first-grade teacher in a class with many black students said, "It never comes up in my class." Asked whether she ever introduced discussion of a racial issue, she replied, "I can think of no occasion."

Some frankly said they determinedly avoided talk of race or racial prejudice, because it created rather than resolved problems. Although the commission clearly felt teachers were wrong in this assumption, Philip Cusick's subsequent research would give support to the teachers' view.[3] In the commission's eyes, teachers failed to understand that black children's poor discipline and belligerence were a reaction to what the pupils considered a hostile environment. The suggested remedy was to educate the teachers:

> That many teachers failed to perceive this [hostile environment for blacks] is a measure of the need for much greater sensitivity on the teachers' part. Interracial tension in desegregated schools is a product of fear, distrust, lack of understanding, and previous isolation. Many

teachers view this situation only in terms of unruly Negro children who need discipline. Some recognize that it is more complex and that teachers need assistance in understanding and dealing with the problem.[4]

When the commission published its report three years after desegregation had begun, it felt educational efforts had worked; Median was cited as a success story. The report claimed that "most parents had accepted integration . . . Virtually all of the mothers interviewed felt that children were doing better work." The president of the Median school board said that by 1968 "the staff and the parents in the receiving schools [were] reasonably adjusted to the situation."[5] The report concluded:

> In summary, the lessons to be drawn from Median's experience are that:
>
> A school system can successfully and voluntarily accomplish desegregation if the community and school leadership are committed to this goal . . .
>
> The scholastic performance of most Negro and white children in desegregated schools has been maintained or improved.
>
> The classroom climate and the sensitivity of teachers are important ingredients of successful desegregation. The process of integration is not complete until the teachers and administrators are adequately trained to cope with problems of interracial tension so that children of both races can accept and respect each other as equals.
>
> White students do not necessarily leave the public schools in large numbers. White enrollment may drop initially, but in Median white enrollment continues to increase. School districts must have assistance from Government at all levels . . . in order to accomplish complete desegregation and improve educational programs.[6]

Subsequent events would show that a number of these claims were premature, while others would be falsified.

Rather than improving, the scholastic performance of children in elementary schools in Median took a sharp and steady turn downward beginning in 1969. During the period 1969 to 1974 the average performance of Median pupils in grade six declined thirteen points (from sixty-six to fifty-three) on standardized reading tests and six points (sixty-six to sixty) on statewide mathematics achievement tests.[7] Observers felt the lower scores were linked to changes in attendance patterns and turnovers in school staffs associated with integration. Contrary to the commission's finding, white students did begin to leave the school system in large numbers in the late 1960s and early 1970s. From a base population of 216,000 students in 1960, there would be a total loss of 61,000 whites and an increase of 14,000 blacks by 1980, more than doubling the percentage of blacks in the city school system from 15 percent to 33 percent. The ingrained prejudices of parents and teachers based on lifelong racial separation would not be overcome by "training" and two-week programs designed to improve teacher sensitivity. Black and white teachers almost universally condemned such workshops as worthless, or in some cases as exacerbating tensions.

Inflated claims for the desegregation effort unfortunately were made on behalf of social programs initiated in the 1960s. Typically, such claims were advanced by white social scientists and government sponsors, eager to justify their projects and to win more funding for them. The intended beneficiaries of social programs, often poor and black, might not so readily agree. More modesty in estimating the impact of the programs not only would have cushioned the disappointment that arose in the 1970s, but would have lent more credibility to the programs and made it more difficult for critics to undercut them. In Median as elsewhere, things were to get much worse before they got better.

Initially, the number of black students at Hamilton increased slowly as the result of changes in junior high school feeder patterns. By 1970, however, the city had consolidated seven public high schools into four, one in each quadrant of the city. Of a total enrollment of 1,100 at Hamilton there were 90 blacks in 1966, 210 in 1970, and nearly 500 by the mid-1970s. Yet it was in the years 1968 to 1971, when the black enrollment was less than 20 percent, that the major violence occurred.

A few years after what students referred to as "the days of the riots," a student editor interviewed the black chemistry teacher who had joined the faculty in 1966. Asked what had caused the violence, she attributed it mostly to "faculty racism." After her comments appeared in the school paper, many white faculty members stopped speaking to her. The wounds were still too raw. Years later some of the white faculty came to agree with her, although they would put it less bluntly. Yes, they felt, they had been racist in the sense that most of them had grown up in or near Median. They shared a culture that taught egalitarian ideals, yet as children they had spoken of "nigger town" without embarrassment and they had had almost no face-to-face interaction with blacks. But, with a few exceptions, they had never been racist in the sense of consciously discriminating against black students.

Some racism did occur. Several senior white male faculty members used the word "niggers" in the faculty lounge. Payne, the principal, rejecting a suggestion that misbehaving black students be expelled more promptly, is said to have replied, "Do you want them out on the street doing God knows what?" It was widely agreed that the librarian had a much harsher policy for black borrowers: "It meant," remembered one teacher, "that a black could have a book if no white student wanted it." One guidance counselor was known to have a low opinion of blacks. A "personality record" attached to students' transcripts provided a space for remarks about "significant limitations (physical, social, mental)." He commonly noted "Negro" as such a limitation, as in the statements: "Mary is a very sweet and reasonable girl. She is a Negro student which may have placed her in a minority position," or "Charles is a Negro student, but is accepted by all as the fine young man that he really is." Students were placed into the college-preparatory course, the general academic track, or the basic track for slow students. As the black population grew from a few students who resembled middle-class whites to scores who wore Afros and carried spike combs in their back pockets, most were placed in the basic track. "Basic" classes were 90 percent black. The college-prep track was less than 10 percent black.

Although most teachers were not overtly racist, current teachers can remember a time when they unconsciously assumed that a black student would perform less well than one who was white. They accepted responses from a black they would not have found acceptable from a white—the white would be challenged, pushed, asked to be more precise or thoughtful. "The worst of it, I suppose," said a math teacher who came to Hamilton in 1965, "is that we treated them.as though they weren't there." A researcher who spent a year in the school toward the end of this period visited a "business math" class that was predominantly black. The students were adding long columns of figures, looking bored. The teacher complained about low attendance on the part of black students. "They don't show up because they really aren't interested in this work. This isn't even the regular business arithmetic class. This is the sub-basic class."[8]

One of the ways in which unconscious bias is most likely to affect achievement is the expectations teachers hold for students. My colleagues and I obtained the records of all the black Hamilton graduates in 1966 and 1967 and compared these with a random sample of whites. We wanted to see whether, when IQ was held constant, there was any significant difference in the grades given to blacks. When blacks in the normal range were compared with similar whites, whites achieved an average class rank of 248 and blacks a rank of 307. Although the sample is small, it indicates that on the average blacks with intelligence similar to whites were given significantly lower grades. Unless one assumes that black students systematically made less of an effort, the "discrimination quotient" seems to have been more than sixty points.

According to their teachers, this cadre of black students was initially quiet, industrious, well-behaved, and eager to succeed. Yet as they increased in numbers they experienced a caste system created in the school. Not only were the basic classes predominantly black, but most teachers regarded teaching such classes as a punishment and some would say, on leaving the faculty lounge to return to a basic class, "Well, back to the zoo." Virtually everyone assumed an assimilationist model of integration: blacks would rise in the system and eventually reach achievement levels comparable to whites. But blacks saw few of their number in the college-preparatory track, and blacks of average intelligence were not expected to achieve like average whites. In a school that was virtually all "college prep" for whites, blacks experienced a widespread sense of failure. The irony of desegregation for black students was that it brought them together with whites only to increase their sense of distance. In predominantly black schools, students of average ability would have felt pride and competence.

A further irony is that by the late 1960s in America, completion of high school was valued less because it was so nearly universal. In what Thomas Green only slightly exaggerates in calling "the law of last entry,"[9] the last group to complete a particular educational level gains the least. Until 1940, when less than half of the age cohort completed high school, the diploma distinguished the graduate and had value in the marketplace. It was no failure not to graduate, for many did not. On the other hand, when nearly all graduate, the diploma offers little advantage, and not having it brands one a failure. The term "dropout" was adopted as a pejorative label only in the 1960s. If blacks were poorly integrated in Hamilton's academic system, they fared little better in the social world at the school. The fraternities and sororities remained all white. In the yearbooks for 1966, 1967 and 1968, no blacks appeared among the superlatives—as "friendliest," "most athletic," or "wittiest" seniors. In the 1968 yearbook there were no blacks in the principal's cabinet, the National Honor Society, the yearbook staff of sixty students, or the school orchestra. Although there were 150 blacks in the school, only one black appeared in the twenty-one candid photographs of school life, and this was a young male in a V-necked tennis sweater. Nine blacks were pictured among twenty students in the Distributive Education Club, an organization for students who would become retail clerks, three on the varsity football team, and six on the track team.

The spring of 1968, shortly after the assassination of Martin Luther King, brought the first public notice that all was not well at Hamilton High. An article in the *Median Herald* reported that classes had been suspended while "some 200 or 300 students gathered in the school's auditorium to talk out racial tensions resulting from misunderstandings between Negro and White pupils."[10] The article closed with assurances from the principal, Harry Payne: "Everybody was very, very happy. Our school is as quiet as it has been since I've been here."

A few weeks later, an organization called Forum was established "to attempt to do something about the problem of racial equality." In almost civics-textbook fashion, the student leader of the group explained, "The reason that Forum is so beneficial is . . . that the students are solving problems of racial equality with their own ideas and forming the means with their own skills. This is student power the way it is meant to be and the way racial problems should be solved, by the leaders of tomorrow, who will hopefully overcome the prejudices of today."[11]

But the residue of three hundred years of racial problems in America would not be solved in a summer. By fall, Payne had resigned and the first of a series of riots had swept through the school. The new principal, William Massucco, a lanky and genial former Hamilton High industrial arts teacher, was liked by everyone. Soon after his installation, the new student newspaper noted that "in the short time he has been in office, he has made students feel half human for a change. New blood was needed to meet the challenge of students who wanted to be in a school, not in an army boot camp under the direction of an old man with nothing to offer but war stories."[12] Massucco, finding this praise too costly to his predecessor, asked the editors to run an apology in the next issue, which they grudgingly did.

The *Picayune Papers* was a newspaper born out of the discussions of racial tensions the previous spring. The editors announced that it was "in no way connected with the policies of the old Hamilton *Record . . .* We are a newspaper for *all,* concerned not merely with what we are told to be concerned with."[13] In contrast to the virtually all-white *Record,* the first issue carried a lead story on the "Soul Generation," sixty students who had formed a new all-black singing group. In a bold photograph that ran across the front page, they announced a new mood by their proud, somewhat defiant, stance and dress— Afro hair styles, dashikis, and African dresses. One of the members of the group explained its purpose by giving an account of a song that they would sing at their first school concert:

> "Cordelia Brown" explains that black people should identify with their own people. Cordelia Brown tried to identify herself with white people— "Cordelia Brown, why's your hair so red . . . Cordelia Brown, why's your hair so straight . . . Cordelia Brown, don't you know you're Black." Black people should be proud of themselves. If you were born with straight hair, keep it straight. If you were born with kinky hair, keep it kinky.[14]

That summer riots had swept through the black ghettos of Detroit and Newark. Hamilton students had seen televised reports of the police "bust" outside the Democratic convention headquarters in Chicago. That fall some of them witnessed Democratic vice presidential candidate Senator Edward Muskie struggling to be heard over antiwar protesters when he spoke in Median. Desegregation brought to Hamilton not only more militant blacks but also more working-class ethnic whites. In a student presidential ballot, Hubert Humphrey outpolled Richard Nixon two to one, but George Wallace received 5 percent of the vote.[15]

Before becoming principal, Massucco had spent a year as acting principal at another school. "I knew when I came back that we could possibly have an increase of racial tension . . . I became acutely aware that I was in the middle of a changing situation." Nevertheless, the first riot, when it erupted in the school cafeteria at lunchtime one Monday in late October, caught him and the faculty by surprise. Chairs were thrown and tables upended; when Massucco tried to stop it, he was clubbed over the head and sent to the hospital with a fractured skull. Most middle-class blacks did not riot. It was the newer black students, mostly from the housing projects, joined by three carloads of their friends, who set off the melee. Initially, the riot was reported by the *Median Herald* as an "invasion" by nonstudents. The superintendent of schools asserted, "This involved a gang of hoodlums, some of whom are known to police." As parents called City Hall, the mayor assured them, "We will not give in to hoodlums."[16] At an open hearing in the school auditorium, however, students told another story. The riot Monday noon was traced to an incident at a dance the previous Friday evening. One of the Hamilton fraternities was holding a "keg party" on the hill behind the school and told several blacks standing at the bottom of the hill to "get out of our school." A black student explained that they considered this a challenge to return "because they were black brothers." A newly elected black member of the school board said that the riot was the "result of overt actions by white students towards black students" and to "tensions from the previous spring" that the faculty had not committed itself to resolving. He added, "I'm not condoning the violence, I'm saying to the community that things below the surface that contribute to these situations should be known."[17]

Racial violence had struck other city high schools, and a pattern of disproportionate police response to black students at those schools was repeated at Hamilton. At Technical High downtown, police forced black students outside the school and cordoned them off more than a block away, while white students were allowed to stand in front of the building. At Hamilton, black students who were not participating in the riot charged that they were roughed up by police, whereas white students who were involved were ignored. One black girl testified that a policeman shoved her against the wall and ordered her to get out of the school. "But I'm a student here, I told him." Until then Hamilton had retained its country club image, and even until 1972 no picture of Hamilton events appearing in the *Median Herald* included any black students. In a sense analogous to the statement of the math teacher quoted earlier, blacks were invisible to the community.

Incidents such as these helped to radicalize the moderate and middle-class black students. As the proportion of poor blacks in the school increased, middle-class blacks were ostracized as "oreos" if they did not join the militants, just as the song "Cordelia Brown" prophesied. Eventually they became the leaders of the protest within the school. As Massucco's successor put it, "What often happened was that the black kid from the better background would pick up the speech pattern of the black kid from the poorer background and become one of the leaders . . . and in order to maintain that leadership would have to cut off his white friends, even to the point of attacking them physically, and that did happen."

In the wake of the first riot, six hundred students and their parents, both black and white, met all day Sunday at a country club near the school to which many of the white parents belonged. The meeting had been organized by the Forum group, under the leadership of the black chemistry teacher, who later summarized the often passionate discussion:

> The [black] students were responding to the way they were treated. You know, it's like these white teachers don't really care anything about me . . . He isn't teaching me anything. You know, it's a handout sheet every day or it's a film every day. The teacher may be making racist remarks overt or subtle . . . [such as] the teacher who tells a student in a college preparatory class not to go into her drawer again without permission in front of the basic students because "they may go in and take things."

White students were able to talk about some of their fears of physical intimidation, of their resentment at lewd remarks in the hallways, and of a growing sense of territoriality in the school, with some bathrooms off limits for whites. Consultants attempted to get white students to empathize with black newcomers to the school. Massucco did a lot of listening: "There was an awful lot of hate involved there . . . and there was some progress. It was brought about by whites and blacks alike being forced to say just who the hell are you and what are you doing? And who the hell are you with all your money? And who the hell are you trying to break up my school? And they really began, I guess, to talk to one another." One student read a poem, and another sang

"What The World Needs Now Is Love Sweet Love."[18] Some felt that the day was a great success and had served to reduce tensions. "I thought it was the greatest thing I've ever seen," a vice principal told a reporter for the *Median Herald* shortly after the meeting.[19] Some teachers who were present knew the struggle was far from over, knew that much had not been said, perhaps could not be said—including that many teachers feared the new black students and the students knew it. Moreover, they realized that the leaders of the black community no longer trusted school officials or teachers, and that fires had been kindled in America that would not easily be extinguished.

Although the school remained on edge, there was no violence for the remainder of that year. Massucco established an "early warning system" composed of a group of black and white students who met with him regularly. Despite frequent scuffles, he kept the lid on. The lavatory light switches were taken out so that students could not douse the lights when a teacher came in to break up a fight. Challenges to a teacher's authority in the classroom became more common, often coupled with a charge of racism, as in this script which a teacher described as typical of everyday occurrences that could easily escalate into trouble:

> *Teacher* (to black student): Please sit down and stop talking.
> *Student:* I was only seeing if I could borrow a pencil and a piece of paper for that quiz you were talking about.
> *Teacher:* You know you're supposed to be in your seat.
> *Student:* But you'll give me a zero if I don't have a quiz paper.
> *Teacher* (slightly exasperated): Sit down. You're supposed to bring those things to class or borrow them before class.
> *Student* (voice rising): Why you picking on me? You don't pick on white kids who borrow a piece a paper.

Black and white students—more typically middle-class whites and poor blacks—experienced the kinds of tensions that the anthropologist Janet Ward Schofield described in her perceptive three-year study of a racially integrated middle school.[20] Well-intentioned whites who offered to help blacks with academic work found that blacks resented the offers, either because they were embarrassed to reveal they were behind or because accepting help meant acknowledging dependence. Whites sometimes misinterpreted friendly black gestures as hostile and were inclined not to respond. Angered by being ignored, black students might continue their provocation until they got a response. Moreover, teachers offered little guidance as they floundered themselves, somehow expecting students to solve these problems on their own. At the same time, with the exception of the riot postmortem, there was no opportunity to discuss the elbow-to-elbow tensions that were building daily in the school. Younger siblings of the Hamilton students who had written editorials condemning racial segregation in the South now complained that black students were "ruining our school." And black students, said Massucco, were just as insistent in pointing out that "they were here to stay; they wanted a piece of the action," and they were not going to be second-class citizens. The preface to the 1969 yearbook was a quotation from the black poet Langston Hughes:

> Hold fast to dreams
> For if dreams die
> Life is a broken-winged bird
> That cannot fly.

The next year brought several new outbreaks of violence. After a memorial service for Martin Luther King, black students rampaged through the school, breaking equipment in a physics laboratory and tearing into the library, where they overturned tables, swept books off the shelves, smashed windows, and tore up floor tiles. This time there was no suggestion that it was an outside invasion. School had to be closed ten times that year because of clashes of various kinds.

The gap between "desegregation" and "integration" was evident to all. Opportunity for informal contact between black and white students was limited to those few minutes while students passed in the halls, during which faculty held their breath. No longer did student honor guides monitor the hall traffic. Now paid aides and a policeman were permanently stationed in the school. Hamilton, like other desegregated high schools in the city, went on "block sessions," which meant that periods were shortened and school ended at 1:00 P.M. so that students could be sent home for lunch rather than risk confrontations in the school cafeteria. Assemblies were canceled for more than a decade. There were no dances.

The tracking system allowed little integration in the classrooms, and Massucco was aware that black students and many of their parents were increasingly critical of the predominantly black basic classes. In Washington, D.C., a federal judge had ordered a tracking system abolished.[21] Massucco did not know what to do. Many of the black students were significantly below grade level, yet the school lacked reading and resource teachers who could enable them to participate in regular classes. He recalled:

> In that era, many of the kids from Mississippi or Florida read three or four grades below grade level. What do we do with them? . . . You do the best you could. They had to be in school, they wanted to be in school and I think many of these poor kids came with the idea they could learn something, and I think some of them did. But they lacked the computing skills, the reading skills—not because they lacked intelligence but because they never really had an opportunity to have a decent education wherever they came from. Now do you cast them off to the winds? No. You put them in the basic classes—some people didn't belong at the high school level.

Actually, most of these black students had not come from Mississippi, but from segregated elementary and junior high schools in Median where their failure was nearly invisible. Massucco's statement was a candid admission by the administrator who had to face the failure and the pain revealed by desegregation. His response was to put the blame elsewhere and to ask for more specialists. All the blame did not lie south of the Mason-Dixon line, and it is not clear that more specialists could have worked a cure in the short term either. The end result was just as Massucco inadvertently put it: Hamilton admitted the students but gave them the message that "some people didn't belong . . ."

As tensions in the school mounted, the principal and vice principals (by now there were two) found that 90 percent of their time was absorbed by disciplinary issues. They had adopted a "get tough" policy, which resulted in higher rates of suspension and expulsion for blacks. Local civil rights organizations brought complaints, and a black assistant principal was singled out for criticism. Tighter safeguards on due process were demanded. Teachers cite the handling of the library trashing incident in January 1970 as a turning point in disciplinary policy. Several students were suspended that day, and action was initiated to have them expelled. At the Median school board meeting a few days later, civil rights leaders complained that the students had not been granted adequate due process and should be presumed innocent until proved guilty. In response, the school superintendent issued a statement assuring the students of their rights. He said parents had been notified by registered mail that students were entitled to a hearing under the provisions of the new state education law; if requested, the hearing would be behind closed doors with students having the right to counsel (to be paid for by the school district) and to call witnesses.

Black students pressured Massucco to drop charges against the three students who had been identified as committing the most damage. Meeting with a large group of students in the auditorium, Massucco agreed that the school and some of its staff had been guilty of racism in the past, but disagreed that violence and destruction of the school was justified. He would not back down. He felt that while some students had acted out of a sense of racial injustice, others were out to wreck the school no matter what. The black student leaders pressed him about his own commitment to racial justice, asking "Which side are you on, where do you stand?" Massucco recalled:

> I said, I can't make the clock go faster. This problem belongs to all of us. Where do I stand? I'm going to tell you. I'm between the guy who came in here at the basketball game the other night, the white guy, who said "the niggers are taking over the school," and the black militant from CORE who came in here and said I was a no-good white motherfucker.

The students obtained their hearing with the superintendent, which lasted two days. In the end, charges were dropped and a few students were transferred to another school. The *Median Herald* summed it up: "Three Students Reassigned in Hamilton Incident."[22]

This was the first stage in a change of consciousness that in the 1970s was to contribute in a major way to a reshaping of the relationship between teachers and students. Teachers began to feel on the defensive, unsure of themselves or that their reprimands following even blatant misbehavior would be supported. Many began to look the other way, to shrink from a challenge, and to avoid bringing a charge because they might not only lose the legal battle, but wind up having to defend themselves.

Increasingly, there was a feeling that no one was certain of the rules, that change had come so rapidly that the old understandings, built on years of informal consensus with a steady middle-class group of families, had been swept away. "We assumed through the fifties and the sixties that we had a set of rules that applied to everyone when in fact they didn't," said Massucco.

> The black community was basically compliant with the expectations of the white community. Then things began to change. Then you get into a situation like Hamilton [where] you say what are the rules? When I first started teaching at Hamilton the kids were sent home if they wore dungarees. I laugh [to think we ever had such a rule]. But [in 1970] there were no rules. We tried anything that worked.

In June Massucco heard rumors that another major riot was brewing. He met with students who told him they could do nothing to stop it. When the appointed day came, Massucco remembered, a police lieutenant on duty in the school was shaking like a leaf. A helmeted riot squad was stationed outside. They swept the school when the fight broke out. Ironically, one of the brothers of Daniel Berrigan, the Jesuit poet and social activist, was at the school that day giving a talk about the peace movement. Massucco resigned soon afterward:

> That day I went home to my wife and I said, look, that's it. I can't deal with this anymore. I realized that whatever the problems were, they were bigger than me . . . I really realized that the community had a big problem and somebody better help these people do something about it. It was beyond my ability.

The new black assistant superintendent in charge of secondary schools chose a principal in a new mold to succeed Massucco. Paul Cunneen was like other Median high school principals in that he was white and male, but unlike them in that he was young (thirty-five), from out of state, had a doctorate in educational administration, and was known for being a liberal and an innovative manager. His previous experience had been primarily in planning and initiating model programs at the state level; he had never been a principal. His charge was clear: first restore order and safety to the school, then improve the academic program. School officials in the central office were aware of the unusual increase in teacher resignations and the beginning of an exodus of white middle-class parents from the Hamilton district. They wanted Cunneen to do something dramatic, and do it soon.

Cunneen began to meet with parents as soon as he was appointed in August 1970. He found that communication had broken down not only between white and black parents but among blacks of different social classes and whites of different backgrounds and areas of the city. Many teachers were fearful and demoralized, although some were encouraged and heartened by his appointment. He hired younger teachers, who he thought might have the resilience to cope with a troubled situation, to replace those who resigned. When school began he saw how segregated the student patterns had become. While waiting for the first bell, working-class whites congregated near the front doors, poor blacks hung out in the cafeteria, and white middle-class and a few black middle-class students drifted into the library or math labs.

Cunneen moved immediately to appoint a teacher-parent committee to make recommendations about the curriculum. He banned fraternities and sororities from using school facilities. He invited students in and "had a rap session with quite a few of them." His philosophy was to make the school serve the students. He wanted to "change the schedule of the entire school and make it student oriented rather than teacher oriented." That involved stripping privileges from what he called the "old guard faculty" who remained—those who might have a telephone in their own room and "who had all the choice assignments—they taught only seniors, advanced students, had the most free periods, never took study halls, this kind of thing." Cunneen gave them a mix of "the best and worst classes." A teachers' union survey in the early 1970s showed that Cunneen had one of the lowest ratings of any principal in the city.

Although curriculum reforms were closest to his heart, Cunneen poured most of his energy into regaining control of the school. The academic year 1970–71 was to be the worst yet. "The school was in chaos . . . and riots in that time were a way of life unfortunately." Instead of breaking up fights, whenever teachers heard a ruckus in the hall, they would automatically lock their door for fear the dispute would spill into their classroom. "There was a true physical feeling of being afraid of the black kids." There were "turf wars over control of the school not only between blacks and whites but also between blacks." Weapons were brought into the school; knife and razor fights were not uncommon. "In an average week I'd probably take away a couple of knives and half a dozen clubs. No guns or explosives, but chains, yes, and lead pipes." Student shakedowns of younger pupils, demanding money or a pen or a bicycle, were common. A few pimps were known to be operating in the school. When his life was threatened, Cunneen had a bodyguard assigned to him. He had a heart seizure and fell unconscious after one particularly stressful period. That was the closest he came to quitting.

> I do recall mornings when I'd been up to 11:30 the night before writing out suspension notices and that kind of thing and I was getting there an hour early to make sure I could open school up, when I felt I was driving to a combat zone. I'd say, God what's the matter? This is not what I went to graduate school for, to fight wars.

One morning at about this time white working-class parents arrived at school ahead of him and chained the doors shut. "They were angry and by God they were going to take over the school. They were going to show them [black students] no one was going to trash their kids." With the help of police, the parents were dispersed and Cunneen opened the school after finding a pair of bolt cutters.

In retrospect, said one social studies teacher, what was remarkable was that such incidents came to be almost accepted. "I remember throwing up before going to work on many mornings. It was a very difficult time. It's hard to recreate the sense of those times, the sense of the constant probability of violence, of the real terror in the cafeteria [then open again]. If somebody dropped a tray the place would just go dead silent . . . It broke some people." The teacher had almost been broken himself. One day the trouble signal sounded—three bells in succession—and he was told to head to the auditorium where the junior class meeting had dissolved into a racial brawl. Later he learned that the incident was traced to a confrontation between Cunneen and a black student who was a member of a group accused of beating up a white student a few days earlier. When the black student was found by Cunneen in the cafeteria, he refused to give his name. In the confrontation that followed, fighting erupted again. Tables were overturned, windows broken, then students ran across the hall to the auditorium where the junior class was holding a meeting to elect officers:

> Well, kids were fighting, screaming all over the place. I went down the right aisle toward the stage and pushed some kids apart. They were bleeding. Going up on the stage I saw a kid who had found the light

controls and he was pulling the circuit breakers. I yelled at him and the next thing I knew I was going down, somebody had hit me on the back of the neck with a microphone.

He sounded a theme that came up frequently in teacher interviews, the notion that there was "no book" to go by anymore: "That does not say the book was always right, the trouble is no one had written a new one yet. We didn't know a lot of times how to act and we did anything to keep the peace—Don't do anything that's going to cause those three bells to go off." Massucco expressed feelings like this as well. No one seemed to know what rules applied; the old world had fallen apart.

Students knew the teachers were off balance, and some would exploit any sign of weakness. One common demand was to leave class for a meeting or a rap session in the auditorium over the latest crisis. A science teacher who had a reputation for being tough recounted a typical incident with a student who wore her down:

> This student insisted he had to go because his friends were depending on him. You always had these discussions going on at the time. Somebody had gotten beaten up or thrown out or whatever. Everybody felt they should support their friends . . . I mean the black students really kind of were sticking together and the white students were sticking together, too. And he was just getting steamed up because I was not going to let him go. So finally . . . I made some deal so both of us could save face.

Cunneen reached a personal turning point the following spring when he realized that it was a mistake to close the school at each outbreak of violence. In effect, he was giving the students the power to shut the school down. He remained firm even when students threw firebombs down the hallway outside the auditorium, setting fire to closets that stored choir robes and costumes. "The firemen came and put up big fans in that area after the fire was out and I said, look, I want to carry on classes . . . and the fire chief understood and he said 'All right, we're going to win this, we're not going to let them close us down.' "

Although no one realized it at the time, the violence would end later in that spring of 1971. As a result of the closing of a vocational high school the previous year, sizable numbers of working-class white students now attended Hamilton. Whereas most of the college-bound middle-class and upper-middle-class whites retreated from physical threats, these ethnic whites were likely to respond and to initiate counterthreats. When blacks at Hamilton planned to avenge their "brothers" who had been attacked by whites at another high school, the ethnic whites at Hamilton got wind of it. They knew the fight was planned for the cafeteria and about forty of them took a stand. A leader of the white students had gone swinging into the blacks with a chair leg. In language expressive of the racial tension of the school, he told a researcher a few months later:

> By the time they got that thing stopped, I think each of the white guys were on one knee. But we had fourteen or fifteen of those coons spread out all over that floor. They were really out.[23]

A sequel to this battle was planned for a few weeks later. About one hundred whites, armed with chains and tire irons, a few of them in hard hats, gathered behind the school at the prearranged time and place. An equal number of blacks came out from the gym. Threats were exchanged, but no blows, before police broke it up. One of the hard-hat whites later claimed with pride that the blacks had "backed off" when the white ranks did not break. In reality, teachers felt, both groups were relieved to have it called off. Although some tension remained in the school for years to come, this was the last large-scale confrontation. The "riots" were over.

The effects on the students were profound. Some liberal white students became racists. Some middle-class blacks were torn apart by conflicting loyalties between the old world they knew and the demands of revolution. Many poor blacks got little or no education in basic classes. A student who graduated a year after the last confrontation said it was hard to explain "what the riots did to personal relationships; they just got lost."[24]

Teachers too were ground down, exhausted, defeated, and confused. Many felt an overwhelming sense of failure as teachers. The strategies that had been effective in the classroom no longer worked. Most teachers lacked the knowledge, the resourcefulness, the imagination, or the energy to teach the new black—often angry—students who sat in their classes. By the fall of 1971, 72 percent of the teachers who had taught at Hamilton in 1966 had resigned, retired, or transferred.[25]

CHAPTER THREE

Let the Students Decide
1971–1979

Everything is all broken up.
—*A student, fall 1971*

T he desegregation of Hamilton High was a true social revolution. It resulted in the deconstruction of an old world and the birth of a new world. By the fall of 1971 the former social and academic system of an elite public school was no longer recognizable. The change was as great as that from peace to war and back again to a different, unsettling peace.

Most of the faculty who had taught at the school earlier had left. The system of faculty preferences and appointed department heads had been abolished and a system of elected chairpersons instituted. The old prerogatives could no longer be assumed and the exercise of traditional authority was in doubt. Under the former disciplinary system, rules had been so widely accepted that the halls were monitored by students; now police officers and paid aides performed the task. The exercise of adult discretion had been eroded by a legalistic system emphasizing student rights, formal hearings, and judicial procedures.

The curriculum committee appointed by the new principal had grave doubts about the tracking system. When faculty members returned in the fall of 1971, they found that Cunneen had abolished it and randomly distributed the basic students in regular classes. Cunneen also began to expand the elective system and to break the former year-long courses into semester or quarter-semester lengths. New tracking resulted, but now by student choice and not by faculty assignment.

The social system of the school had been transformed. Fraternities and sororities had been officially abolished; although a few persisted into the 1970s, they withered away, no longer playing a significant role in the social life of the school. In fact, a researcher who spent the year 1971–72 as a participant observer at Hamilton High concluded that the old social hierarchies had been smashed: "The student population was disparate. [Each group believed] that other groups could believe and act as they saw fit . . . A firm prestige system, which stratified groups hierarchically or which created strong intergroup competition, was not evident."[1] Although classes were more integrated, in terms of informal relations in hallways and cafeteria the school was now almost completely segregated. Whereas the earlier desegregation policy assumed gradual assimilation but condoned a high degree of segregation in tracking, now many black students rejected belated integration of classes and favored a strong separatist stance. True integration was a long way off. A photograph of the 1972 senior class, massed informally on the hill behind the school, showed an almost complete separation of black and white students, with a number of the blacks raising their fists in a black-power salute.

The neighborhood surrounding the school had also changed as middle-class whites moved out and blacks and less affluent ethnic whites bought substantial homes at bargain prices. By 1972 white enrollment had declined by three hundred fifty students and real estate prices in the Hamilton district fell by half. In the period of school violence, some well-informed central-office school officials who lived in the neighborhood were among the first to move to the suburbs. Massucco was the last principal to live in the Hamilton district. Cunneen and those who succeeded him all lived in the suburbs.

Many of the teachers who remained at Hamilton were weary, and many of the students continued to be fearful. But some faculty and students (particularly the blacks) were energized if not exhilarated by the conflict. Some white students who had personal resources and the self-confidence to ride out the conflict also were charged by the revolutionary fervor. The civil rights movement that led to school desegregation at Hamilton and thousands of other public schools across the nation was but one of several powerful movements that reshaped American politics and cultural life in the late 1960s and early 1970s. The protest against the war in Vietnam and student demands for more voice in educational decisions spread down from the college campuses and affected the climate of high schools in the 1970s, especially those like Hamilton that were situated in proximity to a major university. An interreligious center near the school became a focal point for Median antiwar protests. Hamilton student activists used the center's printing press to start an underground newspaper that promoted student rights and supported active resistance to the military draft.

The Hamilton yearbooks in the early 1970s displayed exceptional vibrance and creativity. They also depicted the revolutionary transfer of power to students. The 1971 volume opened with candid photographs of students, instead of the usual formal gallery of school administration followed by faculty. Now the faculty came last. The rise of student power was underscored by many photographs, such as the one of a student holding a sign that read, "Zoo: Do Not Feed the Teachers." A staged photo showed a student in revolutionary garb backing the principal, Cunneen, against the wall at the point of a toy submachine gun. The 1971 and 1972 yearbooks, in particular, featured a grim portrayal of the violence in the school with photographs of barred windows and barbed wire, with police in helmets and riot gear lined up in front of the school. A photograph of the front doors in chains, with a sign taped to shattered glass, captured students' memories of frequent school closings: "These premises are closed when school is not in session." As the distance from the violence increased, some attempts to turn the absurd to comedy were introduced. A page of one yearbook was designed as a board game capsuling recent history. The game begins in 1968 with instructions on the first square: "Go to auditorium and meet your first liberal" and then to "First riot, play catch with chairs in cafeteria." The "Second riot, spring training for football with police," is followed by "First assembly group-therapy session, doctor creates false hopes." The change of social consciousness that was taking place in the 1970s was evident in the rules students had invented for the game: "Pieces of play. Use any object that is fitting to your social standing. Obviously, players with rich parents or good grades must be given special advantages."

Hence, mixed with the pain that had transpired and the further pain that was yet to come, there was a sense of anticipation among some students in the fall of 1971. They understood that the old world had been swept away and a new world was aborning. Although at first it was unclear, within a few years it would be self-evident that a radical change had occurred in the rules defining the interactions between adults and students—a change that would affect every aspect of life in the school. These changes in general gave students more power and initiative, and reduced the traditional authority of adults. Fascinating and complex, the changes resulted from the interaction of many causes, including long-term cultural factors, more immediate changes in policy at local and national levels, and a growing sense of confusion among teachers and staff in the school about their own role as moral agents. Let us turn first to this last topic, the situation of the adults in the school.

The faculty at Hamilton High, like many teachers, were proxies for the whole of society. They were ordered to take the rap, to pay the bill for generations of societal racism. Perhaps only prison wardens were equally exposed to the racial hatred and violence that erupted in the late 1960s. Yet prison guards only kept the peace, whereas teachers were charged both with maintaining order and with educating students. Under siege, and united in their fears, the faculty minimized their differences to maintain a common defense. As the violence subsided and new recruits replaced teachers who had resigned, different political viewpoints emerged. Teachers who had fended off chair-swinging students in the cafeteria favored different policies than those who came after the riots. Faculty meetings became donnybrooks over whether Eldridge Cleaver's *Soul on Ice* should be taught in English classes. The splintering and disarray of the faculty could be seen at lunchtime. Once they all had shared one lounge, but by the early seventies they had split into three groups. Old-guard males gathered in the room where the copy machine was located. These middle-aged white men had fared worst in the challenge to their classroom authority. Some were deeply embittered, and in at least one instance, a teacher regarded as perhaps the most brilliant at Hamilton, alcoholism had resulted. New faculty remember the stares they got if they entered this room, where one's presence had to be justified by battle scars and "war stories." Middle-of-the-road and conservative female faculty ate in the home economics area, and the younger, more liberal faculty of both sexes, including some union organizers, lunched together in the old lounge. A few veterans who had become strong supporters of Cunneen and his reforms, later rejected by most of the faculty, tended to eat alone in their rooms.

The new faculty differed in their orientations. Some were deeply sympathetic to the escalating protest movements. A few had been involved in college demonstrations in the late sixties. They encouraged students to call them by their first names, actively opposed the Vietnam War, and since they smoked marijuana themselves were lenient with students who came to their classrooms in a drugged state. Young female faculty wore miniskirts. The winds of the sexual revolution stirred Hamilton High. Sexual affairs among faculty became more numerous, and an occasional liaison with a student was overlooked. These teachers differed markedly from more traditional faculty in their expectations for achievement, their grading policies, and their tolerance for missed deadlines. They were likely to be lenient with black students, out of what other faculty members felt was misguided and guilty liberalism. They angered older male teachers when they supported protests by female students about sexual inequality in the athletic programs and facilities. One outcome of such differences was that teachers perceived, quite correctly, that they could no longer be sure that another faculty member shared their views about a basic matter of discipline or would support them if they challenged a student misbehaving in the hall. Faculty tended more and more to withdraw from such encounters or not to see them. Hence a car approaching the school was stoned by a group of students in full view of a number of faculty members, and no one attempted to stop the incident.

The administration too gave confused signals about discipline to both students and faculty. A vice principal of this era later explained that it was the period when the school had different standards of discipline for blacks and whites:

> A white and [a] black kid might do the same thing—say walking around the halls cutting classes. The white kid might get a warning and the black kid suspended. And after that it went the other way . . . because all these advocacy groups came in and then the blacks seemed to get a little better of the deal from the standpoint of the rules and regulations of the institution and that's what I'm referring to—one set of rules being applied in two different manners . . . The central office was softpedalling, they were pushing down directives to us at the building level to handle things in this manner or [telling us] don't get too upset over this and so forth . . . and then later we tried to change the system again so

that we could encompass all the kids [under one standard] and we weren't very successful and we're still working on it.

Uncertainty about standards of behavior, erosion of trust between old and young, and parental anger about shifting standards of discipline afflicted other high schools as much as Hamilton. In this climate the Median school board adopted sweeping new due-process requirements in November 1971. Many matters once left to the discretion of the school principals or teachers now were subject to grievance and court-room-like review. This, of course, was not merely a local matter, but a result also of broad cultural changes[2] redefining relations between children and adult guardians, which culminated in the Supreme Court decision in the *Gault* case in 1967 and the *Winship* case in 1970. In *Gault* the Supreme Court established a new standard that juvenile-court proceedings "must measure up to the essentials of due process and fair treatment." The *Gault* decision was later extended, in the *Winship* case, to insist that juvenile courts also meet the standard of proving guilt "beyond a reasonable doubt."

In these two decisions the Supreme Court undid the work of compassionate children's rights advocates who established the juvenile-court system at the turn of the century when ten-year-olds were still tried and sentenced along with hardened criminals. The intention was that a wise and kindly judge would consider a wide variety of evidence in sentencing juveniles who might be straightened out with a stern admonition, referral to a foster home, or attendance at a state reform school. Justice Abe Fortas turned aside this view of a court "in which a fatherly judge touched heart and conscience of the erring youth—talking over his problems, by paternal advice and admonition, and in which, in extreme situations, benevolent and wise institutions of the state provided guidance and help." Fortas turned to sociological evidence to argue that "the essentials of due process . . . may be a more impressive and more therapeutic attitude insofar as a juvenile is concerned." In sum, the Supreme Court was no longer willing to trust the discretion and judgment of the juvenile-court judges. Little time was lost in applying this reasoning to attack the "paternalism" of the school principal. It was not long before all of the tests of due process enumerated in *Gault* were applied to schools, namely: notice of the charges, right to counsel, right to confrontation and cross-examination, privilege against self-incrimination, right to a transcript of the proceedings, and right to appellate review.

In the year following *Gault*, the American Civil Liberties Union published a widely influential document, *Academic Freedom in the Secondary Schools*. The ACLU statement laid down three principles, the first of which pushed academic freedom to a new limit by arguing that freedom implies the right to make mistakes and that therefore students must sometimes "be permitted to act in ways which are predictably unwise so long as the consequences of their acts are not dangerous to life and property, and do not seriously disrupt the academic process." The second principle blurred the line between speech and action, arguing for "a recognition that deviation from the opinions and standards deemed desirable by the faculty is not ipso facto a danger to the educational process." These statements put many teachers on the defensive. Insofar as these principles were restricted to free-speech issues, most school officials and most parents would probably agree with them—although they might not be happy with its relatively strong dismissal of "standards" of the adults in the schools. It was the third ACLU principle that bluntly warned school officials to pay close attention to the *Gault* decision: "Students and their schools should have the right to live under the principle of 'rule by law' as opposed to 'rule by personality.' To protect this right, rules and regulations should be in writing. Students have the right to know the extent and limits of the faculty's authority and, therefore, the powers that are reserved for the students and the responsibilities that they should accept." In every area of discipline the ACLU statement took a lawyerly view of the need to reduce adult latitude and discretion in favor of specific definitions and rules.

The recommendations of the ACLU statement of 1968 became standard operating procedure in many urban schools, as they did in Median, often adopting this ACLU language:

> The teacher and administrator should bear in mind that accusation is not the equivalent of guilt, and he should therefore be satisfied of the guilt of the accused student prior to subjecting such student to disciplinary action . . . Those infractions which may lead to more serious penalties, such as suspension or expulsion from school, or a notation on the record, require the utilization of a comprehensive and formal

procedure . . . [which] should include a formal hearing and the right of appeal. Regulations and proceedings governing the operation of the hearing panel and the appeal procedure should be predetermined in consultation with the students, published and disseminated or otherwise made available to the student body . . . prior to the hearing, the student (and his parent or guardian) should be: (a) Advised in writing of the charges against him, including a summary of the evidence upon which the charges are based. (b) Advised that he is entitled to be represented and/or advised at all times during the course of the proceedings by a person of his choosing who may or may not be connected with the faculty or administration of the school and may include a member of the student body. (c) Advised of the procedure to be followed at the hearing. (d) Given a reasonable time to prepare his defense.

At the hearing the student (his parent, guardian or other representative) and the administrator should have the right to examine and cross-examine witnesses and to present documentary and other evidence in support of their respective contentions. The student should be advised of his privilege to remain silent, and should not be disciplined for acclaiming this privilege. The administration should make available to the student such authority as it may possess to require the presence of witnesses at the hearing. A full record should be taken at the hearing and it should be made available in identical form to the hearing panel, the administration and the student. The cost thereof should be met by the school.[3]

Along with the adoption of similar regulations, in 1971–72 the Median superintendent's Student Cabinet, itself a new body composed of students from all high schools in the city, met and proposed a new grievance procedure. It outlined a five-step process, similar to labor negotiations, in which students could bring a wide range of grievances to arbitration. It was adopted in the fall of 1972 and distributed to all pupils in a student handbook outlining their rights. The prologue to the grievance process noted that it "was designed to provide a method for high school students to resolve legitimate differences or problems between students and staff members. The process does not seek to discredit staff members and administrators, or their position in the schools, but it does recognize that in certain instances a method for reconciling differences is necessary."[4] However, many teachers felt that if it did not discredit them, it encouraged harassment, particularly since the procedure mandated a hearing first with the principal, then with the director of high schools, and finally with the superintendent.

It invited grievance on issues of grading and "when the behavior of any staff member willfully imposes upon a student(s) the ethical, social or political values of the staff member." The statement failed to make a distinction between socialization and indoctrination. Broadly written, it put a chill on a teacher's freedom to set standards in the classroom. How could teachers act responsibly without "imposing" ethical values? It became more difficult, for example, to discipline students for cheating. One of the most admired teachers in the English department, who came to the school in the mid-1970s, is quite liberal in her views. She told of her shock when she first pressed a case of cheating by a neurosurgeon's son:

> The truth is I saw the kid cheating. I saw him with his open book on his lap during a test and by the time I got back to him to get his paper the book was back on the floor. They wanted documentation. "How can you prove it? How did he cheat?" I said I am telling you that he was cheating. But the question now is, "We've heard John's side of the story, what's yours?" As much as I believe in giving due process to kids something grates when I hear, "What's your side of the story?" Somehow it felt like I'm part of the crime . . . The issue is the boy's cheating and now two hours later I'm in the principal's office discussing due process. And that's not the only incident I've had.

The same teacher failed a boy who handed in a term paper he had not written. She had to appear before her supervisor and defend herself repeatedly because "that parent called every day, hired a lawyer, made my life absolutely miserable for four and a half months." The lawyer reviewed all her papers for the whole term to see if the mother's charge that the teacher had shown prejudice toward her son could be substantiated. Finally the boy was transferred to another class. In the case of this unusually dedicated teacher, the effect was not to compromise her standards or to cause her to look the other way at cheating. "I don't think you stop caring and I don't think you stop having values. I think you just pick your fights a lot more carefully." With other teachers, however, there was a tendency to withdraw. A science teacher expressed an attitude we heard in many interviews: "You know what's going to happen. The parents are going to get a lawyer, the kid's going to get off, and you're going to look like a fool."

Some may suspect that the effects we report here are exaggerated. Although educational litigation of all types *doubled* in state appellate and federal courts in the period 1967–1976,[5] new provisions for hearings within schools were not frequently exercised by students or parents. This was true in Median as well, where in the first year students initiated only fifteen formal grievances. But frequency of application of the new procedures does not demonstrate the depth of the psychological change—in both the degree of inhibition felt by adults and the degree of impunity felt by students. Only a few incidents made a broad impact on teachers. The story of a respected teacher who has to meet with lawyers over a case of alleged cheating spreads quickly through the teachers' lounge. Cited repeatedly by teachers in recounting the history of these times was the fact that students who smashed tables and windows in the school library were let off after lengthy hearings with only a school transfer. Concluding that it was fruitless to act, teachers censored themselves. During our observations in the school later that decade, a teacher was visibly upset about a group of students who had verbally assaulted her and made sexually degrading comments in the hall. Asked why she didn't report the episode, she responded, "Well, it wouldn't have done any good." "Why not?" we pressed. "I didn't have any witnesses," she replied. Adult authority was increasingly defined by what would stand up in court. Students were quick to tell teachers, "You can't suspend me." Behavior was regarded as tolerable unless it was specifically declared illegal. Jurisdiction was so narrowly defined in a legal sense that when a student told the principal after lunch that he had been beaten up, the principal asked which side of the street he had been standing on. If he had been across the street, that would be out of the school's jurisdiction and presumably beyond redress by the principal.

Teacher prerogatives were also affected by the challenge to middle-class standards typical of the countercultural movements of the late 1960s and early 1970s. A Median teacher who insisted that a repeatedly tardy student bring a note from her parent each time she was late was told by the parent that no notes would be provided and "to stop worrying my child just because you have a middle-class hang-up about time." Teachers joked that corporal punishment was a relic of the past—except for students who beat up on them. Not so much of a joke, however, was the school board's new regulation that stripped teachers of the power to keep students after school unless the pupil was allowed to call his or her parents: "If parents object to detaining their child after school hours, the pupil *may not* be kept after school." The school board lawyers cited the case of Pierce vs. The Society of Sisters, a 1925 Supreme Court case which struck down the power of the state to prohibit private schooling, saying the state must not maintain a monopoly in education. It essentially gave parents the right to choose the form of schooling they wished for their child. But it had nothing to do with the age-old teacher's punishment of keeping children after school. While the new regulation more directly affected teachers in elementary schools than in high schools, it changed the climate in which all worked and was typical of the series of "shall nots" the teachers felt as a rebuff.

The discovery of the abuse of authority led to aggressive efforts to restructure or challenge that authority in Median, as elsewhere. The tendency to see school officials as adversaries was enhanced by various advocacy groups that encouraged students and parents to use their new rights. A billfold-sized card for the National Committee for Citizens in Education listed parents' rights on a state-by-state basis. In Boston the Educational Coalition published a guide to "Games the System Plays." An article in the *New York Times*, "A Guide for Parents Who Take on the School System," gathered advice from a variety of new experts who spoke of parents as "consumers" of educational commodities. Parents were advised to speak up for their rights and to take a witness along to school meetings as though collecting evidence for a lawsuit. A community organizer urged parents: "Get the facts on the teacher. Take a friend with you to observe the teacher three or four times."[6]

A parallel development was encouraging children to sue or bring charges against parents or adult guardians under new child-abuse laws. The plight of the battered child led to the adoption by 1968 of tough child-abuse statutes in all fifty states. While no one questioned the need to protect children against physical abuse, the eagerness of the state to intervene between parent and child in cases of alleged "emotional" abuse began to draw criticism as child protective service bureaucracies multiplied. According to Albert Solnit of Yale University's Child Study Center, the criteria for what constituted emotional abuse were so vague that the category should be eliminated as justifying coercive state intervention.[7]

Such a criticism applied to Median, where the child protective service gave teachers guidelines so broad as to bring nearly every parent under the net of the service's surveillance. For example, the emotionally abusing parent was defined as including those who love their child "but lose control of themselves when they are angry" or "who may be suffering from a crisis such as a loss of a job." Teachers were warned, "If you don't report a *suspected* case, you are guilty of a Class A misdemeanor and could be civilly liable for any injuries to the child subsequent to your failure to report." In Median allegations of child abuse increased fivefold in the 1970s. The law provided that accusers be granted anonymity and that all complaints must be investigated within twenty-four hours. The child protective service worker serves papers on the accused, notifying him or her that a complaint has been filed in the state's central registry and that a ninety-day investigation has been authorized.

Suits could be brought against teachers as well as against parents, and some pupils taunted, "Don't you touch me or I'll have you arrested." A Hamilton social studies teacher said he began to feel, "Watch out, stay out of the way, don't get yourself in a situation where these people can falsely accuse you." The Median teachers' union published cases of teachers whose jobs had been jeopardized when child-abuse machinery was invoked against them. A teacher in another school district who had restrained a rowdy and abusive student was charged with child abuse. It took months to close the case and expunge it from state records. Another teacher, accused by a student he had physically prevented from disrupting a test in school, said: "Next morning the police came to my home and arrested me. They led me out of my home in handcuffs."[8] By the end of the decade the Median newspaper had published the misgivings of a child protective service worker who broke ranks to complain of the harm that comes from requirements to initiate an investigation "no matter how ridiculous it might seem." Complaints may be made because the "caller has a grudge" or stem from people who "like to play cruel tricks on others, or are too stupid to understand the harm they are doing."

Grievance procedures, new child-abuse statutes, and court decisions limiting school officials' authority to promulgate dress codes were all part of a broad shift in the relations between adults and children that occurred in the 1970s and that raised new questions about what defined the status of child and adult. In Median, for example, it was possible in the 1970s for teenagers to obtain birth control devices over parental objection and to force parents to support them at age sixteen if they did not wish to live at home. One father published an open letter to the governor in a Median newspaper saying that the only reason his daughter would not stay at home was that "we won't allow her to run with her friends." He charged the new laws and support systems for sixteen-year-olds were irresponsible. "As far as I am concerned, the law says kids can do what they please and parents must face the consequences."[9] Many teachers, as parent substitutes, began to have similar thoughts. As new legal rights and formal status equality were being conferred on teenagers, teachers were placed in the paradoxical position of being asked to socialize their equals.

In Median, as in the nation at large, the effect of the increased legalization of the schools, at least in the short run, was neither to improve discipline nor to create a sense of greater justice. It may have assuaged some by giving them the means to address a grievance, and it certainly put a stringent curb on the use of discretionary authority. But its effect on students may have been to increase cynicism about the likelihood of justice being done and to encourage them to use the new rules to beat the system. After a decade of new due-process rules in public schools, a national survey asked students in both public and Catholic high schools about discipline. By a wide margin, students in Catholic schools thought discipline was more effective. More surprisingly, when asked whether discipline was fairly administered, students who supposedly had the benefit of new rules and procedures in the public schools were less likely than their Catholic counterparts (by a margin of 39 percent to 52 percent) to think it fair.[10] Gallup polls also showed parental concern about discipline in public schools rising steadily in the 1970s. It was most often the parents' prime concern.

Not all Hamilton teachers and students responded uniformly to these trends. Some liberal teachers greeted the increase of student rights and decision making with approval. The principal, Cunneen, was ideologically in favor of the student rights movement at the time, although he later came to believe that the overall impact of legalization of the school was harmful. In general, he supported liberalization of requirements both in the curriculum and with respect to disciplinary issues, and he favored a student-centered philosophy. For a combination of reasons—whether sympathy for the student revolution, or a feeling that insistence on traditional standards of discipline could lead one into losing protracted conflicts, or doubt that one's colleagues would back one up—teachers increasingly adopted a posture of non-interference. In such a situation, one might ask, what kind of world do students construct? Here we have the benefit of first-hand observations by Peter Clark, who spent a year of participant observation at Hamilton High in 1971–72 and kept in touch with developments at the school until completing his work in 1977.

Clark describes a school in which radios played most of the day, not only in the cafeteria but also in some classrooms, as long as students sat in the rear of the room and kept the volume low. Seventy-eight percent of Hamilton students said they skipped a class once a week and 46 percent cut classes frequently. Alcohol and drug use "were quite high . . . The general pattern was for beer, fruit wines, or alcohol and fruit juice mixes to be kept in cars and drunk either in the parking lot or on trips away from school."[11] There was open petting and kissing in the halls, and more intense "making out" by couples in cars in the parking lot. Stealing and destruction of school property had increased, and teachers suffered "aggressive verbal abuse"; but "obscene or immoral activity was never an issue which was officially talked about." An exception was this announcement from Cunneen that came over the public address system one day:

> We have a serious problem in the parking lot. A great deal of card playing, drinking, and gambling is going on in the cars. Also there have been some thefts. We can't have this, so I am forced, although I don't want to, to announce some new rules. As of today, no one is allowed to be in a car in the parking lot unless you are in the immediate process of leaving the school grounds. So, if you are caught in a car, whether it is yours, your friend's, or a stranger's, I will have to suspend you from school. Now I mean this; I will enforce it; so don't try me.

Some students interpreted the rule legalistically and sat in their cars on the front drive instead of in the parking lot, arguing they couldn't be suspended because the new rule applied only to the parking lot. For a few days most students only sat on the hoods of their cars, Clark noted, "but the limits of the rule were so vague, the excuses so easy, and the direct supervision so minimal, that within several weeks the behavior of students was very much what it had been before." Some months later students who were concerned about thefts from cars set up video cameras to monitor activity in the parking lot. But that too was abandoned. Even though the students liked their freedom, a poll showed widespread concern about lack of safety in the school. Students cited better discipline as one of the most-needed improvements in the school. One of them told Clark: "A few years ago, you knew if you did something wrong, you'd get your ass busted; but now it takes three, four, five times and they still don't throw anybody out."

Like teachers, students were divided in their responses, however. While some wanted stronger discipline, others published an underground newspaper, *Blasting*, that gave students advice on how to beat the system. In a "Back to School" issue, the incoming freshmen were advised that they could cut classes as much as they wanted because "no one usually misses you." They were told to cover themselves, however: "It's never a good idea to put room numbers on your schedule card. If you must, don't make the numbers clear: make mistakes. This will make it much harder for the office to locate you." Should they get caught or prosecuted, they were reminded of their rights: "If the administration tries to screw you, if there is something that you don't feel is fair about the school system, contact a student group . . . A great deal of pressure can be brought to bear on the system."

Clark's work at Hamilton provides a perspective on the various student subcultures in the early 1970s, the most salient aspect of which was the cleavage between black and white students. In a year of daily observation, Clark did not see "more than a dozen blacks and whites who made an effort to communicate with each other on a regular basis." There was almost no informal interaction between blacks and whites, and Clark, as a white, was unable to cross that barrier. Racial differences were "the clearest, most uniform obstacle to informal student relationships." Militant black students applied strong pressure to avoid association with whites. A popular black honor student and cocaptain of the football team, who had decided to "cross over" the color line, explained:

> One thing about this school that's a real problem is the separation, you know, of blacks and whites. I really felt the pressure [from black friends] . . . but this year I decided I would hang around with anyone I wanted to . . . Some guys called me a Tom . . . but I told them it didn't matter to me [and they] don't bother saying it anymore.

Liberal and radical whites were highly sympathetic to black students. They supported civil rights protests and criticized what they called

the redneck element for using the epithet "niggers." They admired
Hamilton's diversity, yet acknowledged their own fear and ignorance.
One admitted: "Even their language is new. I walk by and I hear one
of them saying 'I'm going to knock that motherfucker upside the head.'
My stomach tightens up; I'm afraid. That fear is a very important
thing at Hamilton."

The fraternity and sorority system collapsed, and some of the traditional clubs petered out. Students lost interest and faculty were less
willing advisers. In the early seventies random selection temporarily
replaced class elections. Sports were racially divided. Basketball and
football were predominantly black, whereas soccer, lacrosse, and tennis were white sports.

Students were acutely aware that now school social life was clearly
divided, not only racially but also between new economic and ethnic
groups of whites. One student told Clark, "Everything is all broken
up," and another said, "There are just too many factions." Unfriend-
liness and distrust prevailed. Clark was most impressed by the lack of
social hierarchy among groups. "None felt the others had to be like
themselves" or expected "others to follow their leading behaviors."
The situation was anarchic and fluid. There were no "shared feelings
across groups regarding the general social orientation of the school."

Clark focused on three groups in the senior class, which he called
the Protesters, the Hardliners, and the Achievers. In a style of research
known as participant observation, he made friends with students in
these groups, spent time in and out of school with them, and as a
graduate student in a nearby university was invited to their parties
and other social events.

The Protesters were a loosely affiliated group of eighty students who
included both countercultural "freaks" and political activists. They
published the underground newspaper, organized a Vietnam Moratorium day, and enjoyed put-ons. Once they placed a red phospho-
rescent strip across a hallway and used a stop-and-go sign to regulate
the traffic there. Alienated from school, unconventional in dress and
hair style, they were critical of authority and politically and sexually
radical. At one of the parties Clark attended, many of them took
drugs and stripped off their clothes. They used mescaline, marijuana,
and amphetamines fairly regularly, with some taking LSD and opiates.
A number smoked marijuana habitually between classes, which, "though

they would not admit it, inhibited their ability in school." Although a few Protesters had high academic averages, most slid by and sporadically exerted great effort on subjects that engaged them.

The Protesters tended to accept vandalism as "expressions of frustration against the school." They were angered by attempts to limit petting in class, by antismoking rules, and by threatened drug busts. "There was a certain amount of paranoia among the group members about getting busted." They were vigilant about student privacy, student rights, and student power. They opposed searches of lockers, pushed for draft counseling, and supported Cunneen's moves to give students more freedom—to allow them to cut regular study halls and go to the cafeteria for rap sessions, for example. "Some of Cunneen's decisions make me angry and suspicious," one of the Protesters confided, "but he's really loosened up the atmosphere."

The Protesters' parents tended to be supportive liberals, many of whom worked at the nearby university. Some parents were antiwar protesters who usually backed their children's initiatives. A few smoked marijuana with their children, and some had no objection to their spending the night with a member of the opposite sex. One student who had a standing parental excuse for skipping school (one year he cut seventy days) told Clark: "There are only two ways the school can control me—through my parents or through suspending me. My parents agree with me, so the school can't use that method." Although no firm evidence exists, many teachers believe that the white exodus included a disproportionate number of conservative Hamilton parents and that liberals moved less readily in the face of racial integration. Parental leadership at the school grew more laissez-faire and more supportive of Cunneen's liberal reforms of discipline and curriculum.

The Hardliners represented 10 to 15 percent of the population at Hamilton High. These working-class white ethnic students were job-oriented rather than college-oriented. In the 1950s many would have dropped out of school at age sixteen, but now they drove souped-up cars to school, in which they sometimes drank beer and played cards at lunchtime. Before desegregation many Hardliners attended vocational high school. These were the students who first physically resisted the blacks during the days of the riots. Some of them spoke candidly about the changing racial composition of the school: "Them Puerto Ricans are just as bad as the Coons, if you ask me," one told Clark.

Three of the Hardliners Clark observed spent much of their time skipping classes, hanging out, and smoking cigarettes in front of the school. They usually spent less than two hours a day in classes. Clark explained:

> With all the official and unofficial unscheduled time available [as a result of open study halls, a lax policy on cuts, and more flexible curricular requirements], they associated with each other, talking of girls, hunting trips, past and future fights, and their Brawlers' football contests. Typically they spent at least an hour a day away from the school building in their car eating lunch, occasionally drinking, visiting a slot car track— a favorite hobby—or taxiing other students around.

The Achievers were a subgroup among the large segment that comprised the white "straights". Other groups among the straights were the remnants of the "frats," the wealthy "social set," and the jocks. Some occasionally used marijuana, and most were neatly dressed, fairly traditional in social and sexual mores, and concerned about grades and admission to good colleges. Class officers would have been drawn from their ranks prior to the policy of random selection by the student council. These students played in the band and were captains of the predominantly white sports teams. They studied in study halls, took calculus and advanced placement in biology, and sought the most challenging teachers. Not activists or change agents, they criticized the Protesters as "freaks" for not getting involved in traditional school activities. They were concerned about the "wall-to-wall garbage" of litter, paper bags, and cups that spilled out of the lunchroom and down the halls. Generally supportive of school rules, they, like the other students, skipped classes that bored them.

An unused, half-painted student lounge symbolized the lack of communication among student groups at Hamilton. After student activists argued that students, like teachers, had the right to a lounge, Cunneen turned over a storage room on the proviso that it be cleaned and refurbished. After a few weeks of activity the room languished for months with partially painted walls and broken armchairs. The lounge project was abandoned when no further students joined in. There was no common ground at Hamilton High.

Traditional teachers felt Cunneen's agreement that students had equal right to a lounge was another bitter reminder of their lost status. A teacher who came to Hamilton in 1976 and who believed that Cunneen had "given the store away" recalled one of the first announcements he heard Cunneen give:

> "Good People"—he always referred to students that way—"good people, we're going to have an assembly this afternoon and its going to be fun. After the bell I want you to get together with your friends and come on down to the auditorium and find any place to sit where you'd like. I want you to be with your friends and to enjoy yourself." Then more routinely, almost brusquely, "Teachers, your auditorium assignments are posted in the office." This was ass backwards, just the reverse of the way it ought to have been.

Although this individual came to Hamilton as an experienced teacher, he was unprepared for what he experienced on his first day of classes:

> The kids were off the walls. They were sitting on the tables, on top of the desks, on the radiators and the window seats . . . When I walked into the room one of the girls said, "Who's this turkey?" She really gave me a lot of lip and when I went to see one of the assistant principals he sort of tried to talk me out of it saying she was really a good kid and didn't mean it. So many came in late. You kept getting interrupted. They would come in fifteen minutes after the bell and you'd look out in the hallway and there would still be a hundred and fifty people out there . . . just milling around. Teachers would just stick to their rooms, lock their doors because it wouldn't be unusual for students roaming the halls to open your door five times during a period, look in, glance around, then shut the door and walk on with no explanation of why . . . It was a constant struggle. During this period I gave a lot of thought to quitting.

He saw that teachers had withdrawn and were unwilling to confront students. After the bell teachers might walk down the hall and tell a student to be in class, but "they wouldn't look the student in the eye, and they wouldn't look back to see if the student obeyed." Teachers had the feeling that they were outmatched physically and that if they complained nothing would be done about it. "We would have a discussion each year about the rules for study halls but there never was any roll call because [the lists] were never accurate and even if somebody was absent the penalty for skipping a study hall was to be told to go to another study hall."

An assistant principal who also came to the school in the mid-seventies saw at once that the adults had lost control because of a combination of many factors. He was particularly struck by the aggressive sense of legal rights mentioned earlier, of students who said, "You can't touch me, you can't push me out, you can't keep me from coming here"—which was not altogether true, although teachers were cowed by the statement and did not want to challenge students. Many of the young people had a subtle sense of their rights and acted on the presumption that they knew what was best and should have no interference in the exercise of their options. "So many times you would hear, 'I'm an individual; I can do what I want to do; I know what I got to do to pass,' and too many teachers bought that." With some exceptions, teachers began to avoid encounters or made only nominal attempts to win compliance. This inconsistency added to students' disrespect for adults, who on one occasion would threaten them with suspension and on another ignore the same activity.

Students skillfully played off one adult against another, just as they might inconsistent parents at home. In fact, a class we observed late in the decade gave a painful sense of students feeling abandoned by adults. In a health class, students discussed how they thought their parents had felt about the birth of their children. They believed the parents had resented having their freedom curtailed. Skepticism was expressed when a student said, "Well, my case is a little different. My parents told my brother and me that they were so happy to have us that they didn't mind giving up their freedom."[12] Several students whose parents had divorced revealed their hurt. The discussion was accusatory toward parents who students felt had relinquished their authority by their own inconsistencies and failures to live by their commitments. Adults are fallible and engaged in power struggles of their own, students argued, and hence have lost any claim to moral superiority. The right of an adult to enforce and impose rules of conduct appeared questionable, and the very nature of rules and norms was seen as arbitrary. Students wanted to decide these matters for themselves.

This view was actively reinforced by some of the teachers and staff, who no longer seemed to know what was right—or if they did, believed that they had no right to impose it. A Hamilton counselor, working with habitual drug users referred to her by the courts or other agencies, told us that she would not approach known drug users in the school:

> Let's face it. It's not a problem if there is no effect on the kid's performance. I mean, who are we to say what's right or wrong? A kid could always turn around and say to you, "How many of the faculty have an alcohol problem or a drinking problem? And yet . . . they continue to teach." They can point that out to you. So who are we to say what's right or wrong?

Here was the collapse of adult authority as a standard for children. Not only did this counselor express no moral authority, she actively concurred in the notion that adults in general deserve no authority because *some* adults have a drinking problem. Pressed about her personal attitude toward drugs, the counselor took no stand, saying that if she said she approved of drug use, the administration would fire her. On the other hand, she did not think she would be believable to the kids if she said she did not use drugs. It was up to the kids to decide. Her technical mentality argued, "Let's face it. It's not a problem if there is no effect on the kid's performance." Only the performance, the score, the end product mattered. She implicitly ruled out questions of character, of responsibility, of desirable conduct.

This view was becoming more widespread as the number and variety of specialists increased in this era. It was the stance of a neutral, facilitating professional who defined his or her job as helping students clarfy their options and make curricular and life choices. If Hamilton High had an unwritten slogan in the seventies, it was "Let the student decide." Let the student decide whether to use birth control, whether to smoke dope, whether to go to class. Our research late in the seventies confirmed what Clark had concluded early in the decade, that there were "no widely shared, positively motivated understandings . . . which influenced the nature of interaction [with] the students."[13] Adults fell back on a purely legal, technical view of their responsibilities, which for many boiled down to a responsibility to house students, to keep the peace, to avoid engagement or demands in the way of either moral or intellectual standards.

The school had become a social service center in which a variety of specialists often treated students as adult clients. Like many urban schools, the staff expanded by nearly a third to accommodate a range of new programs. Some of the academic programs employed reading specialists, teachers of English as a second language, audiovisual and media specialists, special teachers for the mentally or physically handicapped, and teacher aides. But the school also became the center for a variety of nonacademic programs. There were free breakfast and lunch programs for children on welfare, sex education programs, drug counseling, suicide prevention programs, medical advice and counseling for pregnant teenagers, an in-school nursery for children of students, and after-school child care.

Hamilton became more complex as state and local bureaucracies multiplied and new professionals came into the school. Not only was power now shared with the teachers' union, but the lines of authority from principal to staff were more ambiguous. The new specialists often felt more loyalty to professional groups outside the school. And the lines of authority tied to state and federal funding for special programs bypassed the principal. The drug counselor, for example, stressed that she did not fall within the usual chain of command: "Well, let me explain to you that I don't report to the school administration at all. I am directly linked up with a different agency outside the school itself." These kinds of shifts had enormous implications for leadership, for the task of creating a sense of shared expectations within the school. It was much more complex than a problem of wider span of control, for the increased numbers of specialized staff reflected the growth of separate professional cultures within the school. New roles were being shaped and new statuses were sought. Younger guidance counselors, trained in crisis intervention, no longer saw their roles as primarily academic advisers or as disciplinary aides to the principal. As therapists, they were likely to insist on the confidentiality with student clients that characterized psychotherapy with adults. Cunneen put it this way:

> The guidance became . . . involved in personal problems. You know, how do I handle sexual advances of my uncle or my friends . . . And it gets frustrating to me as an administrator when one of the counselors would come to me and say this girl is doing these things but I don't feel I should tell the parents because then I'll destroy my counselor-student relationship. It was hard to know where their loyalties should be because they were school employees; they weren't psychiatrists.[14]

The students' right to choose was most evident in the curriculum itself. Cunneen had abolished the tracking system and instituted a curriculum with many more electives and modular courses that met for only ten weeks. Of the eighteen credits required for graduation, only ten were specified. Hence nearly half a student's load could be drawn from electives that included such new courses as Parenting Today, Black English, Consumer Economics, How to Fix Your Bachelor Pad, TV Production, Fun with Words, Science Fiction, Science and Society, Cinema, Black Voices, Paramedics, and Scuba Diving. Asked to describe a typical student's program of the 1970s, a teacher replied, "I can't imagine what a typical curriculum looked like." Many younger teachers, eager to teach experimental courses they had experienced in college, embraced these broader options, as did a number of the veterans who welcomed relief from teaching required courses that students disliked. More faculty felt the tracking system was ineffective and many hoped discipline would improve with student choice.

Astonishingly, the tracking system was not abolished; instead, students now tracked themselves. This came about in two ways. The best students sought out the best teachers, asked what courses they would be teaching, and signed up for them. Students who wanted to avoid a demanding teacher would do so, and those who found themselves mistakenly in such a class were usually granted a transfer. Second, students avoided advanced math and science courses if their parents did not push them. When we compared the average number of years of math, science, and foreign language taken by both black and white students in 1967 and 1978, we found that tracking actually increased slightly under the elective system. The old tracking system was still in place in 1967, just before the outbreak of violence in the school. But Table 1 shows that while there was an increase in the total number of basic subjects taken by all students, the gap between black and white students expanded slightly. In 1967, whites took an average 3.75 years more of these basic subjects than did blacks—and a decade later, 3.96 years more.

The radical liberalization of the curriculum was at once an advantage and disadvantage. It revitalized some teachers, who created extraordinarily challenging courses for the 10 or 15 percent of the student body who chose them. For other teachers, courses such as Fun with Words or Cinema allowed them to spend congenial, undemanding time with their students. Our classroom observations confirmed Clark's earlier in the decade: "Fragmentation of academic experiences [produced] a sense of discontinuity of adult expectations during the day. Different teachers have different styles and expectations; they rarely share information about the same students so that they can develop a joint understanding about the student's interests, strengths and weaknesses."[15] The two courses just mentioned, Fun with Words and Cinema, could fulfill English requirements. Let us look in on four other courses offered by members of the English department in these years.[16]

Twenty-three students enrolled in Individualized Reading are today, as on most days, reading a novel of their choice. When finished, or if the teacher calls on them, they give an oral report on the book at

Table 1   Average years of foreign language, math, and science successfully completed by white students and black students in the Hamilton High graduating classes of 1967 and 1978. In 1967 N for whites was 43; for blacks, 35. In 1978 N for whites was 40; for blacks, 30.

Subject	Students	Average years of instruction completed by students in class of—	
		1967	1978
Foreign language	All	1.97	2.04
	Whites	2.60	2.64
	Blacks	1.20	1.23
	Black-white difference	1.40	1.41
Math	All	2.21	2.44
	Whites	2.85	3.01
	Blacks	1.43	1.68
	Black-white difference	1.42	1.33
Science	All	2.28	2.83
	Whites	2.70	3.35
	Blacks	1.77	2.13
	Black-white difference	0.93	1.22
Total	All	6.46	7.31
	Whites	8.15	9.00
	Blacks	4.40	5.04
	Black-white difference	3.75	3.96

Source: Random samples of student records for the years cited.

the teacher's desk. Then they choose another novel and return to their seat to continue silent reading.

Mr. Carnova has time before class to explain that his Search for Self course involves "lessons in communications and human nature" and says today's lesson is on decision-making. Texts on his shelf reveal the search-for-identity theme: *Man's Unfinished Journey, Perception, Encounters, Values in Literature.* Students enter after the bell and constantly interrupt roll call with comments and questions. "Are you telling us our grades yet?" He answers patiently, "Your grades will be on the report cards," to which a student replies, "Report cards are for parents." He completes the roll call and reminds the class that the words on the board are for a spelling test Friday. A student shouts, "Right on! Why don't you give us those work sheets on the words?" Another student, obviously mocking one of the teacher's frequent comments, chimes in: "Take you time on that vocabulary, Mr. Carnova," and a chorus of others join the fun: "Take your time on that spelling, Mr. Carnova . . . Take your time on that teaching, Mr. Carnova." He absorbs this good-naturedly, apparently enjoying the ruckus as much as they and calling it to a halt just short of pandemonium.

They are seated at octagonal tables in three groups, and he explains that each group will perform a skit portraying a moral dilemma. Following the enactment they will discuss their own decision if caught personally in that dilemma. Students half-listen and ask several times to have the assignment explained again, which is done. Then Carnova hands out the scripts. One skit portrays someone wrongly blamed for cheating, another points to the effect of cliquish behavior on the person who is left out. The students take about twenty minutes to read and act the skits. But when Carnova attempts to discuss what decision they would make in the enacted situation, students repeatedly stall by attemping to get the facts straight. They never discuss questions of judgment or alternative courses of action. Voting on which group acted best, each table noisily claims victory. For the remaining minutes Carnova passes out dittoed work sheets on decision-making, and the first exercise asks students to write a comment about William James's proposition that when you choose not to act, you are in fact choosing a course of action. One of the boys mutters, "It's a bunch of double-talk, that's what it is," but there is no discussion and the bell rings.

In another class the teacher is attempting to work out assignments for the book the students are supposed to be reading, while they ask "What'd ya get?" as papers are returned. She suggests that each row deal with a different chapter on successive days and wonders aloud which chapter they want to report on. One boy asks what if they "did not read it at all." Another supports him, "Yeah, how many are interested anyway?" She responds, "Well, you have no choice; you have to read it," which meets with the immediate retort from another: "Oh, you're wrong! We have a choice in everything we do!"

In the next period we enter Ms. Gresham's classroom. She is one of the most respected teachers in the school, and the one who protested about the way cheating was handled. She begins today, as every day, with a quick spelling and vocabulary test. Students settle down immediately and the test is completed and collected within seven minutes. Then she asks if anyone minds if she reads aloud from their papers, promising to conceal the writers' identities. "The idea is not to run you down but to give everyone an idea of what other people are writing, how they approach a poem, and the general criticism of the style and the approach." She reads and elicits comments on several papers, then asks students to assume they were grading the first three papers. "Would you accept this paper? Now if you were to rank the first and second, how would you do it? Would they be on a par? Do they sort of measure up to each other? Does one seem weaker, from what you've heard so far?" Picking up the third paper again, she asks, "What seems to be the most glaring flaw in this introduction?" "It's badly mixed up," a student calls out. When another adds, "As a reader you don't know exactly what this person wanted to tell you about," she explains why she agrees.

In this class each minute counts, and our notes run to nineteen typewritten pages. For the next thirty-five minutes the class discusses the three poems they have been asked to read: Gerard Manley Hopkins' "God's Grandeur," Wilfred Owen's "Arms and the Boy," and Andrew Marvell's "To His Coy Mistress." She takes them through Hopkins' poem line by line, examining imagery, phrase, and shades of meaning. Then they turn to Marvell's "Coy Mistress":

Ms. Gresham: Okay, down to business. The word "coy" in the title had a different connotation in the seventeenth century than it has today. Then it meant virginal, pure. And today, what does it mean? It means playing hard to get, and then, perhaps, giving in eventually. There has been a subtle change in connotation. Keep that in mind . . . Now in the first stanza you've got to remember that it begins with a big if. What is the general idea contained in the first part of the poem?

Student: Well, he praises and admires her.

Ms. Gresham: Yes, it's a relatively simple notion of a man admiring different parts of the body of a woman.

Student: It's almost flattery.

Ms. Gresham: Yes, that's the right word. It's sheer flattery. (On the blackboard she writes "1. Sheer flattery . . . *if*") All right. Now, the next stage of the poem turned around a little bit and the significant word is "but." What does "but" suggest over here?

Student: It's not true what was said before, or what was said previously. Now it's not true anymore.

Ms. Gresham: Yes, that's almost correct.—

> Time-winded chariot hurrying near;
> And yonder all before us lie
> Deserts of vast eternity.

What does this suggest to you?

(Many voices calling out at once, she strains to hear, points to students in turn.)

Student: It suggests great speed.

Student: Desert suggests dryness, emptiness.

Student: Time seems to be passing very fast.

Ms. Gresham: Yes, you've got the idea. There is great speed of the passage of time and, also, it suggests sterility, dryness, emptiness, as . you find in a desert. All right. Now the next couple of lines:

> Nor in thy marble vault

Vault, literally, is a grave and when the poet is talking about the beauty of his beloved being buried in a grave, you also hear him saying that she's not going to be so hot to look at any more. Do you agree?

Student: You're right, but it sounds awful.

Ms. Gresham: Awful? Yes, but true nonetheless. It's realistic. And then comes your favorite line, folks:

> Then worms shall try
> That long-preserved virginity
> And your quaint honor
> Turned to dust
> And into ashes all my lust.

These lines are among the most evoked, the most powerful images in English literature. Disgusting, perhaps, but very effective, don't you agree?

(Students engage in exaggerated shuddering and shivering motions and lots of sound effects to suggest worms munching.) All right. The word "quaint" here suggests old-fashioned in a prudy, disgusted sense. And now, the next two lines:

> The grave's a fine and private place
> But none, I think, do there embrace.

Am I just saying this sarcastically, or do you think it is meant to be sarcastic?

Student: Oh, it's meant to be sarcastic.

Ms. Gresham: Do you think it is true?

Student: Of course, because once you die you can't touch anybody.

Ms. Gresham: How many of you are familiar with syllogisms in mathematics?

Student: Oh, give us a break.

Student: We don't know what syllogisms are.

Student: Yes, we know.

Ms. Gresham: Okay, okay, okay. In mathematics, particularly in geometry, you have an arrangement where you start off saying if, if then, therefore. It's a logical progression set up and, then, a conclusion automatically follows. And that is exactly what the poet is resorting to here. You notice that the stanza begins with a "now . . . therefore."

Student: It'll be like proving a theorem.

Ms. Gresham: That's absolutely correct. Now let's look at this line:

> And while thy willing soul transpires

What does that suggest?

Student: It's a reminder that one is going to die eventually.

Ms. Gresham: That's right. You're dying with each breath, and this is what the poet tries to bring to the consciousness of the beloved. In the next line you have the word "sport." It suggests play. Now watch it! You have "amorous birds of prey / rather at once our time devour / than languish in his slow-chapped power." What do "birds of prey" suggest? That you're going to be gentle and slow and polite or courteous? Or, aggressive and forceful?

Student: Aggressive and forceful.

Ms. Gresham: That's good! You don't really get the picture of birds of prey, vultures, having a nice little dinner and using a napkin to daintily wipe the corners of their mouth. On the contrary. What would be the right word to express it?

Student: Horny.

Ms. Gresham: "Horny" is probably right. It certainly expresses one aspect of the feelings that are involved here but I don't really think for a college-style essay you'd want to use that word. So, what would be a more acceptable word, a better word to use. I'd suggest "lustful." Would that be all right? Would that be acceptable to the class?

Student: Okay, if you insist. "Lustful" will do.

Ms. Gresham: The word "languish" in the last line here suggests a southern belle, all dressed up and walking slowly, gracefully. And it's just the opposite that the poet has offered his beloved . . .

All right. Now we are at the final conclusion. The word "ball" here suggests to me at least, something like a string that's all coiled up and has a lot of vitality and energy. Again it brings to mind the lust that the poet has within him. The next line, more or less, confirms this. I'm sure you'll agree. Just pay attention:

> And tear our pleasures with rough strife
> Through the iron gates of life.

Notice the connection between "tear" and "iron gates." Tearing doesn't sound at all like a gentle act or a gentle emotion. In fact, it's just the opposite. The force that the beating world is tearing through iron suggests a lot of energy and force. Now, for the last two lines:

> Thus, though we cannot make our sun
> Stand still, yet we will make him run.

What, really, does this mean?

Student: That time can't stand still and we must make the most of it while we have it.

Ms. Gresham: Yes, in a nut shell, that's it.

A hush fell over the class as the poem ended. Then Ms. Gresham led the students through a discussion of the broad themes of the poem, and the use of imagery and hyperbole. She returned to consideration of its propositional structure and drew out the "if . . . but" thesis that had seduced them with flattery in the first stanza and then undercut it with harsh and realistic imagery. Students felt out these ideas, argued fine points, were engaged, excited. In the last minutes she reminded them of their homework assignment, which was to prepare a careful analysis of the imagery in three stanzas, one of which they would be asked to write a paragraph about in a quiz the next day. When the bell rang, some students hung back to ask questions while others went out the door buzzing.

This, too, was Hamilton High. Some students, often with concerned parents, worked with Ms. Gresham. Others sat in Cinema, Fun with Words, or Search for Self. Recalling those days, a male English teacher said parents began to complain that students could fulfill their English requirements by choosing a variety of courses in which they learned little grammar, seldom wrote a paragraph, and only occasionally read literature. This assumed that they went to class. Under Cunneen, students were aware that "they had three cuts, but they took forty-five."

This awareness grew. Parents saw that the halls were well populated during class hours. A member of the school board discovered that his daughter had cut eighty-five classes in one term at Hamilton and that he had never been notified. At commencement some students hooted and rolled across the stage on skateboards to receive their diplomas. Enrollment at Hamilton declined from 1,100 students to 831 and the school board debated whether a proposed $6 million addition to the school should be canceled. Some students in the Hamilton district were paying tuition to attend public school in the suburbs.[17] A turning point had been reached, and it led to Cunneen's ouster at the end of the 1977 school year.

Joseph Kielecki, principal of one of the junior highs that fed into Hamilton, replaced Cunneen that August. Kielecki, born in one of Median's old Polish neighborhoods, was a twenty-year veteran who had joined the school system as a math teacher after he left the seminary. Unlike Cunneen, he had no doctorate; but he had a reputation as a fighter, a shouter with heart, who had helped restore order and bring two other schools through a period of crisis. "I was known as a voice. I'd stand outside the office on the first floor and I could yell and they'd hear me all throughout the building . . . The kids knew when I was upset." He respected Cunneen's intelligence and his attempt to renew the curriculum. But he felt he walked into a school in which discipline was completely absent. Kielecki thought this was especially true where blacks were concerned, since Cunneen "would nail the white kid to the wall, but if it was a black kid from what I hear he wouldn't. He would look the other way." However, Kielecki also saw that teachers bore much of the responsibility for the chaos. Many were only too glad to leave the blacks loafing in the halls rather than challenging them in the classroom, and they were negligent in reporting cuts because they did not want disruptive students in their classes.

That summer Kielecki invited about twenty Hamilton teachers to his home to ask them what should be done. They soon reached consensus on three things: restore a uniform code of discipline that would treat black and white alike, back teachers up in the classrooms and hallways, and get rid of the quarter-courses. It had become obvious to the teachers that while some good courses had been created, the curriculum as a whole was too soft. Weeks of instruction were lost in having four sign-up and start-up periods during the year. Moreover, said Kielecki, "some of the kids were smart and got there early and got the best teachers; every year they got the best teachers."

On their return to school that fall, students found that quarter-courses had been eliminated, no cuts were allowed, and no hats could be worn in classes. They met the "shouter", who stood in the hall, confiscating radios and skateboards. During Kielecki's tenure, the suspension rate was nearly triple Cunneen's record. Between 1971 and 1973, while tension was still high, Cunneen had suspended fewer than 70 pupils a year. In Kielecki's first year on the job, he handed out 351 suspensions.[18] The cop was back on the beat, deeply resented by students. The showdown came the following June when thirty seniors who had overcut and had failed courses were not allowed to participate in the graduation ceremonies. (Cunneen had allowed all students to walk across the stage and have their names announced, even if they had not completed the requirements for graduation.) Students protested, and the local television station recorded their threats to disrupt commencement ceremonies. But Kielecki held his ground. Some teachers resented his loud-mouthed style as much as the students, but most breathed more easily when he did not cave in.

Kielecki agreed with some of Cunneen's initiatives. Like his predecessor, he enhanced programs in painting, dance, sculpture, and theater. During Kielecki's tenure completion of the long-delayed new wing provided space for a gymnasium, pottery classes, art studios, and a swimming pool. In 1978 the arts and theater programs caused Hamilton to be declared a magnet high school, open to all students in the city. By the end of the decade the first real racial integration was beginning to occur among students who formed a lively theater company. It was now possible to hold dances and plays, which had been suspended for years.

Discipline, however, was not restored overnight. I spent a day with Kielecki in the spring of 1979, a good part of which involved keeping up with him as he toured the halls. Students, though not as many as previously, still loitered in the T where two long halls intersected. Kielecki waded in, hollering, telling them to get to class, threatening to suspend them if they did not. He would grab a student who did not stop when he called out, sometimes giving chase. When he appeared, teachers would come out to tell students to get to class. One suspected that once he was gone, these students would be back and teachers would probably ignore them, believing that the paid aides should attend to such hall-clearing functions unless the students were particularly obnoxious. There was a surly "We'll do it in our own sweet way" kind of compliance on the part of many students, but less and less outright refusal.

In the community, parents were ambivalent about Kielecki's barking, confrontational style. But the perception grew that Hamilton High was settling down, that it was "safe" again. Police cars no longer cluttered the front drive on a regular basis. And real estate prices turned slightly upward, encouraging a few teachers to buy houses in the neighborhood before prices got too steep.

CHAPTER FOUR

The Second Transformation
1980-1985

Racism is gone. There has been a tremendous change. It's
wonderful.

—A Hamilton High teacher, 1985

I f the first transformation of Hamilton High was brought about by
racial desegregation and deconstruction of the traditional authority
structure of the school, the second resulted in part from the enrollment
of two new groups, Asians and disabled students. The rapid maturation
of the mainstreaming movement—which aimed to appropriately place
disabled students in "normal" schools and classrooms—brought a wide
range of new students to Hamilton. Some were autistic, others were
severely mentally retarded. Asians, including a sizable number of Cam-
bodians, accounted for about 7 percent of the enrollment by the early
1980s. There were now five teachers of English as a Second Language
(ESL) and eleven teachers of disabled students. The dislocation caused
by the new students, and by the programs and personnel required to
serve them, was not marked by the violent upheavals of the racial
revolution; but the demands on teachers and students were in some
ways as great.

The Mainstreaming Experience

The stream of disabled students grew slowly in the early 1970s; by
1976 there were about thirty, most of them with conventional physical
handicaps. But by 1980, ninety-three of Hamilton's one thousand
seventy students were disabled: mentally retarded, emotionally disturbed, learning disabled, and multiply handicapped. The school was
being pushed to add a class of autistic students, which would include

some individuals who had spent most of their lives in institutions and some of whom daily returned to group homes or to the Median Institute for the Disabled. Hamilton's principal, Joseph Kielecki, responded to the external mandates and parental pressures, frankly admitting that the new programs served his needs, too: "I'll be honest. Everyone has the right to education, but let's face the other reasons. This high school has an unfavorable racial balance and declining enrollment. To put it bluntly, I need bodies." Yet he was beginning to feel that the school's resources were stretched to the limit and was reluctant to accept the autistic class.

> I just can't handle it with all the pressure I'm under now. We have three EMR [Educable Mentally Retarded] programs and Laura's severely emotionally disturbed class and then the LD [Learning Disabled] and the resource room. I want to start good programs, programs that can work, that can bring the kids together with other kids. The district asks you to take kids and they give you a special ed teacher and nothing else. Hell, if you keep taking classes, that's an additional load on the regular teachers. These handicapped kids, if they're in regular classes, have to be with regular teachers but they don't get any support. The central office doesn't realize that it takes a hell of a lot more resources than just the special ed teacher to run a special ed program in a high school.

In the process of decentralizing special education, the district placed more responsibility on the principal, but Kielecki felt unqualified to direct the program and wanted more help from the central office. He was unsure who was responsible for making mainstreaming work.

Teachers were similarly confused about how to share responsibility with special-education staff for the disabled pupils placed in their classrooms. Some were highly skeptical or frankly opposed to the program, saying in private that schools were not set up to accommodate such individuals. It was too burdensome to have children in school who could not control their bowels. Even those teachers who were inclined to give it a try had all the fears, growing out of ignorance and self-doubt, that parents often have in the early stages of the discovery of a child's malady. Helen Featherstone has described these so movingly: fears that one couldn't cope, that one didn't have enough to give, or even that one could not empathize with a child deformed in certain ways.[1]

In the fall of 1981 Kielecki relented and a class of autistic children was added to the roster at Hamilton. The *Median Herald* ran a story about the class, focusing on a thirteen-year-old who did not speak and had never carried a tray in a cafeteria before:

> Teachers and students at the school are overcoming fears of handicapped people. In Hamilton's classrooms, the students are learning practical skills: how to dress and take showers, and to perform small tasks that may lead to employment in sheltered workshops. Just the idea of going to the bathroom by yourself or learning how to use a screwdriver is new for many of these students . . . Most will never be totally independent. They will probably stay at Hamilton until they are twenty-one.[2]

In the confusion of the early days, disabled students would sometimes be assigned to regular classes for part of the day without the teachers being informed of their special needs. A teacher might wonder about a student rocking in his seat in a compulsive way, or a student who approached a drinking fountain and grew agitated, not knowing how to get the water. Another teacher might face a sudden outburst from an emotionally disturbed girl who was asked to begin a new activity before she had completed a prior task.

Students initially treated some of the new arrivals as freaks, literally parting and making an aisle for them as they made their way down the hall. Philip Ferguson, a researcher who studied the advent of mainstreaming at Hamilton, noted that cruelty and derision were not uncommon then, with a student screaming, "EEK, he touched me," or mocking those with deformities by imitating their speech or walk. A student who was ashamed of the reaction of her peers told Ferguson: "It's the retarded kids who really get brutalized. There's one girl who is always running around crying because they tease her, and another guy whom the students lead on without him knowing they were making fun of him."[3]

As time passed, Ferguson found that "problems [had] lessened" and his observations "revealed a school that seemed at least tolerant" of disabled students.[4] Yet two years after Ferguson's observations another student wrote, "Often I've seen people deliberately taunt students who are classified as mentally disturbed, aggravating them enough that they became upset and make a scene, which onlookers found to be quite humorous."[5] Many students responded with sympathy and a few volunteered to help, but not as part of any schoolwide effort. The students, even more than the teachers, were unprepared for mainstreaming. As in the case of desegregation, the school took no stance and provided no guiding philosophy. Mainstreaming was not talked about; it just happened.

The special-education teachers performed a range of tasks to help mainstream their disabled pupils. They acted as negotiators and advocates, convincing the teacher of a sophomore English class that a neurologically impaired child could participate with appropriate backup (such as being provided with audio tapes of poems she could not read). In many instances the special-education teachers accompanied pupils to class and served as aides and interpreters for the regular teachers. In other cases they met their students between periods to provide encouragement and support, to help with homework, or to clarify a difficult assignment. As one put it: "I try to help them as much as I can. Kind of support them. If they need help, I am here to give it to them. These are my kids."[6] They were responsible not only for teaching "living skills" but for preparing disabled pupils to pass the competency tests the state required for high school graduation. The basic skills developed in a class for neurologically impaired and learning-disabled pupils included "reading and ordering from a menu, restaurant language, computing sales tax, reading signs around town, reading bus schedules." Robert Bogdan visited the classroom the day Ms. Marge, and her assistant, Alfred, were teaching students how to decipher a newspaper advertisement.

> Ms. Marge began, "What we are going to do today is apartments. Remember how to look for apartments in the paper? We started it yesterday. Now open the book to ad #1." Most everyone had the booklet folded to that place. Ms. Marge and Alfred went around checking each one. "Look at ad #1. Does the apartment have a stove and a refrigerator?" Somebody said "No." A few people said "Yes." Ms. Marge said, "Who said no? It says right there that it has a stove and refrigerator. See, it's abbreviated. Remember the list of abbreviations at the start of the lesson. What about pets?" Everyone said in unison, "No pets." Ms. Marge continued, "Remember, don't guess. Look them up."

Mentally retarded pupils are awarded a modified diploma and are excused from the competency tests. Other handicapped students are expected to pass them, although learning-disabled pupils may use calculators and may be read the reading comprehension section. Emotionally disturbed and physically handicapped students take the test without such compensations. Ms. Marge is proud of students who have graduated but thinks the requirements are silly: "To me, it's just a joke . . . The state says this is a reading test and you can read it to them. They are saying pass them any way you want." Like many specialists, she believes that students need more of the things she teaches—in this case, living skills. Although she has worked hard to have two of her students, Louis and Philip, placed in regular English and social studies classes to accumulate the credits required for graduation, she is candid about her preferences: "Lou, he really needs living skills; he doesn't need Shakespeare. The same with Philip. *The Great Gatsby* and *Glass Menagerie*—he needs that like a hole in the head . . . Lou can't even take care of himself so he needs the French Revolution?"

About ten of Ms. Marge's thirteen students attended on any given day. Half spent the mornings in Hamilton classes and the afternoon in a vocational center for training as food-service workers, carpenters, beauticians, and auto mechanics. The others were in regular classes for most of the day. There were field trips too, not always uplifting ones. The disabled students may have felt stigmatized in school. "Sometimes I don't feel good about being here," said a student about her special-education class. "When I come here they ask, 'Why are you going in there? Are you dumb or something?' . . . These are my so-called friends but not my real friends. My real friends don't say anything." Self-conscious about being identified as a learning-disabled student, this young woman flunked the first semester of social studies rather than ask the teacher for individual help. Although embarrassed, she concluded, "I may not want to come but it is worse sitting at home watching television . . . That's too boring." The law that mandated mainstreaming handicapped students put them in a bind by requiring that they be labeled to qualify for special programs. A male student appreciated the help he received but was keenly aware of the onus of being labeled:

> The only problem is that they label you that, and that is the way you are going to be known for the rest of your life. When they look you up

in the school records, there it is. You are that way for life. It wouldn't help you get a job, people seeing that . . . Now, if after being labeled and you don't graduate, then you really got it bad.

An eighteen-year-old student with cerebral palsy who used a wheelchair was "petrified before I came here." She worried that other students would "ignore me or make fun of me" or that they would find out she couldn't read. Her fears were not confirmed—most people were nice despite the occasional affront.

> One kid told me that if I ran over him, he'd beat my white ass but that is not usual. I feel that I am finally in my school. I'm proud to be with my neighbors . . . Last year I was in a junior high [and] I only had one or two friends. I was only out of the resource class one or two classes, English and math. Here it is just like normal. All my classes are with everyone else. I'm treated like everybody else. I'm not different. They accept me for what I am, I guess.

Some teachers opposed to mainstreaming felt that disabled students were better served in specialized classes. A home economics teacher feared that academically inclined students stayed away from her class as special-education students were streamed into it. But even reluctant teachers tried to serve all students, and most regular teachers took pride in the accomplishments of special-education students, even if they complained of the burdens of making mainstreaming work. Teachers noticed the autistic girl who sang in the chorus and the boy with one leg who made the varsity swim team. Their acceptance of mainstreaming was predicated on the backup provided by the special-education teachers, however; teachers were not willing to do an individualized lesson plan for each disabled pupil. Mainstreaming is a good idea, said an eleventh-grade English teacher, but "only if you have somebody like Ms. Marge working with the teacher. It works as long as the disabled students are doing about the same thing or parallel things to the regular kids but to do a special plan in a special curriculum for each handicapped kid is more than a teacher can do." Speaking of a disabled student, Philip, she explained:

> We read plays and novels. Philip doesn't read them but Ms. Marge put them on tape and he could listen. She works hard to make sure that they have what they need to function in the regular class. Of course, he works at a different level. If the kids are doing sentences and dia-

graming, I'd have Philip write simple sentences. The nice thing is Ms. Marge finds out what we are doing. She will provide alternate material if he can't handle what is being done. One time I had them write a play. Philip wrote one. It wasn't up to the quality of the others but he did put it down. He gets his own vocabulary and spelling list from Ms. Marge.

This teacher was generally positive about the success of the mainstreaming program but was troubled about two pupils. One was mentally retarded and the other emotionally disturbed. "They are behavior problems. They don't come. They don't have any motivation. I could do without them." She complained that the special-education teacher responsible for them did not keep in touch with her the way Ms. Marge did. "I have to take time to chase her down and I don't have that kind of time."

Another English teacher was struggling with large classes and the varied needs of disabled pupils. She spoke of the conflicts experienced by many teachers at Hamilton High as they attempted to divine and then respond to the needs of mainstreamed pupils:

I find it frustrating. Some of them are on the fourth and third grade level. Some are doing well but it has to be geared for their level. One problem is always time. You don't have enough time. Now, Bob Porter, I don't know. He is so slow. He just doesn't get things done. With tests, I tell him just to hand it in as far as he got but he doesn't. I have to take him along on a free period and only then do I learn where he's at. Some of them are no problem. Jason Brown, he adjusts beautifully. He has other problems but he is somebody who will really benefit when you give him extra time, you feel like you are accomplishing something . . . Luca is a lovely boy. I have no problems with him . . . Ms. Marge's kids are eager to seek help; they want help but it is an awful struggle for them. They are not relaxed. You can see frustration written all over them. They want to do well but it is hard. Too bad we don't have graded classes. They'd feel better in there. They feel the pressure. Ken should be in a smaller, slower class. He is in with thirty-six. Bob, he is so frustrated. I ask him if he wants to go to Ms. Marge's room and he says no. Maybe they ought to be in their own special class. They have not been laughed at. They are accepted beautifully but I'm not sure whether I should call on them or not. I'd like to see the program continue. We weren't given any help or guidelines. Being experienced, I could handle it but an inexperienced teacher ought to get some preparation. We need explicit goals for each kid. We need a sense of what you should be shooting for.

Teachers in all departments were struggling to learn and understand a new lexicon of special-education language to feel their way with students whose disabilities they did not always understand, to develop cooperative relationships with the special-education support staff, and to integrate disabled students into the life of the classroom. When the special-education teachers first approached the regular staff about mainstreaming autistic students, the widespread ignorance about autism was revealed when the teachers asked, "Are they dangerous?" "Can they talk?" "What's wrong with them in the first place?" "Why do they look at their fingers?"[7] New regulations specified that disabled students could not be disciplined or suspended for misbehavior that was related to their disability. Teachers wondered how to know the difference, what to do when a disabled student "acted out." They universally complained that there was not enough time. Mainstreaming was one more huge task pushed through the teacher's door by a society that turned away and said, "You handle it." Philip's teacher spoke for many:

> My biggest complaint is the size of our classes. We are supposed to have a hundred and ten to a hundred and twenty-five students per day but we have more like a hundred and fifty. There is a lot of overload, especially on the English. Someone told me I should file a grievance but who has the time. In Philip's class there are thirty-three. I teach five classes. I'm the class advisor. I don't even have time to be with my husband and clean house.[8]

The special-education teachers may have had master's-level training, but some made shifts from other roles with only an additional graduate course or two, or after service as a resource-room teacher. They may have had little understanding of the technical terms psychologists use in labeling a child "neurologically impaired" or "emotionally disturbed." They were often skeptical of the official label, as when they would single out a pupil in a class of the learning disabled and say, "This child is *really* learning disabled." In the case of autism, theories of its causality were undergoing rapid change. One of the special-education teachers admitted he did not know much about autism when he started the program: "A lot of the literature had a lot of mixed information. Some professionals were saying they were emotionally disturbed; others were saying something else. It was a very confusing time for me."[9]

What marked nearly all the special-education teachers was their ideological commitment to mainstreaming. They were less concerned with the label than with closely observing a student to figure out what could be done. They regarded the formal IEP (Individual Educational Plan) required by federal mainstreaming legislation as a political document aimed at appeasing all parties. Their job was to figure out the "unofficial IEP"—what would work in a given context. This required making the right match between disabled pupil and regular classroom teacher, where that was possible, and providing the support to make it work. At times the task was herculean. A teacher spoke of his work with a fourteen-year-old autistic pupil, Danielle. She was now able to work quietly under close supervision. When Danielle had arrived from a state institution, "she was literally like a wild animal in a cage, constantly running around the room, screaming . . . No communication at all, no toileting skills, no eye contact, no eating skills." Or in referring to a male student, also fourteen, he explained:

> You have to understand what Josh's behavior used to be like. Three things characterized his acting out. He would take his shoes off, scratch, and spit. Now we have him down to just spitting. So there really has been a lot of progress. Sometimes he'll go two or three days straight without spitting at all.[10]

The special-education teachers devised behavior-modification programs to help some disabled students learn simple tasks. These often required repeated and painstaking work with individual students—in a few cases with the help of student volunteers. For example, two students who worked with Danielle learned how to communicate with her and eventually accompanied her to the pool, helping her into a bathing suit and, after her swim getting her dressed and back to class. As increasing numbers of disabled students entered Hamilton, including many with severe handicaps, more hands were needed to help them. Some of the special-education teachers met with the Median superintendent of schools to suggest that student volunteers were needed in the face of cutbacks of aides at the school. Even if additional paid aides could be provided, the teachers doubted that mainstreaming would be successful in the long run without the willing help of the students themselves. But student volunteers were the exception. There was no schoolwide expectation that students had any obligation to help or would derive any satisfaction from assisting those in need. Both Ferguson and Bogdan, in separate studies of mainstreaming, point in different ways to the absence of a strong positive ethos at Hamilton High. Bogdan concluded that "the kids may be in the school but how special education fits into Hamilton's philosophy, what it values and strives for, its way of doing things, has yet to be conceptualized."[11] Ferguson implied that mere tolerance of disabled students was not enough. He found "an organizational ambivalence at Hamilton toward its disabled students . . . There is no forming vision at Hamilton of how it wants to treat its handicapped students."[12]

The ESL Program

As the name implies, the English as a Second Language (ESL) program was aimed at students born abroad. About ninety were enrolled at Hamilton in 1984, of whom seventy-five were required to take ESL classes. Approximately two-thirds of these were Asians, mostly Vietnamese and Cambodian refugees. A sixteen-year-old girl wrote this story of her journey to Hamilton from South Vietnam:

> Before 1975 in my country there was a big war. The Communists came over South Vietnam. In 1975 they killed a lot of people who worked for the army in South Vietnam. My family had a lot of trouble. My father fled in the mountains, and he lived there for three years. Every week I had to bring food for him . . .
>
> In 1978 the Communists spoke in loudspeakers; they said they will give freedom for people who worked for the army before 1975. When we heard that, we were very happy, because my father came back home. The Communists started to hurt him and put him in jail. My mother cried all days and all nights . . . The Communists began to teach us how to grow rice, vegetables, and a lot of things. We started to work for them all day and when the dark came they wouldn't let us go home. The people began to get sick because all day long we worked outside. We didn't have time to rest.
>
> In 1979, we heard some place had people who lived in South Vietnam who made a boat and started to go to America. Then, my brothers thought I would like to do what they did . . .

We left our country May 5, 1980, on Sunday at 4:00 A.M. We went quietly. Only thirty-six people were in that boat. When we left, my parents said, "Goodbye and good luck." We were very sad when we said goodbye. We turned around and left. "Wait," my parents said. "You have to stay here and pray one time together before you leave us." We went back to pray together and then it was time to go. We couldn't stay. We had to say goodbye again. When we got in the boat, we heard the bell at the church ring.[13]

Like her, a number of the refugees came as "unaccompanied minors" and lived with foster parents or in group homes managed by the Catholic charities in Median. Not all of them had such dramatic tales to tell, but most of them found Hamilton a culture shock. They were stunned by pupils who wore shorts and treated their teachers with an informality that often bordered on rudeness. As an American student at Hamilton put it, "they were not used to romantic interludes in the hallways" and they had to "adjust from [attending] a regimented school to one that is far more lax and chaotic."[14] Nor did the Asian students admire American peers "who use dirty language, fool around, have no respect for teachers."[15] Because reverence for teachers and elders is a prominent feature of Asian cultures, a Vietnamese student was shocked by Americans who "go out and start swearing at teachers and everybody." He was also baffled when a Hamilton teacher wanted to pay him for the wooden nameplates the teacher had asked him to make. This would be unthinkable in the Asian context, where students were expected to make gifts to honor their teachers. And respect for the teacher sometimes put them at a disadvantage because they felt that to ask a teacher for help after class could be an occasion for loss of face—implying that either the student had not been attentive or the teacher had not taught well.

Teachers in the ESL program helped Asian students adjust. Like the teachers of the disabled students, they acted as advocates, counselors, and interpreters for their students. They taught survival skills— how to write one's name and address in English, or how to use the city bus system. They taught basic English, giving counsel and support while the students learned enough to enroll in regular classes at Hamilton (which might take several years). In the interim, students were taught a simplified curriculum in ESL classes.

ESL teachers were divided about this approach. Some believed that mainstreaming students into regular classes from the start was the best motivation to learn English and to reduce the dependence they believed the segregated classes fostered. Others thought a psychological buffer was necessary and pointed to the peer tutoring of one another by ESL students in their study hall. When the students left the ESL study hall for gym or the cafeteria, they moved in small groups and tended to talk in their native language. Teachers said this was not only a function of their desire for conversation and a reflection of Asian group-oriented patterns, but it also manifested a fear of hostility, which many of them had encountered.

In the early days of the program fights between Asians and blacks were common, peaking when the second wave of Cambodian and Vietnamese immigrants arrived. Unlike the first group, who tended to be the children of middle-class professionals and government workers, the second wave came from working-class and peasant families. Asian students themselves split in ways analogous to the earlier pattern of black integration. In 1983 a minor riot broke out between these later arrivals and blacks at Hamilton, who the Asians said had been taunting them. Thereafter the violence subsided, but some tension continued. Interviews with students revealed whites also rebuffed Asians, but the black game of the "dozens," in which group members trade escalating insults, may have heightened anger against blacks initially. Asian students reported that ridicule was common. Epithets such as "ching-chong" and "chink" came to be expected, and students were told to "speak English or go back where you came from."[16] An Asian girl at Hamilton wrote a poem about her experiences:

> They think that I'm stupid
> Because I don't talk much
> Because I don't play with them
> Because they don't like me
>
> Especially I am a Asian girl
> They will laugh of my figure
> They don't have any compassion
> And they always think that they're higher
>
> They don't understand that I'm different
> They don't understand my feelings
> If they were in my place
> What would happen to them?[17]

And how could the majority of the student body understand these first Asians that many had ever met? There were no required history courses to prepare them for Asian culture and little study of current events through the school year. Furthermore, as with desegregation and mainstreaming, the school had done nothing to sensitize the existing students to the background and needs of the newcomers.

As more Asian students left the ESL program and took their places in regular classes, tensions and misunderstandings abated. Some of the Asian students began to see the difference between kidding and insults. As they felt secure enough to leave the ESL table in the cafeteria and travel through the hallways apart from groups of fellow Asians, they started to be accepted as individuals. "They're all rock fans now," an ESL teacher said in 1985.[18] Noting their adoption of vulgar speech patterns, she regretted that Asian students were becoming quite so thoroughly Americanized. She fantasized about how wonderful it would have been if the cultural currents had been stronger in the other direction—if, for example, the Asians' reverence for teachers had influenced their American peers.

The Drug World

Disabled students and ESL students both participated in and were shaped by the culture of Hamilton High, and they also constituted distinct subcultures within it—with special teachers and patterns of socialization. As Herbert Blumer has pointed out, "People may be living side by side and yet be living in different worlds."[19] And although they were not per se part of an academic program, drug users at Hamilton formed another distinct subculture or world of interaction. In the middle and late 1970s "partying" (smoking marijuana) in the halls was occasionally overlooked. By the early 1980s Kielecki had put a stop to it, and drug users moved outside to the smokers' patch behind the school. Students felt that drugs were tolerated as long as they smoked there. One of the most comprehensive studies of adolescent drug use on record was carried out in the early 1980s at Hamilton High and at its feeder middle school by the sociologists Barry Glassner and Julia Loughlin.[20] They and their assistants spent months gaining the confidence of students and interviewed one hundred of them in depth. Some were known drug users and forty were students randomly selected from the Hamilton rolls.

National survey data show that drug use peaked in 1978 with 37 percent of high school seniors reporting that they had smoked marijuana in the previous month. This figure declined to 25 percent of seniors by 1984.[21] Although Glassner and Loughlin drew on a small sample, their survey shows that in the early 1980s 38 percent of Hamilton High students used drugs. Twenty percent of Hamilton's students were classified as light users, meaning that they smoked marijuana a few times a month on average. About 18 percent were heavy users, reporting that they used a variety of drugs regularly or smoked marijuana three or more times each week. Hence it appears that Hamilton's drug use ran ahead of the national average, although not precipitously so. About half the drug users in the sample were male and half female. Two-thirds were white, one-third black. None were Asian. About 60 percent identified their families as Protestant, 20 percent as Catholic, 7 percent as Jewish, and 13 percent as practicing no religion. About 70 percent lived with both parents. Users were less likely than nonusers to think of themselves as "good persons" and fewer of them had role models they admired. About three-fifths of the heavy drug users first tried marijuana before the age of thirteen; however, 90 percent of the light users did not experiment with it until after that age. About a fourth were first turned on by a member of the family—usually a brother or a sister, but sometimes a parent who had been part of the drug-experimenting 1960s counterculture. Sometimes drug use began in school, when someone in a group passed a "joint":

> I met this girl. We were sitting down just having a cigarette, because you're allowed to smoke out back, behind the doors. It's not a rule that you can't. You can. And this girl comes out, and we were just sitting by each other, and then she started introducing me to all of her friends, and then we just started partying. It was like I was one of the gang.

There were marked cleavages between users and other students: 90 percent of the heavy users reported that nearly all of their friends used drugs, whereas three-quarters of the nonusers said none of their friends used drugs. Hamilton students were aware of patterns of drug use among their peers and shared a language for placing students on a continuum from "burnouts" (the heaviest drug users) to "straights" (nonusers). For the heavy users especially, drugs become "the most readily available objects of value for exhibiting and sustaining communal relations." When asked to describe a typical day, two-thirds of the frequent users mentioned drug use.

Questioner: Describe a typical day to me.

Student: I get up, go downstairs, and eat, at about seven. Watch TV, smoke about half a pack of cigarettes. Go to school. Probably goof around all day.

Questioner: How do you get to school . . . ?

Student: Walk. Probably smoke the other half a pack a day walking to school. Um, I go to school, probably goof off. Skip school, go out and smoke some reefer, and then, and then go back in school. Goof around a little more . . .

Questioner: About how often would you say you smoke marijuana?

Student: Whenever I can.

Questioner: Which is about how often?

Student: Three times a day. Nah, nah, nah. Twice a day.

Only 12 percent of the light users, when asked this open-ended question, mentioned drug use. Their use was more likely to occur at a party outside school than during a "reefer break" behind the school on a daily basis. Drug taking for them was a social occasion—sharing, passing the joint, getting high together, laughing. Frequent users might ask others to cut classes with them: "If I could talk other people into skipping, and somebody had a car, we'd maybe go down to McDonald's and pick up some breakfast or something. Or, if nobody had a car, we'd go around back if anybody had any dope, and we'd get high." A Hamilton student who studied patterns of drug use found a "high incidence of class skipping" among heavy users. "It was not just a once in a while occurrence but very regular. The most common reasons for skipping were boredom or the feeling that the class was a waste of time." She found that boredom with school, sex, and complaints about teachers and administrators were dominant topics among these students, with drug use itself the leading topic:

People were constantly discussing who had packed how many bowls [of marijuana] the night before, what kind of trip they had, how many wine coolers it took to get drunk on any given night, and things like that were natural occurrences. No one considered drugs a particularly exciting thing to talk about. Someone might tell how they got high the night before the same way he would discuss going to a movie or eating dinner . . . The attitude was not I live to get high, but rather I enjoy getting high.[22]

Glassner and Loughlin concurred that some of the heavy drug users did not feel stimulated in school: "You know, you were just told, okay, memorize this, look it up in a book, memorize it, write it down, take notes, then you got a test . . . There was really nothing that I had to study hard for and, you know, papers I had to really research, or anything like that. And it was boring." Others admitted they had tuned out: "You just want to smoke it, get high, ha-ha, and that's about it. You sit there and listen to tunes. That's about it. You don't want to work or go to school or do your work." These individuals were more likely to have grandiose fantasies of the future unrelated to working hard in the present. Users said "they would be very rich, own magnificent houses and fancy cars, and be professional athletes, movie stars, business tycoons, and the like." Our student anthropologist found that the fantasies sometimes were built around drugs as well:

A couple of times J. and J. were discussing a tropical island in the Pacific Ocean. They said they would like to buy such an island, declare themselves King, and name it Partyland. On this island they would grow massive marijuana plants. Their house would be built of marijuana leaves and rolling papers, the joints would be lit with the jet plane. The reasoning being that if they had the money for an island they would obviously have the money for a private plane. J. mentioned that they would be so used to getting high it would take a whole sheet of acid to get him high.[23]

Nonusers avoided drugs because drugs "would mess up my system." They were likely to be engaged in schoolwork and to say they had other things to do: "I'm happy as I am. I don't need drugs to make me different." Or: "It's not really my idea of fun to sit around and get mellow. I'd rather work on my art or something like that, or read." Peer pressures mattered: " 'Cause the people I hang around with don't do things like that." Heavy users who were trying to taper off or give up drugs feared the cumulative effects of addiction, noticing that "pot kills brain cells; you start forgetting and getting stupider." Another concluded, "I don't like to get high; it makes people do stupid things, like Harriet and Ivy getting high and wanting to rob people and me being stupid right along with them." Some users said they always tried to "save enough brain" to do schoolwork, or felt they wouldn't have to quit until they got to college " 'cause then you get serious work. You have to use your brain a lot. Not just common sense." But others concluded they couldn't handle the academic load at Hamilton while using drugs:

> I screwed up a lot of my schoolwork doing a lot of this shit too . . . I used to go out before first period and get high with some people. That screwed me up. I didn't feel like doing any schoolwork all day. Just sat in class and slept or something, you know. It didn't do me any good. So I stopped doing that, and I started doing better in school.

Glassner and Loughlin found that heavy users whose parents were divorced usually sought to live with the more permissive parent, yet the students were moving away from their parents' more liberal views. They were emphatic that they did not want to raise their own children the way they had been raised, and especially did not want to allow their own children to get in trouble. "My kids won't be getting high, 'cause I won't allow it; my kid's health is more important." One regretted that his parents "didn't really teach us manners" or how to get along with others. Glassner and Loughlin determined that parental objections to drug use were taken seriously by users, even when the parents themselves were drug users. "When parents object to their children's drug use but use drugs themselves, they still contribute to shaping their children's behavior toward delaying experimentation." It did not matter whether parents were strict or permissive, their preferences were perceived as important to children. Even when drug users complained that their parents were getting too strict, "they also insist that the boundaries between parents and child should not be broken down too quickly." Students wanted their parents to exercise authority and "to restrict adult privileges even when they are ineffective in their efforts." Glassner and Loughlin reported this colloquy with a student:

> *Questioner:* Do you think it's wrong for parents to get high with kids?
> *Student:* Yeah.
> *Questioner:* How come?
> *Student:* Bad example. You know, it's like telling them, this is a good

thing, why don't you smoke pot with me. You know. Instead of having them steer you away from it. It's really not that good.

About a third of all the Hamilton High drug users interviewed by Glassner and Loughlin expressed a latent yearning for more guidance by adults. They would tell their own children to "do well in school, develop good manners, stay away from drugs, . . . behave, make money, be responsible and be moral." Drug users were not the only ones who wanted parental guidance. Strong support later developed in the student body for an organization that would solicit pledges against drunk driving from students and their parents. Nevertheless, most students continued to believe that pot smoking out back was permissible as long as the users behaved tolerably.

Changing of the Guard

A new principal, John Lotito, was appointed in 1982 when Kielecki's health began to fail. Like Kielecki, Lotito was a local product who had been a middle school principal and who had graduated from the same Catholic college in Median. Whereas Kielecki had arrived as an old-style top sergeant prepared to do battle, Lotito struck teachers as the good bureaucrat, a subdued middle manager who would continue the cleanup operation while paying more attention to the curriculum. Lotito wanted to bring a team approach to management of the school and to develop more consistency in discipline. "I view my job more like a general manager of an athletic team where I have to go through and make sure that everybody is doing their thing," he explained in an interview. In the 1970s he had been part of a team of three administrators assigned to take over another city high school following a period of racial unrest. He described a school similar to the Hamilton of that era, where "the students were just literally taking over the school. The administration was unable to say no . . . The kids would come in and say this is what we're going to do and just wear down the administration until they got their way."

In his first days at Hamilton, Lotito was pleasantly surprised to find that the school had settled down. Students were hanging out in the parking lot and the halls, but the school was improving. Some teachers were still reluctant to challenge students who were misbehaving. Senior staff would not confront a student unless they had a personal relationship with that student, nor enforce general norms. "At one point I had to have a faculty meeting to explain to them what my role as manager was and that I was not a glorified hall monitor." Lotito instituted a policy of "sweeps," whereby all teachers were to lock their doors one minute after the regular class bell. Then he and the assistant principals would sweep through the corridors, rounding up students who were not in class. Initially, their names were taken and they were sent back to class; but this angered the teachers, as students filtered into classes even later than usual. So students were detained for a period. It got so that whenever students saw Lotito out in the halls with his clipboard, they would begin to chant "sweep, sweep" and run for their classrooms.

Although Lotito recognized that the Asians were experiencing some tensions, what was astonishing was that the racial hostilities between whites and blacks had dissolved. The changes in the school paralleled the changes in the community. Whites no longer fled, real estate prices rose steadily, and a new residential stability was reflected in the formation of a biracial neighborhood association. Ten years earlier white homeowners feared to speak to black youths who smashed soft-drink bottles in the streets, and they stayed away from a local super-market where black teenagers congregated. Now blacks and whites cooperated in a neighborhood crime watch and sponsored field days that drew parents and children of both races. The parents' association began a People Enrichment Program, which drew adults to the school for evening classes in swimming, the use of computers, and a dozen other subjects. In the fall and spring more than a hundred parents and children turned out for monthly Sunday morning runs followed by a pancake breakfast at the school.

Inside the school, the ease and playfulness between blacks and whites was remarkable. Laughter had returned. A white student entering a dimly lighted locker room could call out to a black friend, "Smile, Jesse, so I can see you." Classroom seating patterns were more mixed than those in the cafeteria, but the injunction against crossing racial boundaries was no longer in force. Some tables were either all white or all black, but four or five in each lunch period were mixed. An anthropology student who analyzed seating patterns in the cafeteria produced a typology of the subcultures in the school based on student maps of seating preferences they had observed.[24] These categories emerged (the alternate names applied to each subgroup are given in parentheses):

Black
White
Black and white (mixed)
Preps (preppies, senior popular people, haughty people, rich, cool seniors)
Druggies (burnouts, outcasts, people of all grades who play guitar or
    drums, smoke pot, drink, and are violent)
Brains (geeks, weirdos, very intelligent seniors, honor society, smart peo-
    ple, ultra intelligent, computer people)
Losers (people without a group, loners, underclass misfits)
Breakers (break dancers)
Home boys (downtown people, south side, the boys, poor blacks)
Theater people (chorus, dance, artistic types)
ESL (foreign kids, Asians, Koreans, Chinese, Japanese, Latin American,
    Hispanics, Spanish speaking)
Poor whites
Special ed (autistic, retards, wheelchairs, handicapped, "slow people—not
    retarded but not right")
Jocks (athletes)

Like racial groups, the sexes sometimes segregated themselves and sometimes came together. The "home boys," poor black students whose families came from the rural South, who wore baseball caps at cocky angles and T-shirts cut off under the armpits to expose skin and muscle, kept to themselves—as did the "breakers," who might wear studded wristbands and even gloves in the manner of Michael Jackson. Middle-class blacks were more likely to cross racial lines. The labels reveal a strong awareness of class identities, although theater people, special ed, jocks, and brains were especially likely to be racially and socially inclusive. Some middle-class and upper-class whites imitated the home boys' cutoffs or chanted their black rap music. Interracial dating was infrequent, but not so rare as to draw special comment; half a dozen interracial couples at the senior prom were not unusual in the mid-1980s. In the 1982 yearbook five interracial couples were selected to represent the most versatile, artistic, athletic, best-looking, and class couple categories. The most talkative, best-dressed, best smile, and funniest were all black couples, and the friendliest, most intelligent, most musical, most unusual, "Mutt and Jeff," and most active were whites. Two of the four senior class officers were black, eight of the sixteen cheerleaders. Gospel choir, basketball, and the Booster Club were virtually all-black, whereas soccer and the science club were mostly white. Football, baseball, track, and lacrosse were mixed. "Racism is gone," said a teacher in 1985. "There has been a tremendous change. It's wonderful. The classes are absolutely mixed; the black kid is as good or bad a student on any given day as any white kid. The old distinctions—expecting a black kid to be a reading problem or a discipline problem—aren't there anymore." She also noted that "kids are willing to tell each other to shut up—and that goes across racial boundaries." Blacks and whites had learned to read each others' verbal and nonverbal language and to shift modes of speech and gesture accordingly. Coming out of a computer class, whites are entertaining black classmates as they read with comic skill a note that a black nicknamed Tron Dee has sent them on the computer:

> Tron Dee in the place to be once again. Because it ain't no thing but a chicken wing. Me and my home boys run this school and every body in it. The reason for this letter is because some of you softies have step out of line. And it is up to me and my boys to put you back in check. And to some of you soft hearted ducks who think you are bad please step forward. Because me and my boys haven't dogged no body in a long time. Now don't have Tron Dee come to no corny library again to waist my time warning you brothers . . . so you better cool it now all you soft ass punks.

These whites who could jive with black classmates would find it hard to imagine the fear that seized white students who heard such language fifteen years earlier.

Unlike the earlier cohort, who first met blacks face to face as high school adolescents, these white students had known black classmates since the earliest grades. A yearbook picture of the class of 1984 showed the students as third graders in a classroom that was one-third black. They had not all lived in the same neighborhood, but they had played soccer together since fifth grade and all gone to dances at middle school. The anthropology student who studied racial interaction in the cafeteria found that integrated seating patterns could be traced to friendships originating in grade school.

Three exogenous factors also played a role in achieving interracial harmony within the school. The first was the sharp change in the pattern of black in-migration. Whereas the proportion of blacks in the Median school system doubled in the 1950s and again in the 1960s, by the mid-1970s the flow of black migrants from the South had stopped and there was even a slight out-migration during the economic recession that occurred later in the decade. Hence, nervous whites who had begun to think that a predominantly black school system was inevitable saw the city public schools stabilize at about 33 percent black. Hamilton High reached a peak of 40 percent black in 1978, retreating to 35 percent by 1985.

The voluntary transfer program was the second factor. The original integration plan had sharply wrenched established patterns of association and resulted in some school closings, some forced mergers, and the redrawing of school boundary lines. There were forty-eight public schools in Median in 1964; thirty-two remained in 1985. Virtually all closings had occurred by the mid-1970s, when the voluntary transfer plan was firmly in place. Under it, white and black parents were allowed, within racial balance guidelines, to choose any school for their children. Blacks could escape the ghetto, and children of both races might be bused.

By 1985 nearly all schools had remained racially balanced for more than a decade. Of the thirty-two schools, only one was more than 90 percent white and two were more than 50 percent black. All four high schools were racially balanced, ranging between 24 and 37 percent black. Although developed to foster racial integration, both blacks and whites also used the transfer plan like a voucher system to choose programs or schools they preferred. Specific schools might appeal to parents because of special programs, perhaps a traditional philosophy, day care, or advanced science courses. Interviews with parents indicated their choices were strongly influenced as well by nonacademic criteria such as safety, perceived climate of the school, or the destination of the child's friends.[25] Thirty-seven percent of all pupils requested attendance at a school outside their neighborhood. A wide range of schools were chosen, and poor parents participated actively in the program. In one inner-city housing project children chose to attend more than a dozen different elementary schools throughout the city. The transfer plan contributed to stability within schools, in that a child did not have to change schools if his family moved. The academic progress of poor children, whose families tended to move more often, was not as frequently disrupted, nor did the child suffer the loss of friends. Finally, both blacks and whites had more confidence in the schools as educational budgets rose. During a period of stable enrollment in the first six years of the decade, the Median school budget increased 72 percent, while the inflation rate rose only 20 percent. The 18 percent loss of federal revenues in this period was more than compensated by a 40 percent increase in city school funds and an 82 percent rise in state aid.

Academic Performance and the Curriculum

The stability and improved financial climate contributed, in addition, to improvement in basic math and reading scores as measured by standardized tests administered to all pupils in the state at third-grade and sixth-grade levels. In Median these scores declined steadily during the years of racial turmoil. Sixty-six percent of Median pupils exceeded the state minimum in reading in 1969, a figure that dropped to a low of 54 percent in 1974. Math scores fell from 66 to 60 percent in the same period. Thereafter, through the remainder of the decade, achievement improved until reading scores returned to the levels before desegregation; math scores rose even higher, with 70 percent of all pupils exceeding the state minimum. The students with these improved sixth-grade scores graduated from Hamilton High in the years 1984 and 1985. There were no comparable tests given to all pupils at the high school level, but subject matter tests were administered to a majority of Hamilton sophomores by the State Department of Education. The results for 1976 and 1984 are compared in Table 2. In that decade, after the completion of desegregation, Hamilton students registered slight, statistically insignificant declines in English and math. The 1984 passing rate in English dropped three points from the 86 percent mark in 1976, and the math rate two points from the 67 percent registered then. Social studies dropped by ten points, but a larger proportion of students took the test in 1984, thereby skewing the results. Hence the sophomore data indicate that achievement was stable, although improvements at the high school level did not appear to keep pace with the foundation that had been laid in the elementary grades.

Table 2   State Department of Education subject matter tests for Hamilton High sophomores, 1976 and 1984.

	1976		1984	
Subject	Percent taking test	Percent passing	Percent taking test	Percent passing
Social studies	54 (N = 151)	83 (N = 125)	71 (N = 203)	73 (N = 148)
English	65 (N = 181)	86 (N = 156)	67 (N = 192)	83 (N = 159)
Math	58 (N = 161)	67 (N = 108)	55 (N = 143)	65 (N = 93)

Source: Hamilton High, basic educational data reports.

Scholastic Aptitude Test results show significant improvement in the same period, however. The mean total SAT for the school declined sharply from 934 in 1967 to 874 in 1978, but rose to 911 by 1985. Although this was 23 points below the level before desegregation, 911 represents a significant gain when one recalls that Hamilton enrolled a much higher proportion of poor blacks in 1985 than it did in 1967. The disaggregated scores, arrayed in Table 3 and graphed in Figure 1, show particularly strong gains for blacks in the latter period. The social composition of the school did not change significantly after 1978, and by 1985 the black SAT had increased by an average of 62 points, outpacing a white increase of 13 points. Blacks made their largest gains in mathematics, where whites declined. On the other hand, whereas white verbal scores declined slightly in the period 1967 to 1978, they jumped by nearly 30 points by 1985. It is almost as if whites lost speech during the years of racial upset but found a new voice, enriched by black idiom, in the later period.

The long view, therefore, shows that blacks initially suffered most from the dislocations that accompanied desegregation, although the subsequent improvement of blacks is probably underestimated because of the changes in the social-class composition of blacks. White students in 1985 actually outscored their peers of 1965 by an average of 27 points when verbal and math scores are combined, a result that was not known in Median. On the contrary, white parents generally as-

Table 3   Scholastic Aptitude Test score means for white students and black
students in the Hamilton High graduating classes of 1967, 1978, and
1985. In 1967 N for whites was 43; for blacks, 35. In 1978 N for whites
was 40; for blacks, 30. In 1985 N for whites was 52; for blacks, 50.

Portion of SAT	Students	Year		
		1967	1978	1985
Percent	All	61	67	75
taking SAT	Whites	74	83	88
	Blacks	48	50	62
Verbal score	All	452	422	440
	Whites	498	495	524
	Blacks	406	348	355
Math score	All	482	452	471
	Whites	536	553	537
	Blacks	428	350	405
Total score	All	934	874	911
	Whites	1,034	1,048	1,061
	Blacks	834	698	760

Source: Random samples of student records for the years cited.

sumed that although Hamilton High had rebounded, it was still far
below the levels achieved in the earlier period when Hamilton was
at the top of the city school system.

The most significant change in curriculum, mandated by the Median
school board in 1981, raised from eighteen to twenty-one the credits
required for graduation. Previously, students could elect eight of the
eighteen required credits. Under the new plan, fifteen of the twenty-
one courses were specified, including an additional year each of math,
science, and social studies. Besides physical education and health, all
students were required to take four years of English, four of social
studies, two years of math, and two of science. Of their six remaining
electives, at least three had to constitute a sequence in some subject.
Systematic testing in the early grades pinpointed children who needed
remedial instruction before they fell far behind. In response to complaints from black parents, planning of a student's high school course
of study was begun in middle school, so that more students entered
high school equipped to take college-preparatory courses. And, as a

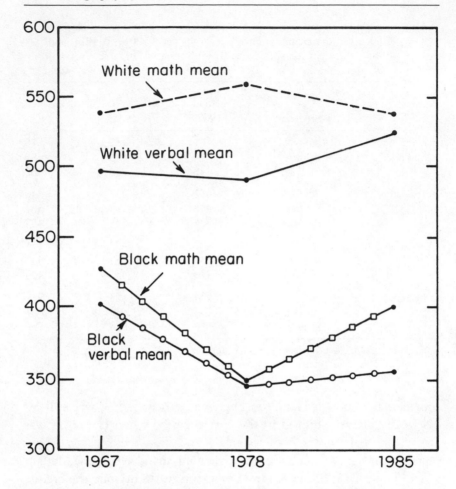

Figure 1   Scholastic Aptitude Test results for white students and black students in the Hamilton High graduating classes of 1967, 1978, and 1985. The scores were compiled from random samples of student records for the years cited.

check on the quality of early advising for black students, high school counselors were prodded to report registration in advanced academic courses by race.

Greater attention to academic achievement produced dramatic results. In 1976 only 68 students, mostly white, took the third year trigonometry course. Although the third year was not required in 1984, most students were then prepared for the advanced sequence and 139 students, including many blacks, enrolled. The mean math SAT score for blacks rose 55 points between 1978 and 1985. A comparison of the average years of math and science courses successfully completed, shown in Table 4 reveals that blacks were beginning to close the gap. We have seen that one of the ironies following the abolition of the old tracking system was that while black scores improved, the gap between blacks and whites actually increased under the expanded elective curriculum of the 1970s, as whites took more courses in math and science. White graduates took 2.5 years more of such courses than blacks by 1978, but the difference narrowed to 1.8 years by the class of 1985. Blacks graduated in 1985 with 5.7 years of math and science, almost double what they had completed in 1967.

In addition to raising the graduation standard, the school board adopted new rules in 1984 requiring students to maintain passing grades in five subjects if they wished to play on athletic teams or participate in extracurricular activities. These requirements made a difference.[26] But an experienced teacher insisted that the new achievements levels

Table 4   Average years of math and science successfully completed by white students and black students in the Hamilton High graduating classes of 1967, 1978, and 1985. In 1967 N for whites was 43; for blacks, 35. In 1978 N for whites was 40; for blacks, 30. In 1985 N for whites was 52; for blacks, 50.

Subject	Students	Average years completed by students in class of—		
		1967	1978	1985
Math	All	2.21	2.44	3.33
	Whites	2.85	3.01	3.90
	Blacks	1.43	1.68	2.83
	Black-white difference	1.42	1.33	1.07
Science	All	2.28	2.83	3.11
	Whites	2.70	3.35	3.62
	Blacks	1.77	2.13	2.91
	Black-white difference	0.93	1.22	0.71
Total	All	4.49	5.27	6.44
	Whites	5.55	6.36	7.52
	Blacks	3.20	3.81	5.74
	Black-white difference	2.35	2.55	1.78

Source: Random samples of student records for the years cited.

could be attributed also to a shift in the consciousness of black students, since average years of math and science completed by blacks exceeded requirements by 1985. During the early years of desegregation, when militant blacks drew a hard separatist line, they mocked studious blacks who did their homework like "whitey," the teacher recalled. He felt that the positive change in racial relations had brought about a shift in the willingness of blacks to be regarded as good students. "It was no longer a bad thing to be—you didn't lose your status or your 'rep' if you took the hard classes and did your homework." Teachers now expected to find some blacks among their best students. By the mid-1980s blacks appeared more frequently in the once all-white honor society, although they still constituted less than 10 percent of the membership.

Although teachers noticed the increased numbers of "good" black students in their classes, they had little awareness of the aggregate gains reported here. Hamilton, like many public schools, reeled on from year to year with little sense of its history and hence little pride in its corporate achievements. The reports published by the Median school system gave no indication of whether the achievement of a given school was better or worse than five years before. Within the school, staff had little time to gather or assess such data. Masses of records were sent "downtown" but no progress reports came back to the teachers. The data that were most meticulously assessed had to do with attendance, because state financial-aid formulas were based on average daily attendance. The most unambiguous directives from the central office concerned prevention of dropout. The best teachers complained privately that they were lectured about the need to keep pupils in school and were warned against failing pupils because failure led to dropout. Their perception was that insufficient attention was paid to challenging students to higher levels of achievement, especially the broad mass of average pupils. The system failed to reward adequately the able majority of teachers who deserved most of the credit for the gains reported here, at the same time that it tolerated low levels of performance—at times shamefully low—by other teachers.

In this respect Hamilton High resembled the world described by Arthur Powell and his colleagues in *The Shopping Mall High School*. [27] Highly motivated students took advanced placement courses and sought demanding teachers. Disabled students and those with special needs were given close attention in small classes. But those in the broad middle—both black and white—often slid by, even though enrolled in the college-preparatory curriculum. More than a few classes fit the flaccid picture drawn by an anthropology student of "a study hall with a teacher in it." The teacher arrived late, gave the students make-work assignments, and left them free to socialize while she corrected papers to hand back in her next class. "As students finish their busy work, they start to talk to friends or walk toward the door to speak to students in the halls, just arriving at school. 'If you don't return to your seat, I'll take ten points off your grade,' she says. The students scoff at this. They move away and await the end of class when everyone masses at the door to leave."[28]

A Negotiated Reality

The increased graduation requirements at Hamilton High had a positive effect in limiting the worst abuses of the elective curriculum. But legislating more requirements or extending the school day would not affect the classroom reality just described. It could make matters worse, forcing more teachers into such postures as a defense against overwork and inadequate time for class preparation. Furthermore, those who propose new requirements should be aware of the ways that students skillfully breach them as they negotiate their real curriculum. Despite initial class assignment by computer, many students not only pick their courses and teachers by negotiating with counselors, but to some extent select each day's menu of classes to suit their mood. This was brought home to me in my first week of teaching at Hamilton High when I was greeted before class by two students who wanted to know what I was doing that day. After I explained that we would be discussing an article by Colin Turnbull, they asked to be excused to go to chorus. Were they giving a concert? No, it was just chorus practice. What was the rule governing such things? They explained that if the classroom teacher said OK it was OK, and that they often were granted such permissions. I let them go, later chiding myself for discounting the value of my own teaching so readily. I made plain the next day that I would not do so again. But I learned that teachers who "didn't have much going on" that day commonly excused students. In many cases school policy made it easy for students to simply duck out. An English teacher who was concerned about frequent absences found that in one month students could be legitimately excused from class on seventeen teaching days for everything from senior pictures to play practice. "Whatever happened to *after-school* activities?" she asked.

Such negotiations were usually amiable, however, compared to the harsh adversarial tone that characterized relations with students in the early 1970s. A teacher in 1985 said, "I now feel I've died and gone to heaven." The imbalance had been addressed in several ways. In a school that had achieved a stable pattern of racial integration, teachers no longer feared they would automatically lose a legal challenge. "Black students know that if they misbehave, no civil rights lawyer is going to be in here defending them," said a black teacher. The children's rights movement had ebbed; teachers felt students were less belligerent. The teachers' union also served notice that it would support countersuits against those who falsely accused teachers of abusing students.[29] The trend toward "emancipation" of high school students was being countered by new regulations redefining the boundaries of adulthood, such as a state law raising the drinking age from eighteen to twenty-one. Hamilton High students had not returned to the respectful and obedient mode of the 1950s and early 1960s, but they were no longer psychologically in charge, either. The revolt was over. An informal equality prevailed and was evident in the interpersonal ease between teachers and pupils. There was more affection, even hugging, and a great deal of playful banter.

For students, equality meant that no adult's authority was taken for granted. It was continually, although amicably, tested. Teachers were not to get uppity "or exhibit a holier than thou attitude," as one student put it.[30] Teachers should express a personal concern about student problems but should back down if the students felt their privacy was invaded. Students wanted teachers to be there for them, but on their terms. They assumed that virtually any item was negotiable. The administration, in order to maximize attendance and keep the peace, also tended to negotiate with students and lower demands to keep everyone happy. Direct adult authority was seldom exercised to correct students or impose a public standard. Assemblies often degenerated into catcalls and semiobscene behavior while teachers watched silently. Trash littered the hallway outside the cafeteria, but it was a rare teacher who suggested a student pick up a milk carton he or she had thrown on the floor. An anthropology student who compared the cafeteria to an "instant village" concluded that "in this village there was no altruism demonstrated, although there were plenty of opportunities. No villagers helped a handicapped boy with his tray. No one stopped one boy from terrorizing another. No one helped when a boy spilled his lunch tray all over the counter. And no one, except the paid workers, even tried to explain the food procedures to the foreign-born students."[31]

Another student who examined the norm of honesty at Hamilton High concluded that cheating in the mid-1980s was widespread and that the best students cheated most because grades mattered more to them and few adults seemed to care whether or not they cheated. In a sense, their behavior was rational. "Seemingly unobserved deceit and outright dishonesty are an integral part of the experience of being a student," she wrote. "It is common knowledge that students forge excuses, copy homework, cheat on tests, skip classes, and regularly lie to staff members . . . This . . . was related to the atmosphere which does virtually nothing to discourage it."[32] In a class discussion, captured on videotape, the students were asked to raise their hands if they agreed with the report. Nearly every hand went up. When queried whether they had been in a class where they knew that the teacher was aware that cheating was going on but turned a blind eye to it, about a fourth raised their hands. As the discussion continued, several students expressed anger toward adults in the school who did not take a stronger stand against cheating.

An orange folder distributed to students at the beginning of each school year was written in legalistic prose. It specified those things that were prohibited, such as gambling, stealing, and other "unlawful acts." But it said almost nothing about a student's obligations beyond observing the law. It did not ask students to improve what they found, to extend a hand to others, to aspire to any ideals or worthy traditions. As noted by Clark in the early seventies and Acharya, Ferguson, and Bogdan in the early eighties, there was no ideal that captured the heart and motivated students to do their best. It was a bureaucratic document that specified the minimum. Instead of implanting a strong positive ethos, Hamilton High "taught them how to play the system and see what you could get away with," said a widely admired teacher. "If you never communicate expectations to students, and you never give them a chance to practice them, you aren't going to have much of a community." Teachers also felt the absence of a positive ethos and the kind of support a solid community provides. Recalling the troubled fate of a younger colleague in her department, a veteran reflected sorrowfully on the fact that everyone, herself included, "had turned their backs" when the novice could have been saved with help. Then, her voice turning bitter, she added: "This faculty is characterized by an attitude of 'you leave me alone and I'll leave you alone and maybe if I find out that you're dying of cancer I might talk to you.' There is absolutely no support system to help you become a better person or a better teacher."

Good communities are characterized by rituals and celebrations that underscore communal values. The rituals at Hamilton High celebrated individuality and freedom. During senior year, despite some opposition from the administration, students celebrated "skip day," when most took an illegal holiday. Skip day capped a series of days in which students came to school in outlandish costumes, including "pajama day" and "beach day." Another tradition at Hamilton High was the sending of singing telegrams on Valentine's Day. Occasionally one went to a teacher, but for the most part the greetings went from one student to another. There were almost no celebrations of community. Pep rallies were poorly attended. Assemblies were rare. On the day following the death of a widely admired student during a school field trip, students were encouraged to talk separately to counselors and were allowed to go home if they wished. Individualized therapeutic encounters were the standard response on such occasions, reflecting the loss of public speech capable of addressing virtues within the school setting. Life at Hamilton was life without heroes—not for lack of heroes but for lack of celebrating them. In the course of our research, we came across the story of a black Hamilton sophomore who lost his life going to the aid of a woman who was being harassed by several men. Hamilton students in 1985, only a few years after the event, know nothing of this student. Nor are Hamilton teachers who played heroic roles during the years of racial turmoil enshrined in student memory. Like many teachers, Hamilton students have very little sense of their own often quite stirring history.

The Student View

The culture of Hamilton High from the students' point of view was revealed in an anthropology class. After reading Sara Lawrence Light-foot's penetrating portrait of St. Paul's, an elite boarding school in Concord, New Hampshire,[33] the Hamilton students wrote essays describing what it would be like to change places with a St. Paul's sophomore. Hamilton students vigorously defended their diversity, freedom, and tolerance. In moving to St. Paul's, they expected to experience a constriction, "a narrower perception of what things are socially acceptable."[34] A major benefit of attending Hamilton was to "get a taste of what other people of different racial, ethnic, and economic backgrounds are like," whereas St. Paul's "seems so isolated from the true life one shall encounter after graduation." Moreover, Hamilton as an institution "attempts to meet the needs of a diverse student body—to help foreign students to become more easily socialized in ESL classes" and to offer special classes for autistic students. They feared becoming like a St. Paul's student who "has probably internalized to some degree the idea that his ways of thinking are superior, merely because he has not had much contact with those of different backgrounds and is thus unable to understand others' views." Hamilton students are "less arrogant" because the school is "less selective." They recognized that blacks (about 7 percent) and some poor students on scholarship attended St. Paul's, but doubted that this provided a "real world" experience compared to Hamilton, which was nearly half minority.

Students also celebrated the freedom they enjoyed at Hamilton. Although they admired much about both the morals and the morale at St. Paul's, some said they resented attempts by Hamilton faculty "to pry into my personal life or to interfere." Another, picking up on a popular lyric, noted "we are able to speak our peace [sic] and say what we have to say in a matter. We don't have a special tradition because the times are always changing." Students in the anthropology class had discussed the meanings of education, socialization, and indoctrination. Some saw dangers of indoctrination in attending a school like St. Paul's because it "blindly follows ritual" and faculty do not "have to give reasons [for what's demanded of students] other than to say it's the tradition." At St. Paul's I would feel "my independence stifled . . . not really given opportunity for healthy rebellion and test-ing." Said another, "I may even become bored by the conformity of my peers." One of the leaders in the class wrote that she would "miss the freedom to question the authority of the rector, after having been allowed to complain to the principal at Hamilton." A girl who had transferred to Hamilton from a private school praised the "great free-dom to meet many different kinds of people and to choose an individual route concerning friends, opinions, activities, and studies."

Yet the Hamilton students felt "there are many advantages to a close-knit community like St. Paul's that may be worth sacrificing a bit of freedom for." They deplored the lack of respect, absence of caring, and hostility that they felt characterized life at Hamilton. The St. Paul's transfer would be "shocked" and "taken aback" by life at Hamilton. Virtually every student essay noted admiringly the mutual respect that characterized relations among students and between fac-ulty and students at St. Paul's. "The atmosphere here might seem more violent and hyperactive; the St. Paul student could not expose so much of his or her own personality and would have to develop a protective barrier," one student advised. "Insults and rough physical contact aren't always meant personally, but it's a way of life at Ham-ilton." A Hamilton soccer player predicted the St. Paul's transfer "would be in a state of confusion and culture shock adjusting to all the dishonesty, profanity, lack of respect of students for students and of students for teachers." A quiet and serious Cambodian student, reflecting on his own experiences in broken English, wrote that the transfer would see Hamilton students "acting a fool like: swearing to teacher, yell around the hall, talking to their friends by swearing, never listen to anyone try to tell them. During the bell ring, they never come to class on time. They skip class and they talk back to the teacher." A female student who had spent a year in school in France admired the norms of "love and caring" at St. Paul's, "while norms at Hamilton tend to be dishonesty, disrespect and in general dis-everything." It was noted that "smoking, drinking, and drug abuse are commonplace at Hamilton" in contrast to closer surveillance and stern admonitions at St. Paul's. Some objected to the fact that St. Paul's students who broke the rules about drinking and drug use had to hear their punishments announced at chapel, but neither did they like the fact that at Hamilton "everyone does it and gets away with it."

Three intertwined themes point up marked differences perceived by students in levels of achievement between St. Paul's and Hamilton. The first was nearly universal in the essays—a fear of ridicule at Hamilton that led to withdrawal from participation in class discussions and unwillingness to take a risk. "No student [at St. Paul's] will have fear of being laughed at and this allows for greater efforts to take risks," said one student. "The certainty of love and care generated there would enable me to come out of my shell," said another. "It would stay with me all my life and allow me to take risks and ask probing questions." Still another stressed that "critical evaluation, not ridicule, would help me correct my faults and become a better person."

The second theme was that St. Paul's had high expectations for all students. You were expected to do your best, to stretch yourself. The least able, as well as the best, students in the anthropology class felt they would be affected by this climate: "I would do my homework," said one borderline student. A student with average grades felt that if she had gone to St. Paul's, "I would be an entirely different person than who I am today. I would work probably twice as hard as I do because I would get pushed to my limit academically, athletically, and socially." One of the best students in the class wrote that the St. Paul's transfer would "learn that getting good grades without actually learning or working is the major goal of many Hamilton students." On the other hand, she believed that the caring faculty at St. Paul's would bring out her best: "At Hamilton I was always classified as a member of the smartest group. There was really no higher you could go because the teachers didn't have enough time or resources to lead you. So I never worked harder. There was no incentive. I could reach my highest with a minimum of work." Hamilton students felt teachers saw them too exclusively in terms of their grade-point averages, rather than as individuals in their "entirety." They felt that once classified as an able student, they were likely to get high grades even when they failed to make any effort.

This was the refrain of the third theme, that high expectations should mean not the same standard for everyone but an appropriate challenge for each student. In the essays and class discussion, the students singled out a passage in Lightfoot's essay that moved them deeply:

> Nine students dressed in traditional ballet garb go through their practiced motions at the bar. Without much talk, the dance teacher demonstrates the next step and then walks around the floor offering individual support and criticism. Suddenly, he claps and says "No." Music and motion stop. One dancer is singled out, "Maria, get your arms down . . . in the same rhythm, open your arms and plié." Maria, a tall, angular Hispanic girl, tries the step again without embarrassment, as everyone turns silently towards her. An hour later, when the dancers are doing complicated, fast-moving combinations across the floor, the teacher singles out Michelle, a pretty, petite Black girl, whose steps have been tentative and constricted. "That's a good start, but take a chance, a risk . . . Go for it, Michelle," he bellows. It is a tough challenge as he makes her do it over and over again. She is awkward, unbalanced, and almost falls several times, but the dance master won't let her stop. As Michelle struggles to master this complicated step in front of her class-mates some watch attentively, without laughter or judgment. Others practice on their own around the edges of the floor waiting for their turn. Everyone, including Mr. Sloan, exerts great energy and tries very hard. Imperfections are identified and worked on without embarrass-ment . . .
>
> As dancers execute the swift steps across the floor, the wide range of skill and talent is revealed. Kara is a precise and elegant dancer whose hopes of becoming a professional dancer seem realistic and promising. Even when she is tackling the most difficult step, she is smooth and graceful. Yet she doesn't escape criticism. Mr. Sloan insists on the subtle, almost invisible points. There is always room for improvement. A very tall and lean young man, who looks awkward and primitive in com-parison, tries just as hard, but never produces a step that even vaguely resembles that one demonstrated by the teacher. No one laughs or grimaces as he breaks down halfway across the floor. The challenge remains: "You'll do it like that for awhile and you'll build up to doing it better . . . It's a very difficult step."[35]

A student who aptly summarizes this as the work of a teacher whose "expectations are different for every person" notes also that the class is not an isolated occurrence but grows out of the overall ethos or climate of the school: "They work to do the best that they can because it is the norm and tradition of the school." Hamilton is a more im-personal environment, where students "become lost in the bureaucratic hustle." Students speak longingly of an environment where "I would flourish" or that would be a "major imprint on my life." Hamilton is characterized by weak norms, high tolerance for the illicit as well as for the variety of human life, and freedom to go one's own way, although often that freedom can degenerate into "the feeling of every man out for himself." Students lament, "There is no feeling of special unity, nothing that binds the school together." It is a school where students search for ideals that can be made palpable and command their loyalty. As one essayist put it, they look for more than coexistence but are not sure what it is that they seek.

First as an observer, and later as a teacher, I came to share the students' view about all that was good at Hamilton High. With them, I was sometimes thrilled by the sheer vibrancy and fecundity of life there. Moving about its halls, I could not help be moved by what the school represented in the way of extending educational opportunities to students of every social class and color and every level of ability or disability. Along with the students, however, I wanted something more than mere coexistence. Their essays pose the problem to be addressed by the remainder of this book. What is it that shapes the ethos or climate of a school, for good or for ill? Does the achievement of diversity in racial and economic terms deny the possibility of developing a strong positive ethos in contemporary public schools? Implicitly, these essays ask, can such an ethos be achieved apart from the privilege and high selectivity that characterize life at St. Paul's, and without the benefit of agreement on a specific religious tradition? Are bureaucratic public schools with weak norms the price we must pay for the progress we have made?

PART TWO

Making a World

CHAPTER FIVE

Why Schools Differ

I'll give the kids a speech the first day and give the dictionaries out and we'll look up the difference between authority and authoritarian . . . because somebody has to make decisions.

—A Hamilton High teacher, 1985

W hat explains the variation in the ethos or character of schools? All schools are somewhat alike, yet in some respects each school is unique. In the first part of this book we saw that the ethos of Hamilton High changed radically over time. The close-knit world adolescents encountered there in 1965 was frayed almost beyond recognition five years later. Then the black separatism of the mid-1970s gave way to racial harmony in the 1980s.

What Is Ethos?

The Greek root of the word "ethos" means the habits of the animals in a place. Joan and Erik Erikson describe it as "the organizing power of the social processes . . . It is a certain spirit . . . almost like what the community is for."[1] Ethos is the sharing of attitudes, values, and beliefs that bond disparate individuals into a community. Ethos varies greatly from one school to another. In one school, expectations will be high and children will be engaged and learning avidly; in a school a few blocks away, teachers may waste a quarter of the hour before getting down to business, homework will not be collected regularly, and many pupils will be absent.

These differences in ethos have significant impact on a child. I visited the public schools in Harlan, Kentucky, some years ago. One day I walked up a washed-out mountain road to call on a family. The children peered at me shyly from their shack propped up on cinder blocks. There were seven of them, barefoot and poorly dressed. The next morning I saw one of the youngest, Jay, in his one-room school, a few miles down a winding road past heaps of coal slag. It too was a shack except that, unlike Jay's house, it had some paint on the clapboards. Inside, a young teacher whose blackboard instructions suggested that she might have trouble passing a grammar and vocabulary test, did her pleasant best to teach Jay and his classmates. A few books lay in the corner near a wood stove and there was little in the way of enrichment materials.

In the afternoon I visited the middle school, a substantial brick building attended by Jay's sisters and brothers. This looked more like a mainstream American school. It gave evidence of several new federal aid programs, including one staffed by two "reading specialists" who sat in the back of a classroom reading *Watchtower,* but I doubted their influence on Jay's family.

This youngster's life seemed bleak, and the schools within his reach offered little hope of significantly improving his prospects. Yet certain schools could affect him powerfully. If Jay were sent to Brookline, Massachusetts, for instance, to live with one of his aunts, he would enter a different world. Even if his aunt did not reside in an affluent section of Brookline, but rather in one of the crumbling border sections abutting the Boston city limits, he would still be absorbed by a radically different intellectual, social, and aesthetic school culture. His classmates, many of them Jewish, would be two or three years above the national average on standard tests of verbal and mathematical ability. Whereas in his one-room school in Kentucky he might never have even seen a violin, here every third grader would be given one and would learn to play some simple tunes on it. By the time Jay entered Brookline High, he might be speaking a different language in terms of his cognitive capacity in English, as well as in French or Spanish. Some of his teachers would have degrees from prestigious universities and would encourage him to think of college choices, since nearly all of his classmates would continue their education. In moving to Massachusetts, Jay would be entering a state that spends almost twice as much per pupil for education as Kentucky.[2]

Of course, Jay's aunt and the quality of his home life with her would be critical in his adjustment to the school. It would matter a great deal if, on the one hand, his aunt had left Kentucky to become an alcoholic waitress who worked nights, or if, on the other hand, she had joined the armed forces, seen something of the world, become a teacher who loved literature, and developed a circle of friends who brightened and enlarged her life. She might then have more capacity to nurture and discipline, adult qualities that influence a child's success in school. We have ample evidence from both British and American studies confirming the importance of simple rules and sanctions in the home by adults who are there to enforce them—rules to limit television viewing, establish curfews, and set aside time for homework. Such parental supervision explains more of the differences in juvenile delinquency rates than do differences in social class.[3]

James Coleman's remarkable survey, *Equality of Educational Opportunity*, argued that the combination of social class and family background explained the most significant differences in cognitive outcomes among schools.[4] The principal finding of Coleman and his coworkers was that schools, at least as then constituted, had little effect on overcoming the disadvantages children brought from home. This was popularly interpreted as meaning that schools had no independent effects, which Coleman himself never said. He would agree, for instance, that without schools many children would never learn mathematics or understand the principles of science. He simply pointed out that schools seemed powerless to reduce inequality in the cognitive deficits between groups of pupils. The children and the values they brought from home were the dominant influence in establishing the ethos of the school. If you wanted to change the climate, Coleman argued, you needed to change the pupil mix.

A major redirection of this stream of research came in an ingenious study by Michael Rutter and his colleagues, *Fifteen Thousand Hours*, which focused attention on the action of responsible adults in shaping the ethos of the school.[5] Unlike Coleman, who surveyed students and teachers at one particular time to discover the correlations between the inputs of schooling and its outputs, Rutter followed the same twenty-seven hundred pupils from the end of elementary school through twelve different secondary schools in South London. Rutter would say that it might be of the utmost significance which high school Jay attended, or if his aunt could afford to send him to a Jesuit or a Quaker school rather than a public school. The research of the Rutter group shows that it is necessary to have a core of able pupils around which to create a favorable climate or a positive school ethos. Then the school can absorb many poor and difficult pupils while achieving successful social and cognitive outcomes. Rutter showed that climates do differ markedly in schools with similar intakes of pupils, and that these differences in intellectual and social climate have real effects on student success (as measured by exams or whether pupils end up in trouble with the law). A primary school child who is identified as potentially troublesome at age ten has a 48 percent probability of delinquency if he goes to secondary school A, but only a 9 percent likelihood if he goes to secondary school B—although both schools enroll roughly the same proportion of "difficult" children.

We began our work with Rutter's study fresh in mind. My colleagues and I conducted year-long field studies in five schools characterized by very different climates. In each of these schools we focused on the struggles of the teachers and staff to improve the ethos of the school. And we uncovered a complex network of authority relations that shaped the climate of a given school.

The Concept of Authority

There is much confusion about the concept of authority, and we all should get out our dictionaries, as did the Hamilton teacher quoted at the beginning of the chapter. Americans are especially likely to conflate authority with authoritarianism, although the latter is meant to denote a repressive or even totalitarian climate. The United States, born in the Enlightenment, has accented liberty, and progress has often been falsely equated with a decay in authority. "Between the collapse of authority and the search for its substitute falls the shadow of modernism," wrote John P. Diggins.[6] American writers on education have been disparaging of the concept of authority until recent years, when its significance was rediscovered. Hannah Arendt noted this hostility toward authority in the midst of the cultural revolution of the late nineteen sixties, remarking that "the necessity for 'authority' is more plausible and evident in child-rearing and education than anywhere else," and she found it characteristic of those heady days "to want to eradicate even this . . . extremely limited form of authority.' "[7] Christopher Hurn traced the way a generation of sociologists and writers assumed a "critical, if not a wholly condemnatory, stance toward the traditional, and previously universal, function of schools: to mold the young into socially approved styles of beliefs, thought and action." It was not the "decline in school's power to regulate behavior which has been problematic but the persistence of what is often seen as questionable authority."[8] Still, every social organization must strike some balance between authority and liberty. An absence of liberty leads to tyranny and of authority to abusive license. As Arendt remarked, "Authority implies an obedience in which men retain their freedom."[9]

But whether the cultural currents flow toward buttressing authority or freedom—and the pendulum of discourse has recently swung again toward the need to augment the authority of the teacher and the school—the reality of authority relations not only demands our attention but is the key to understanding the question posed at the start of this chapter. For it is the way that teachers and staff exercise their intellectual and moral authority that critically shapes the ethos of the school. We shall examine the complex factors influencing that utilization of authority, but we turn first to the concept itself. What is authority, and why is it necessary?

There are two principal justifications for the authority that must be exercised in every school. The first is substitutive. Insofar as they are adults responsible for minors, teachers must act in the best interest of those who are not yet fully equipped for self-rule. This is as true in the moral realm as in the intellectual. A teacher of mathematics is exercising moral authority when she reprimands a student who ridicules another's groping to understand a difficult proof. And she exercises intellectual authority when she asks students to accept a proposition that they are not yet in a position to understand. The aim is not to inculcate blind obedience—which is what an authoritarian wants—but to lead students toward growth and eventual autonomy. Substitutional authority is exercised in proportion to the age and wisdom of the child. The need is greater at age five than at fifteen, but fifteen-year-olds also require guidance. It is impossible to specify in advance how much each child needs at any particular point. Rules may guide but cannot cover the application of every case; the judicious exercise of authority depends on the practical judgment of persons in unique circumstances.

The second justification of authority, its essential and primary function according to philosopher Yves Simon, is to assure the united action of a group aiming at a common good that cannot be obtained without cooperation.

> The best method of ascertaining whether there is such a thing as an essential function of authority is to consider a community of adults, intelligent and of perfect good will, and to inquire into the requirements of the common life of that community . . . This community, however small it may be, must be regulated in its common action by decisions which bind all members. How will these decisions be made? They can be made unanimously, but the unanimity is not guaranteed. There is no steady principle which could indefectibly assure this unanimity. Any member of the community under consideration can disagree with the others as to the best course to take in the common action. In case of persistent disagreement, either the unity of action of the community will be broken, or one judgment will prevail, which means that some person or some group of persons will be recognized as having authority. I say: a person or a group of persons, because the decision which is to prevail can be issued by a single individual, or by a majority vote of the whole community, or by a majority vote of a selected group within the community as well: as far as the principle of authority is concerned it makes no difference.[10]

Groups that endure after forming common aims work out the means of making progress toward their goals. Under the means of coordination adopted, certain persons are empowered to act in specific ways to further the aims of the group. That power to act, legitimated by the group, is what we call authority.

Legitimation, which Max Weber defined as the "rightful use of power," is what distinguishes authority from coercion or pure force. Weber, in his classic formulation, distinguished three types of "legitimate domination." The first, both historically and logically, is *charismatic authority*, "resting on devotion to the exceptional sanctity, heroism or exemplary character of an individual person, and the normative patterns of order revealed by him." Charismatic authority lies in the group's voluntary and immediate response to the person. He or she need not be a good person; Hitler as well as Jesus exercised charismatic authority. But if the normative patterns are not to die with the personality, charismatic authority must be continued by other means. Thus it usually devolves into one of two other "pure types," *traditional authority*, grounded in "an established belief in the sanctity of immemorial traditions and the legitimacy of those exercising authority under them," or *legal-rational authority*, rooted in "a belief in the legality of enacted rules and the right of those elevated to authority under such rules to issue commands."[11]

The Zulu chief and the Oxford don are good exemplars of the exercise of traditional authority. The emphasis shifts from the specific competence required to exercise authority within the legally defined sphere of a given office to personal loyalty owed to the traditional leader, chosen in ways sanctioned by the tradition, which may limit succession to an elect group or to those related by blood. Once selected under governing traditions, the person in authority generally has wide discretion in giving commands as long as they can be justified within the terms of the tradition. If a command is questioned, the rationale is likely to be that "this is the way these things have always been done"—or the way the founder or his or her disciples would have wanted it done. The positive aspects of such forms lie in the discretion of means to accomplish purposes, and the strength of the bonds that develop between master and disciples (or the head and those loyal to him or her). The possibility of bribery on the one side and exploitation on the other also exist. Traditional forms may suffer from ossification through limitations on appointments, the continuation of irrational though ancient practices, and the corruption of discretion into abuse and favoritism.

Modern corporations and bureaucratic organizations are examples of the legal-rational form of authority. In them authority can be traced to the rules governing appointment to the "office" individuals occupy. Sometimes the authority of the expert is subsumed under the form because of the legal criteria governing appointment to such roles in modern societies, or the authority of the expert may be treated as a separate category. The strength of the legal-rational form lies in its capacity for developing fair and consistent procedures and for carrying out complex activities through specialization of tasks and hierarchical control. The corollary weaknesses lie in a cancerous elaboration of rule and legal procedure and the death of personality. At its worst, bureaucracy suffers from the entropy of a closed system, forgetting original purposes in an all-consuming effort to keep the organization manual up-to-date.

Actually, the types are often mixed. In Japan both corporate organization and government organization are characterized by a traditional emphasis on personal bonds of loyalty to one's superior within the bureaucratic organization, so that services rendered go far beyond those nominally defined by one's position. And as we shall see in the next chapter, the public-school teacher in America is an amalgam of charismatic, traditional, and legal-rational sources of authority.

Authority Relations

Now let us consider a schema of authority relations in a school. There are four components of these relations, which I visualize as the layers of a fruit taking nutriment from the soil. The seeds of the fruit represent the teachers and staff who are responsible for the school's daily functioning, whose commands and personalities shape the school for good or for ill. They have a primary but far from exclusive responsibility for the ethos of the school. The exercise of their authority is conditioned, constrained, or amplified by the other components. What the responsible adults can achieve is determined to a large extent by the second layer, the family mix, represented by the flesh of the fruit. The understandings and dispositions children bring from the home, and the attitudes and behaviors of families toward the school, are elements of the family mix. The third layer, the skin of the fruit, comprises the policy matrix—all those policies made by agencies or persons external to the staff which affect the interactions of the adults and children in a given school. The soil is the fourth layer, that deeper and slower-changing set of influences I call the cultural ground. School policies transported to another culture may have very different effects because the basic orientation and ground of that culture may be inhospitable.

To extend our metaphor, the American high school of 1900 was like an avocado. Its center of adult power and initiative was unified and virtually impregnable, its middle layer of students fairly homogeneous, and its skin of external policy thin and clearly defined. The high school of 1950 was like a cantaloupe, a middle-class fruit with a considerably larger student body. External policies such as regents' examinations and curriculum guides in the more progressive states had enlarged somewhat, but at the center adults still held considerable autonomy for action and initiative. Even though specialized, the staff hung together in a net of connective tissue. Like a watermelon, the high school of the 1980s has a thick rind of federal and state policy, a greatly expanded and diverse student body, and often no well-defined center. The teachers and specialists, like watermelon seeds, are dispersed throughout, and commands—often in conflict—issue from a variety of locations.

Of course all such depictions are exaggerations, and historical transitions cannot be demarcated so distinctly. In fact, *each* type of high school exists today. If we think of the watermelon rind as an accretion of bureaucracy, court orders, union contracts, and new measures of accountability—nearly all of which were by-products of efforts to correct injustices—the metaphor is most apt for urban schools. The cantaloupe can still be found in many rural and suburban areas, where the student composition remains fairly homogeneous and community consensus acts as a buffer to litigation-prone interest groups. In search of the avocado, we must leave public education and enter the world of private schools. The students at Hamilton High were acutely sensitive to these differences when they vicariously transported themselves to St. Paul's.

Let us take a closer look at each of these layers of influence, beginning with changes in the policy layer, then turning to the family mix, and concluding with a discussion of the cultural ground. We shall postpone until the next chapter the ways in which these elements combine to affect the exercise of authority by the teachers and staff of the school.

The Policy Matrix.   All schools exist within a particular policy matrix—that web of rule, regulation, proscription, and requirements that sets constraints on what schools may do and shapes the interaction of adults and children within the school. By policy matrix I mean specifically the network of rule and regulation that is external to an individual school—external in the sense that the staff of the school has no power to make or repeal such policies. The policy matrix establishes the official world within which the school exists and within which it must develop its own practices, including its rules and policies. The internally developed practices represent the exercise of the moral and intellectual authority of the adults in the school. In the case of public schools, the external policy matrix includes all those policies developed at federal, state, and local school district levels.

Private schools are free of much but not all of the regulation that binds public schools. Some states regulate certification of teachers who may teach in private schools, and most specify health and safety regulations for such schools. Publicly funded programs require adherence to regulations and stipulations governing the use of those funds in private schools. Many private schools must also be responsive to an external policy matrix by virtue of their affiliation with a system of broader church or sectarian governance.

Nonpublic agencies and organizations can be considered part of the external policy matrix that affects both public and private schools. Textbook publishers and the developers of curriculum materials have had significant influence on both subject matter and the way it is taught. Similarly, large testing organizations (the Education Testing Service, for instance) have shaped teacher goals in both public and private schools. Advocates, such as Ralph Nader's Public Interest Research Groups, have pressed class-action suits that have had an impact on schools. Foundations have funded model enterprises or paid for new services that have subsequently affected policy or led to a reorganization of schools, as did the Ford Foundation's sponsorship of the decentralization of New York City's public schools. Teachers' unions have negotiated contracts limiting class size, specifying the length of the class day, and defining the roles of paraprofessionals. Although officers of these organizations are not publicly elected or publicly accountable, they constitute private governments that form part of the public-policy matrix.[12]

Although there are probably more similarities than differences between the schools of Montana and Massachusetts, state policies affecting education differ greatly. Despite efforts toward equalization that I shall say more about later, states diverge widely in average expenditure per pupil, and district policies within a state may further color those disparities. States differ, for example, in the level of educational preparation they require of teachers, the length of the school day and school year, the years of mathematics or science required for graduation, whether corporal punishment is permitted, and whether standardized tests are mandated for all students in basic academic subjects.

Within states, school districts establish varying policies. While the state may establish baseline requirements for high school graduation, some districts may stipulate an additional year of mathematics, add a requirement for computer literacy, or specify some form of sex education. Although the state's laws may permit corporal punishment, a particular district may prohibit it—or allow it only under particular conditions. A school district will usually establish its own curriculum guidelines, perhaps developing specific district-wide tests based on its curriculum. A district may choose its own form of school organization and establish its own staffing levels and requirements for hiring as long as state minima are met. Districts may develop a variety of policies to meet a state law mandating racial balance. (Median emphasized a volunteer transfer plan, whereas another district redrew the school boundaries.)

The policy changes that most radically reshaped the world of Hamilton High and thousands of schools across America grew from massive efforts to extend equality of educational opportunity. Schools have long been the locus of the slow revolution in America, the means of creating social change through improving the opportunities for the next generation rather than consummating radical reform in the present generation. We can trace to the nineteenth-century common-school movement efforts to reduce disparities and extend opportunities. School reform, especially the movement toward centralization, the professionalization of administration, and the development of a more standardized curriculum was part of the program of the administrative progressives in the early 1900s. Efforts to reduce inequities between schools in a given district spread by the 1960s to include demands to equalize levels of expenditure among the districts within a state and for federal legislation to address imbalances among the states. In recent decades the scope of reform has been enlarged from efforts to address inequities within the educational system to efforts to use the schools as a means of achieving broader social reforms. Americans did not attempt large-scale programs of residential desegregation, seeking instead to break down age-old racial prejudice through changes in school attendance patterns. The War on Poverty hoped that equalizing cognitive outcomes in the schools would eventually equalize income opportunities; there was less emphasis than in some Scandinavian countries, for example, on using tax policy to redistribute income directly. Americans established new school policies to mainstream disabled and severely handicapped children who in the past had been treated as pariahs, and the schools became one of the principal means for attacking sexual discrimination.

These reforms did not just happen as the culmination of an inevitable momentum. They grew out of powerful reform thrusts, especially the civil rights movement, which showed, as did protesters in Median, that the schools were themselves implicated in the preservation of inequities. The revelation resulted in loss of trust and dissolution of the consent on which the authority of local school officials had rested. The old pattern of local control was broken and its loss, combined with the necessity of centralization in order to equalize opportunities, paved the way for a major realignment of the polity in American education. The historic logjam on federal aid to education was breached with the passage of the Elementary and Secondary Education Act in 1965. Although the federal government was still a junior partner in educational financing, putting up only about 10 percent of the total funding base for education, it provided an important stimulus for development of federal education policy and threatened school districts with loss of funds unless they complied. State assumption of responsibility grew proportionately, so that by the 1980s combined state and federal funding accounted for more than half the total dollars in most school districts. Acceptance of those dollars meant acceptance of accountability to centralized powers at state and federal levels. Within the school, this trend hastened a shift from traditional forms of authority that had evolved under strong personalities in particular localities to more bureaucratic, legal-rational forms of control. Educational agents within the schools increasingly realized they were the coordinators of policies made elsewhere. Historians David Tyack and Elisabeth Hansot furnished a capsule history of the period, which indicates that what happened at Hamilton High was no aberration:

> Decisions by federal and state courts set limits on religious ceremony and instruction, prescribed how students could be suspended and assigned to special classes, required help for limited-English-speaking pupils, guaranteed freedom of expression for teachers and students, revised school finance, proscribed sexual inequities, and ordered desegregation. State governments demanded new forms of "accountability" including tests of minimum competence for promotion and graduation. Federal and state governments created dozens of new categorical programs, each with complex guidelines and reporting requirements. Pressures from local

protest groups and mandates from higher governments increased citizen participation in decision making . . . Often protestors and their supporters—popular writers, social scientists, foundation and government officers—portrayed local educators as unjust or ineffectual foot-draggers. On educational leaders, it seemed, rested the burden of remaking society, and the inevitable failure to do so undermined their authority.[13]

Nonpublic schools were not unaffected by these trends, but they had the freedom to respond to them in their own fashion at their own pace. For example, private schools—Roman Catholic schools especially—also became more racially integrated in this period, with the exception of a minority of "white academies" formed to frustrate desegregation mandates. But they did not have to respond virtually overnight to court mandates, new clienteles, or new teacher-selection patterns. The private schools were able, for the most part, to maintain traditional authority structures relatively free from the growth of bureaucratic centralization that was taking place in the public sector. The maintenance of stable relationships between school and families was a critical aspect of the strength of the private sector.

The Family Mix. Each of us is shaped by the family into which we were born, and each school is to a significant degree a creature of the families from which it receives its students. The family mix influences the character of the school in three ways: (1) through the dispositions, capacities, and orientations children bring with them to the school, (2) the degree of change in the family mix from year to year, and (3) the bond that exists between the school and its families.

Recent work by Michael Rutter and others emphasizing the independent effect of schools on the achievement of children has been a useful corrective to the dominant stream of research portraying the school as a virtually passive receptacle. Yet, while balance is needed, the earlier findings should not be discounted. Countless studies have shown that the family's socioeconomic status has a strong influence on the achievement of the child. Whether the status is measured by the occupations, incomes, or educational levels of the parents, children from higher-status families tend to stay in school longer, have better grades and standardized test scores, and win more academic honors. Achievement tends to beget achievement, and a school that draws a large proportion of such children (an upper-middle-class suburban high school, for instance) will score high on these measures.

But the studies are correlational. They do not explain the wide variation in achievement within a particular high school or between two brothers in a wealthy family. Sarane Boocock, in a thorough review of the literature, concluded that the empirical evidence indicates that there is little difference among families in their valuation of achievement.

> Most children and their parents value success and recognize formal education as an important ingredient. What differs is the degree to which a general yearning is translated into a workable set of life goals and strategies for reaching them. Parents of school achievers not only expect more and communicate this to their children, but they also teach them the behavior needed to fulfill their expectations.[14]

The Coleman survey found that identical proportions (86 percent) of black children, mostly poor, and white children, mostly middle class, said they wanted to obtain an education beyond high school. But the numbers diverged when the children were asked if they had read a college catalog or talked to a college representative.[15] Reginald Clark carried out a careful investigation of the kinds of family teaching that lay behind the school success of high-achieving poor black children. He found that the parents of these children prepared them for school by grooming them for the student role. "The interpersonal communication patterns in these homes tended to be marked by frequent parent-child dialogue, strong parental encouragement in academic pursuits, clear and consistent limits set for the young, warm and nurturing interactions, and consistent monitoring of how they used their time." These parents read aloud to children, played rhyming and spelling games, discussed newspaper articles, and "taught language skills and social skills that enable the children to negotiate the classroom successfully." They maintained high expectations and "held strong positive feelings about the necessity of schooling for their children," which included a willingness to put their children's growth and development ahead of their own. They set rules for completion of homework, monitored television watching, and maintained contact with the school in order to guide their children toward good teachers and counselors.[16]

Clark confirms an earlier study of lower-class white youth by J. A. Kahl, which showed that high achievers headed to college had parents who were dissatisfied with their status and encouraged their children to do better. And R. H. Dave also showed the benefit of parent interest and help with homework.[17] It was once fashionable to fault such studies as "blaming the victim." If teachers or school officials cited them to absolve themselves of responsibility for the educational fate of poor children, they would indeed deserve such an accusation. On the other hand, it is undeniable that the kind of social capital just described is not solely a function of social class, and that schools that draw many such children are at a strong advantage. Those with few children so prepared face difficult challenges. We have seen that Rutter's research showed that the ethos of a school is influenced by the presence of academically able children in substantial numbers. Rutter concluded that a nucleus of able pupils may be a necessary ingredient of a strong positive ethos. A majority of such pupils is not required, but a "reasonable balance," perhaps a quarter or a third, is needed.[18]

Pupil turnover, or the rapidity of change in the family mix, also affects the ethos of a school. Frequent changes of school, with the resulting loss of relationships, adversely affect a child's emotional development. And intellectual development is often thwarted by loss of continuity of teachers and supportive services. Time is lost in repetition of diagnosis and placement. The pupil must fumble through new textbooks, curricula, and procedures. A few score or more of such transfers can be absorbed without notice, but massive changes can be as disruptive to the school as is frequent change for the individual child. Schools, too, build up social capital that includes knowledge of particular children and families, balance in faculty and specialized personnel, development of courses, and curricular options. During the period of rapid and massive change at Hamilton High, the resources of the school were strained. Even the best teachers were affected by the high turnover.

The third aspect of the family mix lies in the nature of the bond between the school and its families. The authority that the school exercises rests on the consent of the parents and guardians of its pupils, and through them on the consent of the pupils themselves. In the heart of the civil rights protests of the 1960s, the loss of consent was dramatically symbolized by public-school boycotts in many major American cities. The formation of the Catholic parochial school system in the late nineteenth century was also a protest against what were perceived as Protestant public schools, and fundamentalist Protestant parents today are withdrawing children from what they regard as godless public schools.

Consent may be active or passive. Schools do collect families with certain dispositions—or lack of them. Active choice of a public or private school is meaningful: thus it is important for schools to know what common bonds and orientations currently attract parents or must be created. Where there is active consent, some element of choice and positive identification with the school exists; parents are actively cooperating with the aims of the school. Ideally, the school represents a covenant between the teachers and parents in behalf of ideals to which all subscribe and by which all are bound. Today this is more likely with private schools, which often represent a particular tradition or set of values. Since the continued existence of these schools depends on attracting the tuitions that sustain them, their leadership must form bonds with those who share the tradition or value orientation the school represents.

Strong ties need not be the exclusive property of the private sector. Certainly the founders of the common school in the United States had a strong sense of covenant. Parents at Hamilton High in the 1950s had a sense of covenant that is characteristic of many immigrant parents today—a covenant based on support of the school as a means of social mobility and as preparation for entrance to desirable colleges. It is also possible to speak of a restrictive covenant, as in the case of whites-only private academies or of affluent suburban schools in select townships that have erected such high walls through zoning and other measures that there is no need of the former, restrictive real estate covenants. The creation of a sense of active consent in a positive sense is a critical function of school leadership, a topic to which I shall return.

Most American public schools are characterized by passive consent. There is weak agreement with the general purposes of the school, but cooperation is minimal and trust is low. The school may be a facility where one negotiates better teachers or a different program for one's child, but not a community that evokes active participation or positive identification. The dominant attitudes of families are benign skepticism combined with intelligent consumerism.

The Cultural Ground.   Cultural patterns are the deep ground influencing the forms of socialization in the family and attitudes toward schooling. Patterns of culture shape the actions of teachers and school officials, enhancing some policies and frustrating others. We are seldom aware of how much our culture has taught us until we leave it. American consciousness of cultural differences was raised forty years ago with the launching of Sputnik, which led to popular comparisons such as *What Ivan Knows That Johnny Doesn't* and more scholarly accounts like *Two Worlds of Childhood: U.S. and U.S.S.R.* [19] A second wave of such studies has followed in the wake of America's heightened sense of economic competition with Japan. The most thorough comparisons of achievement were carried out under the direction of Torsten Husen for the International Association for the Evaluation of Educational Achievement, known as the IEA. These results have been reported over a period of twenty years, beginning in 1967. [20] The greatest difference appeared between industrialized and agricultural or developing societies. Students from nonindustrial societies, where a book is a rare object in many rural villages, tend to achieve at the third-grade level in reading and arithmetic after seven years of schooling. The variance was not as notable among the industrialized nations, but the differences were significant. The United States ranked at the bottom of twelve nations in average achievement in science and mathematics when the scores of a cross-section of pupils completing high school were compared. In order to compensate for differences in selectivity among national systems of education, the top 4 percent of students were tested in mathematics. The U.S. ranking moved from twelfth to ninth; Japan was at the top. Although social-class variables continued to explain much of the variance within individual countries, they did not explain the sizable differences between countries. Children from families at the highest occupational and education levels in Sweden, Australia, and the United States scored at or below the level of children from the lowest social class in Japan and Israel. And the Japanese have continued to maintain a stunning superiority in achievement through the secondary level, even as they have surpassed American retention rates: about 90 percent of all Japanese children completed high school in 1985, as compared with approximately 75 percent of Americans.

Some of the differences between Japanese and American children are attributable to different school policies. For example, Japanese children spend more hours per day in class and have a longer school year than do American pupils. But cultural differences are also implicated. Two developmental psychologists, Robert Hess and Hiroshi Azuma, observed and tested Japanese and American children from ages three to six and again in grade five. They found that the mother's style in dealing with her preschool children affected the children's later performance, and that mothers in the two countries differed in the ways they motivated and disciplined children. If a child misbehaved, an American mother was likely to say, "I told you not to do that. Stop it." Japanese mothers went beyond interdictions, to appeal to a child's feelings. Asked what she would say if a child refused to eat his vegetables, one Japanese mother in the sample responded that she would tell him to "think of the feelings of the potatoes and the carrots; they are waiting to be eaten. Do you dare throw them in the garbage?" Hess and Azuma concluded that "Japanese mothers are almost unconsciously trying to capture every opportunity to orient children to feel what others feel, to be good guessers of what others are thinking, to regulate their responses being mindful of others' thinking."

Whereas the American mother is more likely to tell the child what to do, the Japanese mother "realizes much more the importance of the relationship she has with the child, lets the child know what's expected, and uses the strength of that bond as a motivating force." When children were timed in the performance of tasks testing various cognitive skills—such as feeling an unseen object to match it with one in clear view—Japanese children proceeded more slowly and carefully. Americans were quicker but made more errors. Performance on these tasks at age five correlated with school performance later. Harold Stevenson also found that the high achievement of Japanese children could be traced in significant measure to cultural differences rooted in child-rearing practices. In a study that involved observations of first graders and interviews with fifteen hundred mothers in Japan, America, and Taiwan, Stevenson asked the mothers how they explained differences in achievement among children. Japanese mothers tended to attribute it to effort. American mothers were both more likely to rate their own children as having high ability and to attribute differences to ability. In line with their feelings about effort, American mothers gave little weight to homework, whereas Japanese mothers attached great importance to it. And in fact, despite a longer school day, Japanese children spent twice as much time on homework and engaged in more reading for pleasure than did Americans.[21] Both studies provide scholarly documentation for a phrase widely used by the Japanese themselves to explain the success of their educational system—*kyoku mama,* the notion that every Japanese child has a "Jewish mother." Most Japanese mothers do not work outside the home and invest themselves deeply in the role of being the nearly full-time educational manager of their children. By American standards, it is a starkly chauvinist society that rests on a radical division of labor between the sexes.

Although schools in Japan consciously adopted American patterns of reorganization under the postwar reforms directed by General Douglas MacArthur, both pupils and teachers bring to those patterns a cultural orientation toward the primacy of group life that is rooted in the feudal era. For the Japanese, the work group takes precedence in many respects, even over one's family. Japanese use the word *uchi* to mean the place of work, organization, or school to which they belong, and *kaisha* to express group consciousness. The social anthropologist Chie Nakane explains that when *kaisha* is used to denote one's place of employment, it does not refer to a contractual relationship in the Western sense. "Rather, *kaisha* is 'my' or 'our' company, the community to which one belongs primarily, and which is all-important in one's life. Thus in most cases the company provides the whole social existence of a person, and has authority over all aspects of his life; he is deeply emotionally involved in the association."[22]

This orientation was evident to me on a trip to inspect Japanese schools in the fall of 1985. In every railway station were masses of orderly, cheerful Japanese students arranged in serried ranks and dressed in school uniforms, which are an outward badge of the *kaisha* students feel. During my visit late one afternoon to a high school in a poor section of Tokyo, a student was caught shoplifting in a record store a mile away. The shopowner called the principal, and a teacher was dispatched immediately to pick up the boy. I asked the principal what would be done with the boy. The principal replied that he would confer with the teachers to receive their guidance. He knew there had been other problems. It was a difficult case. The boy's parents would be called in to talk it over, and if satisfactory progress could not be made the principal might have to suggest to the boy that he withdraw from the school.

The incident revealed much. The shopowner did not call the police or the parents, as might have happened in the United States; he called the boy's *uchi*. There was no recourse to legal process within or without the school. (There are twenty times as many lawyers per capita in the United States as in Japan.) Just as the average Japanese knows that in the wake of an airplane disaster the president of the firm will assume personal responsibility and call on each bereaved family to offer apologies and reparations, the shopowner knew the principal would assume responsibility. The principal, for his part, would not think of acting unilaterally but turned first to develop consensus about a course of action with the other members of the *uchi*, the teachers, without whose cooperation he would not feel he could act or have any hope of success. There is no word in Japanese for "leadership" in the sense the word is used in the West; all such matters are conceived as reciprocal relationships between superiors and inferiors, each of whom owes the other loyalty and respect. Finally, as a last resort, the principal suggested withdrawal—and it was no more than a suggestion, though one carrying great weight. He knew that loss of group identity is a very great punishment, although not as severe as in the case of an adult, for whom one's *uchi* is usually a lifetime commitment. This kind of commitment combined with the participatory work structures characteristic of large Japanese firms has been shown to raise morale and dissolve competing loyalties based on class, unions, or specific occupation.[23] Japanese children likewise feel strong loyalty to the school as *uchi*, and the IEA studies reveal that among the industrialized countries Japanese children expressed the most positive attitudes about school, whereas American children expressed the most negative.

It is not surprising that in a culture with such a powerful orientation toward smooth group functioning, Japanese classes are nearly twice the size of those in America. Here more emphasis is placed on the individual, with a corresponding development of more individualized teaching. One of the paradoxes of the recent reform movement in both countries is that the Japanese are concerned about loss of creativity, while Americans are paying more attention to Japanese models fostering achievement. It should not be assumed that the paternalism and group orientation of Japanese culture produces rigid or authoritarian classrooms. I saw a great deal of easygoing cooperation among pupils in the schools I visited. Sensitivity to others' needs facilitates peer teaching. The outstanding mathematics achievement of Japanese children does not emerge from rote teaching, according to recent research by Jack and Elizabeth Easley.[24] In the elementary schools they visited in Japan, challenging problems were posed to whole classes and pupils were given several days to solve them in collaboration, including help from older children in other classes.

Whole-class teaching is more common in Japan, and respect for the teacher is high. The word *sensai* for teacher is a term of respect in Japan, analogous to "rabbi" in Jewish culture. In the mid-eighties, teachers in Japan earned 2.4 times the per capita income, compared with 1.7 times per capita income in the United States. There were five times as many applicants for teacher positions in Japan as there were openings.[25] Teacher status is high. In visits to more than a hundred elementary schools in the United States, I have never seen a faculty room like a typical one in Kyoto. There each teacher had a sizable desk, often with telephone, where he or she could confer with parents or prepare classes. A parent wanting a conference in this country hopes to catch the teacher in the classroom and either stands or else sits in a pupil's chair. American teachers will grab a few minutes between classes to have a coke or a cigarette, or to correct papers in the faculty lounge, where they often sit around a long crowded table or balance papers on their knees. There may be no phone there at all, and teachers may compete with students to use the single phone in the office.

Americans might do well to emulate Japanese standards of teacher pay and recruitment. But reformers should not make facile assumptions about the replicability of educational achievement in a country where citizens willingly separate their garbage into six categories, as do the residents of Tokyo. Culture is not destiny, but it is a critical determinant of the ethos of a school.

CHAPTER SIX

The Teacher's Predicament

It is not a fit position for an adult to be in. We have no more business being entertainers than being cops.

—*John Holt*, Freedom and Beyond

In the last chapter we examined the elements of the authority system that shape the ethos of a school. It was a view from the outside, so to speak. Let us now shift our perspective to that of the actors in the center of the system—the teachers in a particular school. By looking more closely at the grounds of their authority, we shall be able to state with greater clarity the contemporary problems inherent in the exercise of that authority—and to suggest the remedies that are needed.

Problems of authority have come into public view over the past decade in polls showing that teachers are increasingly at risk in the classroom. A 1979 survey revealed that one of every twenty teachers in the nation had been physically attacked in the previous year, and one-fourth had suffered property damage while at school. In a 1982 *New York Times* poll of a randomly drawn sample of 5,702 teachers in New York State, 40 percent report that violence is a daily concern; a third of New York City teachers and 15 percent of those elsewhere in the state said they had been assaulted.[1] Teachers increasingly used sick days as "mental health days" to cope with stress and overload. Of course violence is not new. Teachers on the American frontier often had to take on the biggest boy in the class. And schools that served immigrant children of diverse cultures and expectations in the nineteenth century were not always models of civility. But the need for hall guards, turnstiles to frisk students, and the practice of teachers in some New York City schools of always going to restrooms in pairs were new, as were the variety of lethal weapons confiscated from students, sometimes to be returned to them by the courts.[2] I do not wish to dwell on the dramatic issue of school violence, but instead to examine the nature of the teacher's authority in relation to contemporary realities.

Teaching has never been easy. Like a parent, a teacher can never be fully prepared for the demands on him or her; and like a parent, one is bound to fail when one's efforts are measured against lofty standards.[3] Individuals of extraordinary talent have been crushed in the schoolroom. D. H. Lawrence, who taught seventh and eighth graders, found that school was "mean and miserable—and I hate conflict. I was never born to command . . . Think of a quivering greyhound sent to mind a herd of pigs and you see my teaching." Matthew Arnold, with a poet's voice and a school inspector's eye, warned those of "purely studious habit, who betake themselves to this profession as affording the means to continue their favorite pursuits; not knowing, alas, that for all but men of the most exceptional vigor and energy, there are no pursuits more irreconcilable than those of the student and the schoolmaster."[4]

No doubt these writers left teaching for some of the same reasons that teachers have always quit. The stresses are endemic conflicts that grow out of the universal requirements of the task: to establish the minimum order necessary so that education may take place, to gain the trust of pupils, to motivate and engage the students with the subject in ways that ensure that they will learn. In classroom observations, in interviews, and—most revealingly—in the diaries that a few conscientious teachers kept for us, certain conflicts and dissatisfactions seem to be universal themes of teaching. One is the feeling of being overwhelmed by the emotional demands and needs of children, as revealed by this excerpt from a teacher's diary:

> Back to school after two snow days—good to be back although I have a slight flu. Mary looking wan from weeks of strep and family turmoil. Ralph, with bad cough and sore throat and looking feverish, pulled me close to him and said they'd won the custody case I testified in last week. Althea, full of anxious chatter about their moving date in three weeks. Frannie and Carol both on medication which requires reminders to be taken periodically. Chris brings friend who speaks no English to visit for the day. Fei's mother weeps from homesickness for Taiwan. All this

while taking attendance and collecting lunch money between 8:35 and
8:45 A.M.

An almost constant theme is the guilt teachers feel over their failure
to meet the intellectual needs of all children. Diaries are filled with
references to teachers' being brought up short by students they know
they failed to serve or to reach. Teachers in their private musings are
also torn with conflicts between the way they would prefer to teach
and the demands of prescribed curricula. An experienced teacher put
her lesson plan aside after she walked into class one morning to find
that a boy's dry-cell battery had overflowed during the night and spilled
acid on his desk. The class spent the morning researching the topic
to find out what could have caused this accident, how dangerous the
acid might be, what words such as "corrosive" mean, and so on.
Students went to the library, called parents, consulted science texts.
This particular teacher prefers to teach this way, but in her diary she
worried that she might have "wasted" a day that should have been
spent preparing slower children in the class for competency tests. "How
do you assure that all kids get their skills taught in all areas?" And
even for able, experienced teachers, the task of establishing a good
working environment requires relentless vigilance. Teachers are vul-
nerable to emotional kamikaze attacks and are well aware of the ability
of even one student to upset a whole class.

As Dan Lortie has noted, some teachers resent any outside interference, but most have good reason to be irritated by petty instructions
issued over a loudspeaker.[5] Interrupters frequently make condescending assumptions that a teacher would welcome any relief from her
duties and hence regard her classroom as fair game for any fad or
presumed civic cause: Fire Prevention Week, drug education, flamenco
dancing, nutrition, water conservation, and Storybook Week. The
classroom is constantly subject to invasion. Not that it should be
sealed against all inspection, but teachers, like other professionals,
should have some say about when even parents should be allowed to
come into the class to observe their performance.

These diaries and interviews with Hamilton teachers confirm what
Seymour Sarason has found in working with teachers at his psychoed-
ucational clinic at Yale—that teaching is often lonely, repetitive work
in which a teacher is incessantly asked to give and ends the day

emotionally drained.[6] While the tensions discussed above are the perpetual dilemmas of teaching, the balance between getting and giving has grown more disproportionate in recent decades. Expectations, complaints, even lawsuits have multiplied, while rewards have diminished. Responsibilities have increased as authority has weakened. We have seen that authority rests on the legitimate consent of those who willingly render obedience to another in order to accomplish some worthwhile end. In the case of the teacher, that end is the development of educated persons who are capable of critical reflection and moral action. Thus teachers have a special responsibility not to abuse authority. The teacher's task is to create an orderly context for learning and to win obedience in such a way that externally imposed constraints become freely chosen internal disciplines. In the remainder of this chapter we shall see how that authority is derived. It is both individual and social, that is, it is both personally earned and socially conferred.

The Individual or Personal Aspects of Authority

Foremost among the personal factors is the teacher's own intellectual ability and competence in the subject to be taught. In the aggregate, by the mid-1980s, there were signs of a reversal in the long decline in the intellectual caliber of those entering teaching. But the downward trend had been evident for more than a decade. Of nineteen fields of study reported by the American College Testing Program for enrolled college freshmen, education majors placed seventeenth on math scores and fourteenth on English scores. On the reading test, only majors in agriculture or home economics and clerical office fields ranked below education majors. By 1979, high school seniors who said they wanted to enter teaching averaged 392 out of a possible 800 on the verbal portion of the Scholastic Aptitude Test. Unfortunately, apart from such tests of general aptitude, few solid data exist about the knowledge base of most teachers. Although a number of states introduced mandatory testing of teachers in the last decade, most of these ignored specific tests of competence in the subject to be taught. They consisted primarily in tests of basic reading, spelling, and arithmetic skill combined with evaluation of teaching methods and practices. Hence we have no reliable guide to whether biology or mathematics teachers know more or less than their counterparts a generation ago. Some evidence does exist that more intellectually able teachers have left teaching in disproportionate numbers as a result of worsening conditions. And the success of the feminist movement in raising professional horizons for women has probably had a significant impact on the teacher supply. This was especially true of talented women who attended elite colleges. In the early 1960s, four times as many Smith College graduates went into teaching as into business; by the 1980s, the reverse was true.[7]

Classroom observations provide ample illustrations of these trends. A rural school teacher asked children to fill in the blanks in the following sentence: "In the ninth century A.D. (blank) was imported into Japan from (blank)." The words to be filled in were "culture" and "China." The teacher knew very little about either culture or China, or what it would mean to "import" it. The most awkward moments in any class are those when a teacher cannot explain the concepts the students need to know. We observed a teacher who had a textbook list of societal institutions that he wanted students to regurgitate. He wanted them to say things like "family," "education," "government." But when one student suggested "orphanages," the teacher could do little more than point out that it was not on the textbook list. In contrast, down the hall an English teacher with an obvious love and deep knowledge of the language was fully at ease in dealing with a question that arose spontaneously about the difference between the words "lonely" and "alone," and other cognates. We tend, however, to have exalted notions of good teaching based on our models of the very best teachers experienced in our own youth. It is naive to assume that a knowledgeable teacher in tune with his subject is all that is needed to capture the interest of students, and that once that interest is captured, problems of order take care of themselves.

While the subject is the ground that lies between teacher and student, the teacher's knowledge of the terrain is not all that is needed to cross it. If there is a problem, usually it is stated in terms that the "teacher knows the stuff," but cannot "get it across." The teacher seems to lack the intuition or art of presentation that engages student interest. This could be a general failing or, as in the case of some teachers at Hamilton High when abruptly confronted with underprepared black students, a deficit that appears in relation to a specific student or group of students. The teacher may be unable to summon the empathy to understand how the material must appear from the inside of the student's mind, or how to convert it from an irrelevant inert mass to something whose meaning the student can understand. But the problem goes beyond questions of method and imagination to deeper qualities of character. The teacher must have a capacity for engendering trust and an ability to engage in the creative confrontation that is at the heart of all good teaching. She must have the courage to make demands on a student, to insist that he rewrite the same paragraph until it begins to make sense and do work that is often difficult for him—and sometimes boring. The teacher must sustain the student in an engagement with a subject that has its own logic and is independent of the student's impulses or subjective will.[8]

Teachers may undercut their own authority as they reveal their moral qualities or lack of them in hundreds of telling ways each day. Other students in a class held in a high school library could hear as clearly as we did the student who cursed another as a "stupid fat bitch," while the teacher went on as though nothing had happened. Teachers who do not respond, who do not listen, who fail to prepare themselves responsibly for the day's work, reveal that they do not care and that they do not fully respect their students. Pupils will give them little allegiance. A teacher who takes advantage of or ridicules a student may earn an immediate laugh from some, at the cost of long-term resentment by many. Perhaps teachers reveal their moral attitudes most vividly in the expectations they have for students. At Hamilton High a chemistry teacher opened her presentation to the class as related in this excerpt from our field notes:

Mrs. Curran laid great emphasis on the format and the method used in recording and reporting experiments. She also emphatically stressed that no one should ever use another student's lab report and try to pass it on as his or her own. She asked the kids to think for a moment about the need for honesty in science: "If a scientist is not 100 percent truthful and meticulous, then think of all the disasters that could occur in a pharmaceutical laboratory, for instance, which results in medicines which are either contaminated or whose effects are not certain." She said that since they were in her class and were going to be performing as scientists on however elementary a scale, she would expect this as a prime requisite—"honesty, truthfulness, and meticulous care. Was that understood?"

On another occasion after a particularly difficult task, Mrs. Curran explained her philosophy:

> I give the kids assignments well in advance. I don't give them busy work. I make it very clear that what they do really is significant—it is necessary for them in terms of understanding the next page or concept and if they don't do it, then it is detrimental for them. I don't play games with my students, so I don't expect them to play games with me either. Science, in itself, means some kind of discipline.

Other teachers at Hamilton communicated quite different expectations by overlooking cheating, habitually arriving late for class, or failing to return papers that were necessary for understanding the next concept.

The teacher's own conception of his or her role is the third aspect of individual sources of authority. Each teacher's view of that role grows out of a unique amalgam of influences—their own experiences as a pupil, formal training, philosophical bent, mentorship, and early teaching background. For some—not Mrs. Curran—the conception of the role gives very little weight to moral authority. Teachers differ greatly in their sense of intellectual authority as well—the degree to which they will accept an imposed curriculum or someone else's version of what their subject is and how to teach it. They vary in the clarity of their conception and the confidence with which they exercise their authority. In our scores of interviews it was evident that many teachers do not possess a definitive view; on the contrary, they are confused and ambivalent.

The Social Bases of Authority

The differences in the personal qualities and character of teachers are so evident to anyone who has visited schools that one tends to trace all variations in authority directly to the teachers. But authority is socially conferred also, and one of its most important sources derives from the esteem accorded by the community to the role. Teachers have never been near the top in any ranking with other professions such as medicine or law, which can be more selective at entry because the rewards at exit are more exalted. Yet there have been signs of an even further decline of teacher status in recent decades. More than one-fourth of the teachers who took lower-status jobs during the cutbacks forced by New York City's financial crisis of the mid-1970s turned down their old jobs when matters improved. They remained in sales and secretarial positions and continued work as bank tellers, saying they liked having a decent lunch hour, along with a job relatively free of stress and physical danger. By 1985 teacher pay scales began to rise. But for more than a decade previously, teacher salaries had not kept pace with inflation and had fallen in relation to other occupations. The average teacher in 1980 earned about four thousand dollars less than a plumber and only a few dollars more than a government clerk.[9] This is in marked contrast to the esteem in which teachers are held in Japan, for instance, where beginning teacher salaries rank among the top 10 percent of all entry-level government positions. Perhaps the surest sign of the drop in status is recorded by the Gallup polls, which over the years have asked parents whether they would like to have a child take up a teaching career in the public schools. In 1969, 75 percent of all American parents said they would be pleased if a child became a teacher; this dropped to 67 percent in 1972 and to 48 percent in 1980.

It is interesting to speculate on this loss of regard for teaching as a worthy occupation. No doubt parental opinion was influenced both by an awareness of other—and better-paying—options for daughters and reports of increased violence in schools. But something else has happened. While the pedestal may never have been very tall, teachers until recent decades have enjoyed a general respect. One might occasionally run across a mean or embittered teacher, but most were presumed to be decent if not altruistic. Although the halo of authority dimmed for many in public roles in the 1960s and 1970s, teachers came in for special criticism. A wave of best-selling books, such as John Holt's *Why Children Fail,* James Herndon's *The Way It's 'Sposed to Be,* and Jonathan Kozol's *Death at an Early Age: The Destruction of the Minds and Hearts of Negro Children in the Boston Public Schools,* protrayed teachers as insensitive, often authoritarian, and racist. Neo-Marxist and revisionist interpretations of schools, such as Colin Greer's *Great School Legend,* suggested that a high percentage of classroom failure was necessary to the functioning of the American system. Teachers were seen as the agents of a capitalist society in which the intent all along was to ensure that a good share of the student body fail in order to provide a steady supply of workers for the laboring class so that others could be marked for power and success. Charles Silberman referred to this line of reasoning in his *Crisis in the Classroom* when he argued, "Schools fail less because of maliciousness than because of mindlessness."[10]

As this account of Hamilton High has shown, school assignment and tracking policies in Median, as elsewhere in the North, were often racist, although few teachers were consciously so. On the contrary, most struggled and came to grips with their unconscious racism in ways that were often painful and wrenching. Our observations confirm the findings of other researchers who determined that most teachers had the courage to confront the ills that were revealed by the racial revolution in America and attempted to expunge any trace of prejudice in their response to pupils. A careful study by Emile Haller and Sharon Davis of thirty-seven New York teachers found that teachers' perceptions of a student's family background did not influence curricular placements. Analysis by Ray Thompson and colleagues of teacher-student interaction patterns in twelve mainstreamed classrooms showed that teachers were fair in their responses to handicapped, high-achieving, and low-achieving students. Jean Carew and Sara Lawrence Lightfoot discovered little evidence of racial or sexual discrimination during a year's careful observation in two racially integrated urban schools. On the contrary, they saw teachers who worked hard and seemed to derive satisfaction from helping children to learn and grow.[11] This is not to deny the existence of unconscious racism—as evidenced in our earlier analysis of grades for black and white students at Hamilton High. But our own research does not support the harsh and condemnatory portrait of teachers drawn by Kozol and the others noted above. While a few teachers are marked by deep prejudice, most are decent and compassionate. Certainly the teacher's loss of esteem in America cannot be wholly or even largely blamed on the romantic writers or neo-Marxist critics of the recent past, but it can be said that a great libel has been committed.

Another major source of social authority is derived from the teacher's role as a moral agent representing the community. Willard Waller wrote in his classic study that "the teacher has a special position as a paid agent of cultural diffusion . . . and the teacher's position in the community is much affected by the fact that he is supposed to represent those ideals for which the schools serve as repositories."[12] But when the American public school was "delocalized" and became increasingly responsible to the policymaking powers of the centralized modern state, it fell under the sway of what Basil Bernstein has called "the ambiguity of the central value system" of industrialized pluralistic societies.[13] As the policy matrix shifted from authority grounded in local traditions to a more impersonal legal-bureaucratic order, teachers found it difficult to define the source of their moral authority. They could no longer depend on community consensus. In what was for many years a bible of classroom management, W. C. Bagley addressed the young teacher who wanted to know what to do when she or he had lost control of the class:

> There is no explicit formula that will cover each specific case, but one general suggestion may be given: *Get order.* Drop everything else, if necessary, until order is secured. Stretch your authority to the breaking point if you do nothing else . . . Remember that your success in your life work depends upon your success in this one feature of that work more thoroughly than it depends upon anything else. You have the law back of you, you have intelligent public sentiment back of you.[14]

In the past decade many teachers came to recognize that neither the law nor the parents were behind them. What happened in the 1970s at Hamilton High was not unique. Teachers often thought the law reflected distrust of their judgment or intentions, and was a weapon for disciplining them rather than their students. Where the law once upheld the teachers' right to exercise reasonable corporal punishment, they could now be threatened with a suit for child abuse or with dismissal. One of the advantages of the method in our study is that we were often present in schools at critical moments, and our repeated visits to five schools where we spent a year observing classes established a rapport with faculty that led to their speaking candidly and spontaneously with us. At Clydesdale High School a teacher known to be one of the best in the school explained that he had to cancel our interview because a fellow teacher had been suspended for striking a student:

> I don't know whether you know about it, but a very serious thing has happened—a teacher has been suspended for protecting himself from a student and if he's dismissed, it will be the last straw—teachers, as a

group, will have given away everything! As it is we have very few ways of asserting our authority over students. And now when students get to know that we can be chucked for something like this, that will be it. I'm not for hitting students. In fact, I'm very against it but that power should be given legitimately to a teacher in case he judges a certain situation as meriting a physical response. I know the teacher—he's a music teacher—and he's a wonderful person. He's a gentle soul. You know, he is like one of those people who fifty years ago would have made an ideal father—his notions of discipline and care for children are exactly like those held by parents of fifty years ago. And so, he didn't mean any harm to the kid. The kid had been giving him trouble for months now, and he didn't mean any harm but when the kid rose against him, he protected himself. And for that he has been supended.

The incident touched a raw nerve with many teachers in the school; not one agreed with the suspension. This comment was typical of many: "For God's sakes, what is happening to the world when a teacher is suspended for defending himself? Teachers aren't supposed to have any authority any more over disciplinary matters . . . Teachers are really unhappy—they're insecure because they don't know how they can discipline students next without putting their jobs in jeopardy."

Some of the examples we encountered were so bizarre they seemed like persecution. A respected female teacher in an elementary school we studied was notified that she was being investigated by unidentified parties and with unspecified complaints, except that "some parents" had charged her with sexist practices. Since her colleagues saw no evidence of them, they were flabbergasted. It developed that an employee of the local Human Rights Council, who had used a stranger's telephone after a minor auto accident in the vicinity of the school, fell into conversation about school matters while waiting for aid to arrive. When the local resident learned of the Human Rights employee's interest in discrimination on the grounds of sex, she said her child had told her that her third-grade teacher had used a preponderance of male examples in a recent spelling test. This was the basis for a formal charge of sexism, with two notifications to the principal before the true basis of the complaint was revealed. Although the charge was found to be false, it brought confusion and humiliation to the teacher and undermined staff morale. For what next might they be charged? One could argue that the schools were simply going through a period of adjustment to a new set of justifiable mandates, and of course that is true. The fecklessness of many administrators in their overresponsiveness to some complaints, as in this case, worsens the situation. This incident was widely discussed by teachers in the school and helped to shape a new climate of opinion that shifted the teachers' perception of the authority with which they could act.

We did not have many opportunities to observe interactions between teachers and parents, and had to rely on reports from teachers. In their view parents grew less supportive in the recent rights-conscious era; vocal parents were too quick to tell teachers what they could not do, and supportive parents seldom emphasized that they stood behind the teacher. The most frequent teacher refrain about parents was a longing for the day when parents would assure the teacher that if their child needed a whipping in school, he would get another when he reached home. We suspect this is more than nostalgia. Teachers reported widespread rebuffs in trying to win parental cooperation on disciplinary matters, encountering difficulty even in making parental contact. Recall the teacher who was reprimanded by a parent for her "middle-class hang-up about time" because she sought parental cooperation in overcoming the child's habitual tardiness. A high school teacher who worked out careful contracts with students who were severely below grade level, agreements that she wanted parents as well as students to sign, was told by one parent that she was "fascistic."

These parental climates vary greatly from school to school, and poll data show that the vast majority of parents want to keep in touch with teachers and be consulted about their children's progress. What has changed in the aggregate is that parents as a whole may now be more educated relative to teachers and thus are likely to be more critical of a teacher's performance. After the Gallup polls began asking citizens to rate their local public schools in 1974, the grades generally declined for a decade, with 48 percent giving schools an A or B rating then and only 31 percent doing so in 1983. Subsequently, the school reform movement, with its emphasis on increased standards and higher salaries for teachers, may have generated an upward trend, with 41 percent grading schools A or B in 1986.

The third source of teacher authority is derived from the generalized set of norms and expectations held by the staff. The authority of any one teacher in the school is affected by the consensus or lack of it achieved by teachers in that setting. Can a teacher who approaches a student causing a disturbance in the hall expect to be backed up by colleagues? Do other teachers in the school assign homework regularly and expect it to be turned in the next day? Or does a laissez-faire attitude prevail? Do teachers in general tell students they owe it to one another to do their homework so that each can contribute to the discussion of the assigned reading? In his study of twelve London comprehensive high schools, Michael Rutter showed that it made a great difference whether new teachers were aware that more senior teachers were checking up on them and were concerned that they were abiding by school norms with respect to matters such as homework policies. Rutter and his colleagues found that schools had better outcomes when the staff shared standards on disciplinary matters. Asked what the school's response would be to common problems such as stealing or cutting classes, the individual teachers in some schools gave very different answers. In other schools there was broad consensus among teachers and between teachers and administrators about what would be done. Both discipline and test scores were better in the latter.[15]

The loss of consensus at Hamilton High, reflected in the faculty's splitting into three separate locations for lunch, had disastrous consequences for discipline. It was heightened by the rapid turnover of staff in the years following integration. But most public schools, even those that did not undergo the changes of racial desegregation, encountered difficulty maintaining staff cohesion and consistency after the unprecedented expansion of the 1960s. In one decade, as a result of the postwar baby boom, the number of high school teachers nearly doubled from 575,000 to about 1,000,000. Some of these new teachers were influenced by the radical battles on campuses in the 1960s and 1970s and were disposed to question established authority. They shared to some degree the notion that competition was immoral and that hierarchies of any kind were to be avoided. If they did not quite want to establish a participatory democracy with students, they were reluctant to assume the usual disciplinarian role, or to cooperate with other staff in maintaining the established code—sometimes with good reason, sometimes not. At Hamilton some faculty smoked marijuana with students, whereas others believed pot smoking to be a reportable offense.

The social policy that produced the broad diversity among pupils at Hamilton High also produced a diversified range of specialists to serve them, which further complicated the problem of maintaining consensus within the school. From 1953 to 1985 the number of specialized staff more than tripled as psychologists, social workers, remedial specialists, teachers of the disabled and mentally handicapped, guidance personnel, sex and drug counselors, ESL teachers, teacher aides, and a variety of other personnel were added to the staff. Each of these specialists came with his or her own unique perspective of what was in the best interest of the child. Their training and socialization into a particular field of expertise could put them at odds with teachers—and with one another—about what ought to be done in a given case. Our field notes are replete with tensions between teachers and specialists, although teachers recognized, especially in the case of disabled pupils, how dependent they had become on the skills of specialists. In the short run—perhaps for a decade or two—these tensions have increased and will continue to do so. There will be more cases like that of Muriel Forrest, a psychologist in Edgemont, New York, who was fired by her school principal for refusing to cooperate with the school's committee on the handicapped. The committee was composed of teachers and other staff who evaluated handicapped and developmentally disabled children and decided what specialized instruction they needed. The principal argued that Forrest was hired as a consultant to the committee to help them with difficult cases. She took the position that "my clients were the children."[16] Forrest was backed by the American Psychological Association, which took her case to court and argued in effect that specialized expertise gives psychologists an exclusionary right to make certain kinds of determinations about treatment if professional standards are to be upheld. Forrest believed that the school disregarded her diagnosis of children in order to avoid expensive, mandated services. The school principal ordered her to avoid labeling children as "neurologically impaired" and asked that she condense and simplify evaluation reports that other school staff found too full of jargon and technical terminology. It took more than two years of litigation to settle the complex issues of the case.[17] However upsetting such dislocations may be in the short term, in the long run they are the inevitable adjustments characteristic of the division of labor within all modern enterprise. The teaching profession is undergoing a transition that parallels the transformation that occurred in medicine when the family doctor was absorbed into a team in a highly technical medical complex. It embodies a shift from what Durkheim called the mechanical solidarity of interchangeable parts to the more complex interdependence of specialized functions typical of organic forms.[18]

This discussion is germane to my next point, which is that a teacher's authority is also socially determined in the degree to which the teacher's role is circumscribed. A teacher's autonomy may be reduced as the shift to organic interdependence occurs, but the authority of the enterprise may increase if the specialists working in teams produce better outcomes, as they have on the whole in medicine. In education, the patterns of cooperation are still evolving and the benefits are more difficult to assess.

Unionization has increased teacher autonomy by protecting teachers against arbitrary dismissal and freeing them from the kind of rigid moral oversight that once forbade female teachers to marry and prescribed what they should wear and whether they could smoke in public. Unions have not generally succeeded, however, in creating the kind of autonomy achieved by the professions of medicine, law, or engineering. Teachers have not gained control over entry, licensing, promotion, or tenure as have the major professions, a point to be developed in Chapter 8.

With respect to what is taught, the autonomy of teachers has been circumscribed by new curriculum specialists and technocratic managers. This is the latest stage of developments that had their origin in the scientific management of schools that began more than a century ago. What Raymond Callahan called the Cult of Efficiency and historian David Tyack described as the search for the One Best System were movements initiated in the nineteenth century by a new breed of scientific managers.[19] They sought to reform what they regarded as inefficient rural schools and to systematize the ill-disciplined growth of education in the cities. The first generation of scientific managers began to impose a bureaucratic uniformity on the expanding urban schools. They invented the so-called eggcrate school, the now-familiar long corridor with its spine of classrooms, grading children by age and teaching them a uniform course of study through textbooks appropriate to each grade level. They sought to eliminate ward politics as well as lay control of village schools. The new managers would now run the schools in a more scientific way:

> Convinced that there was one best system of education for urban populations, leading educators sought to discover it and implement it. They were impressed with the order and efficiency of the new technology and forms of organization they saw about them. The division of labor in the factory, the punctuality of the railroad, the chain of command and coordination in modern business—these aroused a sense of wonder and excitement in men and women seeking to systematize the schools. They sought to replace confused and erratic means of control with careful allocation of powers and functions within organizations . . . Efficiency, rationality, continuity, precision, impartiality became watchwords of the consolidators.[20]

In many urban schools of the late nineteenth century a Prussian order developed in which pupils literally toed the line, standing with their toes against the edge of a board and their feet spread at a precise 45-degree angle as they gave their recitation. In Oregon Frank Rigler, superintendent of Portland schools in 1896, insisting that teachers carefully adhere to the specified curriculum, met with them on Saturday to rehearse their lessons, going through the textbook page by page, telling the teachers which questions to ask and which answers to accept. There was increased emphasis on testing pupils, both for purposes of sorting and as a check on the degree to which the curriculum was being followed. Teachers joined the public outcry when each child's score was printed next to his name in the newspaper at the end of the year. Although publication of scores was discontinued, testing practices were not—and the tests became the property of the central bureaucracy.

As with most rapid reforms, systematization of the schools provoked a countermovement. When Stanford Professor Ellwood Cubberly was asked to undertake a study of the Portland schools in 1913, he concluded that since neither teachers nor principals had the chance to make decisions, the result was a "uniformity that is almost appalling." The curriculum that Rigler drilled into teachers was "vivisected with mechanical accuracy into fifty-four dead pieces."[21] Paul Hanus, a professor of education at Harvard, drew similar conclusions from his study of New York schools in 1912.

The second generation of reformers like Cubberly and Hanus, the so-called administrative progressives, still sought the one best system, but the emphasis was on better training for teachers, cooperative leadership on behalf of improved efficiency, and a more complex, differentiated school system that resulted in the shaping of the American comprehensive high school with its vocational, business, and academic tracks all under one roof. They were joined by the pedagogical progressives who were guided by John Dewey's ideas of the "project method" and "meeting individual needs." They pushed for less overt control of the teacher and were the forerunners of those educational critics who in the 1960s appealed for informal or "open" classrooms and more child-centered forms of teaching. This alliance of administrative and pedagogical progressives, united in their rejection of a rigid top-down system, held together for more than half a century. Teachers accepted certification requirements, more and longer periods of training, professional forms of supervision, general curriculum guides, and some systemwide testing. Class sizes were progressively reduced to more manageable proportions and teachers secured protection against arbitrary dismissal. They were granted considerable autonomy in the classrooms if they kept order and stayed within the general boundaries of the curriculum.

Eventually, voices began to be raised against the "life adjustment" curricula in the 1950s, although the progressive alliance did not begin to come apart until the launching of Sputnik and the ensuing fear that American schools had slipped disastrously behind the Russians, particularly in mathematics and science. New curricula in the physical and biological sciences, and later in the social sciences, were developed primarily by university scholars, with token participation by school teachers. These curricula were then to be installed in the schools on a large scale. The importance of these developments lay not so much in the details of the curriculum as in the establishment of the principle that the task was too important to be left to the judgment of ordinary classroom teachers. At its best, this kind of curriculum development could allow the teacher a richer choice of materials; at its worst, it meant that experts installed a kit in the classroom that teachers were asked to operate precisely as stipulated. The aim was design of "teacher-proof" curricula by those who seemed unaware of the condescension of the phrase.

A significant turning point was reached in the 1960s with the passage of major new federal aid to the schools. This legislation constituted a tremendous lever for the reform of education—in fact, the most significant outcome may have been the change in the process of reform. The federal government brought a new set of actors, primarily applied social scientists, to both the design and the evaluation of educational programs. Many felt social science had finally come of age; there was a new confidence in the possibilities of social engineering to help reform the schools and break the cycle of poverty.

As the federal government developed new programs, it also earmarked new monies to strengthen state departments of education, bringing those departments into closer alignment with federal purposes and forms of evaluation. The funding brought new equipment and provided increased help for poor children in slums and rural areas. But evaluations of the programs often brought back the disturbing news that inequalities between children in slums and children in suburbs remained as large as ever, and that short-term gains in preschool programs such as Head Start seemed to fade once children entered regular primary schools. Efforts redoubled to design programs that could work (or, some hoped, couldn't fail). Some of the designers had a tendency to place their faith in technologies of instruction for which the military were often the model. If poor blacks could be taught to read and perform effectively at Fort Dix, New Jersey, why couldn't they learn by similar methods in public schools across the Hudson River in Harlem? The idea was to bring the military experts together with the school people in hopes of hastening the transfer of technology. Forgotten in these exchanges was the reality that the military was a perfectly controlled environment—that was what made it so appealing to the cybernetically oriented social scientists. They could design self-correcting systems and appropriate feedback loops. There was little acknowledgment of the low level of functional literacy required for most military jobs; of the nature of the control exercised over instructors, to say nothing of recruits; nor of the distinctions between development of a critical intellect or moral choices in a democratic school and training to be a tank driver.

Yet many aspects of the military approach appealed to educators frustrated in their efforts to create changes in the system. They wondered, Could the school function more effectively by setting educational goals in terms of highly specific objectives and operations, by developing programs that were tied to specific demonstrations of competence, by adapting computers and other self-correcting programmed devices as substitutes for the usual supplements to classroom instruction? The educators hoped such programs would prove to be more cost efficient, for once tbe initial development cost had been paid out, the systems could be widely disseminated. Computers could operate at a low cost per student after the teacher had gone home, and these systems had accountability and control built into their functioning. As the pupil interacted with the machine, the computer kept a record of the student's progress.

It was not simply a matter of new technology, but of fresh attempts to apply more rational management techniques to education. The schools, under pressure from the business community to do so, were encouraged by the federal government and by the military's alleged success with the new techniques. It was the Defense Department, for example, that developed the Program Planning Budgeting System (PPBS) in an attempt to target costs on specific objectives and hence to obtain what was described as a "bigger bang for the buck." When the Johnson administration, assuming that the nation could afford both guns and butter, increased spending by startling amounts for both the war in Vietnam and for innovative social programs, it naturally sought to apply similar management techniques to both areas. Some high Defense Department officials went directly from the Pentagon to the old Department of Health, Education, and Welfare to show how PPBS could be made applicable to education. State departments of education began to apply the new accounting methods and attempted to build economic models of the functioning of the educational system.

Of course, in any attempt by one group to model the activity of another tensions are likely to occur. Because a model reduces the felt reality to a series of abstractions, it is vital to ask how the reduction is accomplished. In the case of education, the matter is particularly difficult because educational goals are broad: to develop intellectual skills and impart a body of knowledge, to educate moral and aesthetic sensibilities, to help children get along in a group, to learn what it means to be a human being. This presents a dilemma to the rationalizer, who wants to control the system, to provide a model so that one can connect changes in specific program inputs to desired out-

comes, such as increased math scores. Poorly defined and diffuse goals
are the enemy of those who want, in Philip Coombs's words, to tighten
"the relationship [between] outputs and inputs" in the educational
system.[22]

The central tension in such a process grows out of conflicts over
goals that are grounded in different views of the nature of the educational process, and therefore the weight that should be given to the
accumulated experience and practical wisdom of the classroom teachers as compared to the evaluation models being imposed from above.
Although they rarely verbalize it in these terms, teachers feel their
tasks are being defined by the new rationalizers in language they find
repugnant and that often misses the heart of teaching. In Michigan,
a state that has taken the lead in developing new systems of accountability, Frederick Ignatovich, Philip Cusick, and James Ray compared
the value orientations of a sample of teachers with officials in the state
bureaucracy who were developing new management systems.[23] The
values of the teachers were virtually the inverse of those held by the
rational managers. Teachers seek to create a feeling of community
within the classroom, "to instill in students a feeling for the classroom
as a collectivity in which each could obtain recognition and satisfaction," and where students learned a sense of mutual responsibility in
the observance of common norms. This did not mean that academic
achievement was of no importance, but that it was a value to be
developed in concert with other values—in fact, it might not be
attainable otherwise. Teachers felt they first had to create what Dan
Lortie has described as "cordial, disciplined and work-eliciting relationships" between themselves and students, and among the students
themselves.[24] Much of the teachers' efforts seem to be designed to gain
the personal respect and affection of the students. The new managers
of instruction, however, characterized teaching as a "delivery system."
In interviews, Ignatovich and his coworkers found that the administrators "view learning as the acquisition of a set of discrete and meas-
urable skills" and "espouse a rationalistic approach to instruction."
They believe that means are separable from ends and that the learning
process "should lend itself to being formulated as a series of clearly
defined rational procedures which, since they are stated abstractly,
can be applied universally and evaluated from without." The attempts
to rationalize classroom procedures and outcomes in Michigan have

"fomented considerable stress between those administrators and teachers," the researchers concluded.[25] The new top-down "management-by-objectives" has led to the specification of more than a thousand curriculum objectives in some school districts and overwhelming record-keeping burdens for teachers. In addition to prescribing particular teaching techniques, elaborate allocations of a teacher's time have been mandated. In some California school districts, teacher evalation forms specified the precise percentages of time that teachers should allocate to each activity—20 percent for information giving, 9 percent for oral reading, 1 percent for discipline—and teachers were rated on their confirmity to this prescribed schedule.[26]

Of course, improved technique is not the enemy of education; computers may be helpful in instruction, and new ways of assessing the competence of students may constitute genuine improvements. The difficulty arises in at least two ways with overrationalization, or what Manfred Stanley has called the spread of the technological conscience. [27] The first danger is the tendency to think of all problems as amenable to improved techniques and more careful specification of goals and tasks, to see all of education as a matter of devising technical solutions to instructional problems. In this sense, army training films on the assembly and disassembly of a rifle are a parody of what we mean by education, and the tragedy would be to have a system of schooling in which students could not appreciate that it was a parody. It would be a system in which everyone might be able to "function" in his or her role, but in which there was no place for the development of critical intellect so that one could question the nature or ordering of the roles.

Second, it is necessary to limit the process of technical rationalization of the curriculum within an institution recognized as essentially cultural. We should recognize the teacher as a proper cultural agent who needs a basic measure of autonomy and trust in order to be truly educative. We must understand that education rests on the practical wisdom of a teacher working in a particular context with a unique mix of children having complex needs. The teacher must be free to devise appropriate means to broad cultural ends; she is not a drill instructor working from a manual. Highly standardized and rationalized methods of instruction—computer assisted, for example—have a place, but that place is certainly secondary to the judgment of a teacher. Is it appropriate, for instance, to install a curriculum in which the entire language exchange between teacher and pupil is programmed, as it is in the Direct Instructional System for Teaching Arithmetic and Reading (known as DISTAR), which was developed by Siegfried Engelmann and Carl Bereiter at the University of Illinois in the 1960s and later published by Science Research Associates, an IBM subsidary? A *New York Times* reporter, who visited a Mount Vernon, New York, school using the DISTAR approach, wrote:

> To walk through the lower classes of Lincoln School is to pass through what appear to be small rehearsals for a major production. Teachers are dealing with small groups of children, typically a half dozen, in what appear at first to be fingersnapping reviews . . .
>
> Mrs. Kay's children read to her rhythmic clapping. She asks a question in the same cadence, and the response comes back in unison. There are individual questions but they, too, are answered in a singsong manner (at least at this level) as small fingers move along pages . . .
>
> Down the hall, a small group of second-graders listen to a question— "What did Troy have?"—and answer as one: "Troy had walls." "Why did Troy have walls?" "To keep enemies out". . .
>
> Mrs. Montalbo, the reading and mathematics supervisor, spoke of the Distar "script" as less conducive to exploration than other reading systems "which are more dependent on the teacher's perception and observation." But "Englemann wanted it that way," she said. "He didn't want to leave success to the teacher's judgment."[28]

The Distar system makes Superintendent Rigler's efforts in Portland in 1896 look obsolete indeed. Rigler met with his teachers on Saturday to review the textbook with them; the Distar system ensures that today's teachers follow a precise script from minute to minute. It is conceivable, though mercifully not yet the case, that such systems could grow to encompass most of the school day; indeed, it is already possible to teach the entire primary math, reading, and language arts in this way. The "product manager" for Science Research Associates, whose job it was "to talk to customers to help solve implementation problems," agreed that "teachers often react negatively to the program because we lay it out in minute detail . . . The intensity of the program is hard on the teacher," he added "Some say they've never worked so hard!" He expressed the technicist's dream only slightly disguised as sympathy for the bedraggled teacher. In our fieldwork we found that the arrival of programs like DISTAR most troubled thoughtful teachers, who sometimes sought transfers or quit, whereas less able instructors were eager to embrace a system in which "the preparation is done for the teacher." Ironically, as superior teachers leave and as the quality of recruits declines, the pressures for adoption of such "teacherproof" methods increases.

The danger is that designers of such systems fail to consider the metaeffects on intellectual and moral development of a rote and sing-song style of instruction. There is a proper, if limited, place for routinized instruction just as there is an appropriate use for a technical film that explains how to prepare a slide for viewing under an electron microscope. But the DISTAR technology moves us toward a version of education in which someone else decides what the teacher ought to be aiming at, specifies the exact procedures, and embeds the whole process in a prescribed language. It may indeed produce some short-term gains (DISTAR teaches many students to decode well), but it sacrifices larger goals: other cultural values are sidetracked in behalf of single-minded and intense pursuit of increasing the score, and reasoning skills are in a decline that is becoming apparent in today's high schools.[29] But my object here is not to make a judgment about a particular program that is hardly the norm, but to illustrate the tendencies within the process.

If those tendencies drive good teachers out of the public-school system, then we have grounds for concern. And it may not take a program of DISTAR's rigidity to do so. A respected teacher who left the public schools wrote:

> The most exciting advantage for me in the private school setting is the opportunity for curriculum development. Although public school teachers do have some freedom and authority in developing curriculum, there are definite state or district guidelines. If I want to start division and multiplication in first grade and delay fractions until fourth grade (as in the school I now teach in), I could not do so in the public schools, regardless of the brilliance of my rationale . . . the public school curriculum is often completely inappropriate for the grade level to which it is assigned. We use very few texts, work books or dittos. It's amazing how the elimination of these three items frees the teacher to invent and create exciting and innovative ways of approaching curriculum.[30]

Although the courts have held that elementary-school and secondary-school teachers do not enjoy the same academic freedom as college faculty (on the ground that school boards have a right to set basic guidelines in light of the school's socializing function), the independence of teachers within these broad guidelines must be respected. One cause of the stress many teachers are experiencing grows out of a loss of reasonable autonomy and a sense, as one teacher put it, that "nobody trusts us to do the job right." In 1986 five hundred teachers who had left teaching in the previous five years were asked why they had quit. Sixty percent cited low salary, 17 percent cited lack of administrative support, 15 percent complained of discipline problems, and 14 percent left because of "lack of input, independence and freedom."[31]

Finally, the social authority of the teacher derives also from the general status of adults in the society.[32] As Glenn Gray has written, "It was Aristotle who pointed out with the simplicity of genius that education is a process of age instructing youth."[33] But, as we saw in Chapter 3, the relative statuses of children and adults have been thrown into cultural confusion in recent decades, and teachers of adolescents can no longer assume much deference on the basis of age. The history of children's rights has been one of progressive liberation of the child from the imposition of values by either the school or the family. The 1970s constituted a high-water mark of the movement in which extensive new rights were conferred. Children in some states, for example, were empowered to divorce their parents. Thirteen-year-old girls could obtain birth control devices over the objection of their parents. In New York sixteen-year-olds could obtain court orders to live apart from parents and receive welfare support from the state. A Ukrainian mother, whose twelve-year-old son was separated from her and her husband because he did not want to move back to the Ukraine with them, complained of her plight: "Who really tells the children what to do? Are the children the parents and the parents the children?"[34]

At Hamilton High teachers experienced a shift from the old individualistic American attitude of "Ain't nobody the boss of me," to a more hard-edged threat, "Don't you dare touch me or I'll have you arrested." Teachers grew wary and defensive, hesitant to exert their authority out of fear that they would become embroiled in lengthy legal proceedings that could end in a draw at best. The 1980s brought some readjustment as the nation entered a more conservative era. The legal drinking age was raised in several states and protests were lodged against free distribution of birth control devices to minors. Threats of legal action by students grew less frequent and became less burden-some. Teachers breathed more easily, although those with long memories knew that the relationship between teachers and students had changed profoundly.

The Effects of The Loss of Social Authority

When social authority weakens, the burden of establishing authority rests more firmly on the individual teacher. The response to this situation on the part of many is to leave, or to wish that they could leave. Some who stay are embittered or resentful. In the late 1970s Katherine Newman interviewed eighteen teachers who had taught for more than twenty years and found that most of them wanted to get out of teaching but could not afford to. They felt the rules of the game had altered drastically in the 1960s. They longed for the rewards and satisfactions they had felt when they began teaching in the 1940s and 1950s.[35]

In our fieldwork we found demoralized teachers sometimes engaged in a poor form of individualized teaching, letting students work in class for the whole term on any project they chose with little guidance and few demands as long as they kept quiet. More common, perhaps, was the teacher who plodded wearily on, covering the material and not seeing or hearing, as illustrated in this excerpt from a research assistant's field notes:

> I went to Mr. Farr's earth sciences class and sat in back of the room where I found myself next to two boys who were constantly bickering with each other. Pupils kept coming in long after the bell had rung. Mr. Farr waited a while and then faced the class and said to them, "Silence, boys; quiet, boys. Tom, Linda, settle down, settle down. Quiet, girls. Quiet, boys. Today we're going to deal with metallic and non-metallic clusters. Quiet, girls. Please. Let us have some quiet now." But kids went on talking with each other, some very loud and disturbing, others more private and low-keyed. There were twenty-nine students in this predominately black class. Two girls had their hair brushes out and were vigorously brushing their hair. The two boys sitting on my left near the window discovered a big cardboard box. One of the boys took a marker and wrote across it in large letters "Linda sucks!" Meanwhile the teacher went on trying to get the kids to notice the difference between anthracites and sulfur and to explain to them how rocks and

other minerals were graded on a hardness scale from zero to ten. Somebody from the other end of the class had seen the boy taunt Linda and nudged her. Linda shouted across the classroom to the boy and said, "Stop that now! You learn to behave!" Mr. Farr continued but I was so affected by this experience that I was in no mood to visit another class. I guess what happened in this class was tolerated and accepted as though it was an ordinary, almost normal feature.

With the social supports undermined, teachers who did not give up were forced to draw on their personal reserves. They tried to win over students by the force of their personality or by offers of friendship. In this sense public schools sometimes became unwitting free schools, that is, teachers were forced to rely on forms of authority that were embraced by the radicals who formed alternative schools in the 1960s to escape what they felt was the rigid and stultifying authority of the public school. The irony is that a whole generation of reformers closely associated with those schools now lament the loss of authority. One's personal coinage is soon expended, and the theme of exhaustion is heard again and again. A decade after his indictment of public schools in *How Children Fail*, John Holt asked why free-school teachers who had "taught for years in conventional schools without getting exhausted, saying all the time how they hated the narrowness, the rigidity, the very discipline, were now worn out." He compared these teachers to a waiter trying to please a rich customer who found fault with every dish. In other words, teachers were trying to please children who no longer had to accept what teachers offered. Holt concluded: "It is not a proper task or a right relationship. It is not a fit position for an adult to be in. We have no more business being entertainers than being cops. Both positions are ignoble. In both we lose our right adult authority."[36]

One of the most careful sociological studies was carried out by Ann Swidler, who spent a year at two experimental "free" schools in California. She found that teachers were likely to invoke intimacy or appeal to friendship when they needed student cooperation. Teachers engaged in "self-revelation, pleas and reminiscences designed to gain sympathy by exposing the teacher's vulnerability." But these personal appeals did not always succeed. On the contrary, Swidler found that teachers were wounded when they threw themselves on the students' mercy and were rebuffed. Ironically, although students preached an ideology of equality with teachers, when they were given responsibility to decide matters, students showed that they believed "they should be disciplined by the teachers, made to show respect for elders." The end result was again exhaustion. Teachers lasted only a year or two, complaining that "the school was consuming their whole lives." They felt they were under constant pressure to maintain a personal mystique:

> This fact meant that it was in their interest to be unpredictable, exotic, and complicated. At the same time, many of the teachers' needs were very prosaic. They wanted students to do the ordinary, unexciting, routine things like attend class, participate in school activities, and occasionally do assignments. Teachers then found themselves in the dilemma of gaining prestige only by encouraging the unusual or exciting, while depleting their scarce reserves of influence when they tried too hard to get students to do precisely those unexciting things that make a teacher's life easier.[37]

We encountered teachers who were similarly exhausted by the effort to woo each class. One of the Hamilton teachers asked us, "Do you know of a job, any kind of a job? I'm ready to quit. The best are leaving, the rest are burned out." Some talented teachers who stayed at Hamilton took a different stance, however. They were highly confident of their own abilities and had earned reputations as demanding, knowledgeable teachers. They made their own rules and made them stick within the confines of their own classrooms, although they often affected an air of glorious unconcern about what happened in the hallway as students came late, skipped classes to smoke dope, and left early. But by setting a high threshold in their own classes, they ensured getting the students they wanted, which often meant these teachers established an unofficial tracking system in which the best students got the best teachers and the less able got the mediocre and withdrawn. The more capable teachers sometimes become "performers" or character types, who relish their image as taskmasters. The competition among them to win the allegiance of a limited number of the best students creates a poor environment for younger teachers.[38] There is less trust and less sharing; the new recruit is less likely to be extended a helping hand.

The relationship between the individual and the social sources of authority is complex. A school or a society that relies primarily on individual sources of authority will produce a generation of burned-out and withdrawn teachers. On the other hand, schools that depend too heavily on the glue of social or institutionalized authority may become rigid or authoritarian. A balance is needed, and any defect in one source produces a strain in the other. There is a further complexity to consider—the withdrawal of talent from teaching. The erosion of the social bases of authority has meant that schools are less pleasant places to teach and to work, and no one is more aware of the fact than the students who sit in high school classrooms. Patterns of recruitment are affected, for those high school graduates who might otherwise be drawn to teaching turn away from it. Also influenced are the decisions of newly employed teachers debating whether to quit or to stick it out after suffering their first rebuffs. The evidence is that many of the best are leaving. Finally, it is important to note that college graduates with teaching certificates have absorbed in formal training less than half of what they need to know in order to become good teachers. Most of that is learned on the job. And the school with a strong positive ethos not only attracts able recruits, it plays a significant role in making good teachers out of those who arrive with the best intentions but few skills. Those schools with good norms and shared expectations for pupils are also good places for young teachers to learn their craft. What are such schools like and how are they created? These are the questions to which we turn in the next chapter.

CHAPTER SEVEN

Creating a Strong Positive Ethos

They want us to do something important, to make some
impact, to do our best.

—*A student at the Sturgis School*

In a delightful essay in *Harper's* several years ago, Frances Taliaferro
pointed out that the fictional literature about education can be
divided into proschool and antischool novels. It is a bald distinction,
but it works.

> In proschool novels, school is the seat of order and civilization, the
> clean well-lighted place where conventions are learned and values ac-
> cepted. It is the cradle of hierarchy and the nursery of striving; prizes
> and demerits are justly given, the class has a top and a bottom, and the
> Head, in his (or her) wisdom, separates the sheep from the goats.
>   Antischool novels assume that school is the place where we learn the
> conventions of oppression and hypocrisy. Here, as elsewhere, the best
> lack all conviction: management is in the hands of oafs and bores.
> Survival requires conformity, or even submission. The trophies are brum-
> magem, the Head is a fraud, and all right-thinking readers must find
> the goats far more interesting than the sheep.[1]

Tom Brown's School Days is the classic representative of the proschool novel, in which the hero defeats the loutish bully and slowly
demonstrates the strength of character that wins the true friendship
of honorable peers. After depositing his eleven-year-old son at the
school, Tom's father reflects on his hopes for the outcome of Christian
nurture at Rugby: "If he'll only turn out a brave, helpful, truth-telling
Englishman, and a gentleman, and a Christian, that's all I want."[2] In
the antischool novel, anarchy defeats a corrupt old order. The hollow
sentiments of character training turn to ashes in the mouths of those

seeking to preserve venal privileges. The teacher is viewed as anything but moral—witness the porter's comment about Paul Pennyfeather in Evelyn Waugh's *Decline and Fall*. After Pennyfeather has been convicted of indecent behavior and "sent down" from his Oxford college, the porter observes: "I expect you'll be becoming a schoolmaster, sir. That's what most of the gentlemen does, sir, that gets sent down for indecent behavior."[3]

Although Taliaferro's eessay, inspired by Elizabeth Bowen's introduction to one of the great proschool novels, Antonia White's *Frost in May*, drew largely on British precedent, we can think of American equivalents: Louis Auchincloss' *Rector of Justin* as representative of the good school and just head, J. D. Salinger's *Catcher in the Rye* aimed at the hypocrisy of the school society. Even more interesting to a social scientist, however, is the way that this distinction captures stereotypical views about private and public schools in America. The analogy is inexact, but some interesting patterns and reversals of patterns can be discerned in both the stereotypes and the data about private and public schooling.

Two Schools That Make an Impact

In the late nineteenth century and for much of the twentieth century, the American public school has been seen as the virtuous source of democratic character, whereas the private school has been treated as the antischool, a breeder of class privilege and antidemocratic spirit. In their aptly named volume, *Managers of Virtue*, David Tyack and Elisabeth Hansot argue that the consensus animating the creation of public education in the nineteenth century was not unlike a moral crusade. The common-school movement was led by citizens of Horace Mann's generation "who both shaped and represented a widespread ideology that stressed civic and moral values that they claimed could only be maintained through public education. The nation could fulfill its destiny only if each rising generation learned those values together in a common institution. This was the dominant theme in the rhetoric of consensual persuasion."[4]

The Protestant-republican ideology that Tyack and Hansot saw undergirding the founding of the public schools was also evident to the Lynds in their study of "Middletown" in 1929. While the public schools do not teach religious beliefs directly, the Lynds observed that "these beliefs tacitly underlie much that goes in the classroom."[5] The discussion of John Dewey and the Progressives linked the success of public education with the survival of democracy itself. Lester Ward, one of the founders of American sociology, argued for exclusive state control of education on the grounds that private education tends to increase inequality and "the less society has of it the better."[6] In *Philadelphia Gentlemen* E. Digby Baltzell saw the development of private boarding schools as the means of shaping a distinctive upper class: "These fashionable family surrogates taught the sons of the new and old rich . . . the subtle nuances of an upper class way of life."[7] Catholic schools were often seen as serving another kind of class interest: a narrow and sectarian set of beliefs taught in a rigidly authoritarian atmosphere that was inimical to democratic beliefs. When large-scale racial desegregation programs were begun in the 1960s, it was charged that private schools, especially the Roman Catholic parochial schools, further offended democratic aims by providing a refuge for those who wanted to avoid attending school with blacks.

Thus the broad stereotypes served to reinforce public education as the school of the democratic social order, whereas private education meant basically either schools for snobbery or bastions of Catholicism indoctrinating immigrants with the formulas of the Baltimore catechism. The real moral vision was held to be that espoused by the common-school reformers. The public school opened its doors to all comers and classes, whereas the private school preserved the divisions of class, race, and religion.

Today these stereotypes have given way if they have not been smashed altogether. The public school seems to have lost its sense of moral crusade as it grew and bureaucratized and became more officially value neutral. The growth of metropolitan areas after World War II resulted in an elaboration of urban and surburban public-school systems, highly stratified by race and social class, sometimes maintained by gerrymandering school boundaries. A few years ago, at a time when the average tuition for National Association of Independent Schools was $3,700, the Greenwich, Connecticut, public-school system decided to open its doors to nonresidents to fill empty classrooms. The tuition would be that of the average per-pupil expenditure: $4,000.

Meanwhile, in the private sector, many of the old elite schools had democratized and were sponsoring scholarships for blacks and urban poor. The most impressive shift had occurred in the Roman Catholic schools, which were the most heavily concentrated in urban areas and which accounted for two-thirds of all students enrolled in nonpublic schools. While some parochial schools closed as upwardly mobile Catholics moved to the suburbs, many parish schools remained open and served the urban poor, including non-Catholic blacks as well as the new Hispanic immigrants. About a fifth of those attending Catholic schools were officially defined as minority students, according to a 1983 survey. Of these 8.8 percent were black, 9.1 percent Hispanic, 2.1 percent Asian, and 0.04 percent Native American.[8]

This reversal of the conventional wisdom was documented most dramatically by James Coleman in the wake of his 1981 study of public and private schools.[9] Coleman and his associates surveyed 58,000 students and their teachers in 1,015 public and private high schools and concluded that it was the Catholic schools that now most nearly fit the ideal of the American common school. Although Catholic schools draw fewer blacks than public schools (about 6 percent by Coleman's estimate in 1981 and 8 percent in two 1983 surveys, as contrasted with 14 percent in public schools), there is less internal segregation in Catholic schools in both racial and economic terms. That is, within the Catholic sector black and poor students are distributed more randomly, whereas in the public sector suburban schools tend to be predominantly white and urban schools heavily black. Coleman also found that student aspirations in Catholic schools are less class based, that Catholic students are more likely to say that discipline is fair in their schools, and that poor black students appear to learn more in Catholic than in public schools (a finding that has been challenged by critics of Coleman's report).[10] Coleman traces the variations in school policies that he believes undergird higher achievement . . . policies to require homework, to establish discipline, and to reduce absences. His report says much less about how one achieves the consensus within the school that is reflected in consistent policies.

Our own research was contemporaneous with Coleman's. While he was conducting large-scale surveys, we were intensively studying a small sample of public and private schools through participant observation methods. These schools, including Hamilton High, were selected because they seemed to have very different climates for learning. Our aim was to discover how good climates are formed—or what I later came to think of as the question of what shapes the ethos of a school. But before we turn to a discussion of the elements of a strong positive ethos, let us look at some of Coleman's data.

Listed in Table 5 are the responses of students to questions that reveal broad differences in disciplinary climates, or ethos, among several types of schools. The first three columns report results from public, Catholic, and other private schools that are non-Catholic (including Lutheran, Christian, Jewish, and nondenominational schools). The

Table 5   Percentage of affirmative responses to questions on perception of discipline, fairness, and attendance by students in public, Catholic, other private, and "high-performing" (H-P) public and private schools. Time spent on homework and television watching was also queried.

	Type of school				
Question	Public	Catholic	Other private	H-P public	H-P private
Effectiveness of discipline is excellent or good*	42%	72%	58%	52%	79%
Fairness of discipline is excellent or good*	36%	47%	46%	40%	62%
Teacher interest rated by students as excellent or good*	12%	25%	41%	15%	64%
Students often do not attend school	46%	8%	16%	28%	3%
Students often talk back to teacher	42%	23%	22%	26%	9%
Students often get into fights with others	27%	9%	6%	15%	3%
Average hours of homework per week	3.7	5.6	6.0	5.6	9.1
Average hours of TV watching per week	4.2	3.7	3.2	3.2	2.2

Note: This table was constructed from data in James Coleman, Thomas Hoffer, and Sally Kilgore, *Public and Private Schools* (Washington, D.C.: National Center for Education Statistics, 1981), pp. 119–135. Responses to questions marked with an asterisk are from seniors; all others are from sophomores.

last two columns refer to high-performing public and private schools. Each represents about a dozen schools having the highest proportions of their graduating classes listed as semifinalists in the 1978 National Merit Scholarship competition. The high-performing public schools tend to be affluent suburban schools, and the private schools are weighted toward elite boarding schools.

Although the public schools have experienced enormous growth in guarantees of student rights, along with new legal procedures to back them up, students in these schools are much less likely to feel that discipline is effective. More important, significantly smaller percentages of public-school pupils feel that discipline is fair or that their teachers care about them. Compared with Catholic schools, those in public schools report that they do about two hours less homework a week, watch more television, skip classes more frequently, and witness twice as much back talk and fighting in schools. One should not overinterpret the data from the small samples represented by the high-performing schools, yet the differences are striking. Essentially, students in high-performing private schools respond as enhanced versions of those in Catholic schools, with particularly impressive percentages reporting discipline is effective and fair and that their teachers take an interest in them. The high-performing public schools show a sharp distinction in one way that we might expect, equaling the Catholic schools in hours of homework per week. Discipline is seen as much less effective than in the Catholic schools, however, and the perception of fairness and teacher interest is nearly as low as for public schools in general.

If we let the reported hours of homework represent the norm for the intellectual climate of the school, and the response to questions about discipline stand for the moral or social norm within the school, then it would seem the average public school is weakly normed with respect to both intellectual and social climates and the Catholic school is strongly normed on both. The high-performing private school is exceptionally strongly normed on both. The high-performing public school, on the other hand, is strongly normed on the intellectual but weakly normed on the moral and social dimensions.

Recognizing that these are very gross interpretations of the data— interpretations with which Coleman himself might not agree—what produces schools with strong intellectual and moral climates? My colleagues and I were granted a year's access to two private schools that were strongly normed on Coleman's measures. The Sturgis School, an upper-middle-class nondenominational school for girls, covering grades kindergarten through twelve, would qualify as a high-performing private in Coleman's categories. Saint Teresa's, an inner-city parochial school, would fit the profile for Catholic schools, although it spans only grades kindergarten through eight. In both schools we were given extraordinary freedom to visit classes, to examine files and student records, to sit in on discussions and evaluations of students, and to interview teachers, students, and staff. We attended social events, parent meetings, school plays, and in some cases were invited to student and teacher homes. Sturgis, located in an eastern seaboard city, had been founded to prepare girls for entrance to highly selective colleges, and it continues to serve families whose median income exceeds $50,000 a year. Saint Teresa's families are on welfare but all make at least a token payment on the $350 a year tuition. ("There's dignity in that," the principal explains.) Tuition at Sturgis is more than ten times that amount, but we were struck by the similarities in the ethos of the two schools despite the class differences.

We may never be certain whether Coleman's findings are school effects or are the results of collecting like-minded children who come to school disposed to behave and to achieve. In looking at the ethos of the successful school, we shall in effect be asking, If the school is doing something right, what is that something? Our answer is that the school does indeed do something right, but that it does it in interaction with parents, and in part because it is a collection agency. But it does more than simply collect: it collects and educates and enhances.

The ethos represents the enduring values or character of the school community: the spirit that actuates not just manners, but moral and intellectual attitudes, practices, and ideals. In the case of a private school, it is the ideals represented by the parents and founders of the school or of the agency: for example, the church that took the leading role in its founding. As Tyack and Hansot pointed out, the civic and moral values underlying the common-school movement originally constituted a powerful ethos for the public schools. In some instances, as Burton Clark has shown, the ethos was reshaped or restated in more powerful ways by second founders, who assumed leadership later in the life of the institution and elaborated a new saga or life history of the school.[11] In that sense, the ethos of the school is personalized by references to those founders or second founders who represent the revered values of the institution.

Schools with a strong positive ethos are led by those who clearly enunciate a character ideal. Judith Smilg Kleinfeld was struck by the way Eskimo students from a particular Catholic boarding school stood out in her classes at the University of Alaska at Fairbanks. When she went to the school to observe, she found that the leadership repeatedly enunciated an ideal of responsibility to others and stressed the development of character and intellect in a caring community.[12] As in our urban Catholic school, this orientation was emphasized not only in catalog rhetoric but at every important juncture in the life of the school. Much effort is spent in communicating the ideals for which the school stands, and in encouraging a dialogue with a public about those ideals. There is a deeply embedded belief that education is inseparable from the concept of what constitutes a good life and a good community. These ideals are sometimes embodied in a formal statement of aims, such as this declaration by the faculty of Phillips Academy at Andover:

> In a community such as Andover, all must commit themselves to the goals of the community and to loyalty to each other. Since education at Phillips Academy is both intellectual and humane, the students and faculty derive mutual support from sharing of themselves and their ideals . . . Yet the happiness of everyone in the community depends on consideration and awareness, restraint and candor, discretion and shared joy. Collaboration toward these imprecise but worthwhile ends is an expectation which all in the academy hold.[13]

Ideals are most often conveyed in less formal ways, by example and by story, especially stories of exemplary students, or founders or patron saints, or former heads or beloved teachers. For example, a typical article in the newsletter of a Quaker school we visited celebrated the retirement of a respected teacher, Palmer Sharpless:

> Palmer came to George School with a good sense of who he was and what he wanted to accomplish. This frame of reference was nowhere more evident than on his application for employment: "I believe in frankness, earnest effort, honesty, daily reference to ideals, constant and unselfish devotion to the common weal. I plan to fight any injustice, discrimination, or foul play that I meet in my daily community contacts. Only through endeavoring to better our own community will brotherhood and peaceful living ever be realized for mankind."[14]

Intellectual and moral virtue are seen as inseparable. The aim is harmony. A good school is not one that is merely "effective" in raising test scores. While intellect is important, maximizing test scores cannot be assumed to be the highest aim; rather, harmonious development of character must be the goal. There needs to be concern for rigorous academic education but also for qualities of endurance, resilience, responsibility, resourcefulness, and social responsibility. Teachers must have equal concern for mind and for character; schools should be neither morally neutral factories for increasing cognitive output nor witless producers of obedient "well-adjusted" youngsters. There must be a balance in both the life of the student and the life of the school. Like a good parent, the school does not want to squeeze a student too hard to raise his or her grade average at the expense of other aspects of development. Publications often feature craftspeople—artists, musicians, carpenters, chefs, mechanics, or gardeners—because they provide a concrete way of talking about intellectual and moral virtues. As my colleague Thomas Green has pointed out, "To possess a conscience of craft is to have cultivated the capacity for self-congratulation or deep satisfaction at something well done, shame at slovenly work, and even embarrassment at carelessnes." This sense of craft shapes our concern for excellence. "It is what impels us to lay aside slovenly and sloppy work simply because of what it is—slovenly and sloppy."[15]

References to the spirit of the place were made frequently in both the private schools we studied. Teachers expressed a belief in the saving power of the community and exhibited great reluctance to expel or give up on a difficult student. As one teacher noted, "I can't let go of our 'rescue fantasy.' " At the same time, teachers recognize that it takes time for the ethos to make its imprint on the student. As a nun remarked of a recalcitrant younger pupil, "It takes a few years to make a Saint Teresa's student." And older students recognize that it has formed them. "They've done so much for me; they molded me," said one Sturgis junior. "They want us to do something important, to make some impact, to do our best." Evidence that the ethos "takes" shows up in surprising ways, such as a classroom discussion of *Walden* which brought forth the criticism that Thoreau should not have isolated himself at Walden Pond because "it was his duty to do something for another, to serve other people." In the hands of a good teacher, this statement became the occasion for a discussion of the ways in which dissenters may "serve" the long-term interests of a community.

Adults make plain that they are responsible for shaping and maintaining that ethos, and that how they do so makes a difference in the lives of all in the community. That sense of responsibility is fostered by detachment from bureaucracy. Teachers are not waiting for curriculum guides, nor are principals reading "directives." They are mutually creating and sustaining a world. Principals also teach, and may in fact return to full-time teaching after their stint as principal. Teaching is more likely to be regarded as a vocation than as a step in a bureaucratic career.[16]

The ethos is also evident in the high expectations teachers have for students. A first-grade teacher told us, "Each day we make a point of asking them, 'What did you read last night?' " Another teacher who was trying to describe her first year at the school explained, "You always felt you had to give your best, there was an expectation that you would never slack off. I can't pin it down. It was just there." In one class we visited, a nun told a student, "Now that you've gotten 82 on this test, I'll never accept anything less than that again." In discussing a troublesome child, another nun told us that the mother had committed suicide, then said, "I can point to any child in this room and give you a sad, if not tragic story. But they still have to be educated."

There was a reluctance to accept excuses, an expectation that people would get down to work. Teachers are role models for students and create expectations by the way they approach their own job, by how quickly they get down to business, and how seriously they take their work. Absenteeism was extremely low at both schools. A nun who was ill insisted on reporting to work; when the principal saw her, she sent her home. After two hours' rest at the convent, the teacher returned to class, saying, "I'm well enough to teach now."

The foregoing also makes plain that the ethos is reflected as much by what people do as by what they say. Teachers are expected to be available beyond usual office hours, to be scrupulous in writing letters of recommendation. Students in both schools are taught not only to be sensitive to the needs of others but to serve others in volunteer projects in nursing homes and hospitals. Even in difficult situations deadlines are to be met; students who are up most of the night getting ready for a play are not excused from handing in their history paper, and they are told that tiredness is no excuse for sloppiness. Both schools emphasize schoolwide rules of behavior and standards of conduct. As the principal of the Catholic school put it, "The rules of the game should not change from grade to grade." Order should not be a result of obtaining compliance at the cost of crushing spontaneity; it should be the expression of freely chosen worthwhile ends. Students are aided in acquiring those norms when reasons to observe rules are frequently given: you should not be late to class because you are disturbing the learning of others; you have an obligation to do your homework and be prepared for class not only for your own benefit but because it is part of your obligation to your classmates and to the progress of the whole class; courtesy to others consists not only in remaining quiet but in actively listening to what is being said. The degree to which norms have been internalized is evident when children are left to their own devices. When a class of Sturgis second graders was told they would have twenty minutes to wait in the hall before they could use the gym, one girl turned to the others and said, "Let's tell stories." They formed into a group, sitting on the floor, and without any prompting from the teacher the first girl began her story.

The ethos is also expressed in judgments about whether norms are met, and the kinds of sanctions attached to those judgments. We paid special attention to those times when teachers were making judgments. At both Sturgis and Saint Teresa's, faculty spent hours discussing individual pupils. At Saint Teresa's, problems that particular students were encountering were often introduced by the principal for discussion in faculty meetings. At Sturgis all the teachers responsible for teaching a particular grade gathered twice a year to evaluate the progress of pupils in that grade. In these reviews each pupil was discussed for ten or fifteen minutes. It is important to note that *every* pupil was discussed. One of the characteristics of these schools was that they paid as much attention to the average student as to the high or low achiever, whereas at Hamilton High (like many large public schools today) the average student was likely to be more or less invisible. In such schools handicapped students may have individually prescribed programs, troublemakers are watched, and teachers may notice that a student in the top college-bound track has taken a nosedive—but the broad middle mass is likely to be faceless. If one's aim, though, is to save a soul or imprint a character ideal, then every soul is equally worth saving and each imprint deserves equally close inspection.

At Sturgis the inspection began with a report on the student's scores on standardized tests, but the discussion rapidly evolved into a general appraisal of the character of the child in which the grades achieved were but one indicator. The discussions were parentlike in their concern, in that higher scores were not held to be unalloyed good, but something to be considered in relation to optimal development of the child as a whole. Here are some excerpts from our field notes on a review conducted by the tenth-grade teachers:

> The art teacher gave her a 92. She said, "Sandra is very unusual. She does beautiful detail work and knows what she is doing. She's naive but has a lot of style. Her personality really disturbs me. She gets so negative if you give her a suggestion. And then afterward I find she doesn't want me to come near her work, which is limiting for her if I can't help her out. It limits her possibilities. Sometime this almost borders on rudeness. She has a rare talent but somehow she just puts you off." Then others nod in agreement and the biology teacher said, "Yes, that's true. She's very defensive and really shy. She does respond well to humor, and if you can kid her about her work, she loosens up a bit."

We were impressed with how carefully teachers prepared for the reviews, making written comments about every child. They knew an amazing amount of detail about each, in class and out.

Teachers did not always agree in their remarks. In fact, they felt free to express their disagreement, to admit their preferences and biases. It was taken for granted that only if the teachers themselves were honest in their reactions to a child would they be able to learn much from the discussion. Putting one's assessment in writing before the meeting encouraged this diversity. For example, this exchange occurred among sixth-grade teachers:

> "She can be so unpleasant and inconsiderate of other people's feelings," said the homeroom teacher. "It's not that she's inconsiderate," another teacher replied. "She considers it carefully. She *intends* to wound them." The others laughed and then the math teacher commented, "That must be why I like her. She can be very enchanting. Of course, she's just passing in my class." Then the homeroom teacher brought the discussion to a close, "Well, so much for being enchanting."

The teachers were interested in the emotional and mental development of the child and in a wide range of qualities and virtues, including honesty and courage. And their judgments applied to both the individual and the community: the student was expected to meet

the standards of the community, but the community was also responsible for meeting the needs of the child. A troubled girl was described
as an anguished complainer who was growing increasingly self-absorbed
and isolated. A teacher responded: "Let's break this thing if we can.
Why is she so miserable? We really need to talk to her. We need to
get her to believe that she's a serious, capable, worthwhile person."
The assistant head of the school, who had discussed some of the family
problems the girl was having, summed up with a plea, "Please watch
out for her—help her balance her life, help her in that fragile balance."
(This dialogue reminds us of another characteristic these schools shared—
both were led by women and had virtually all-female faculties. This
is not to argue that male faculties are uncaring, but to suggest that
these women, to use Carol Gilligan's language, spoke "in a different
voice." Although headmasters of all-male schools are often quite sensitive to boys' needs—one thinks of Frank Boyden at Deerfield or
Endicott Peabody at Groton—the male schools usually exhibit a stag
quality markedly different from both coed and female schools. We
know of no study on the topic, but in our experience male principals
in both public and private schools are disposed to be more rights
oriented. Female principals tend to conform to Gilligan's typology in
being more concerned with maintaining emotional ties and connections.)[17]

In these schools the adults stand unambivalently in loco parentis,
and, like good parents, the teachers and staff exercise a caring watch-
fullness, concerned with all aspects of a child's development. Cooperation between parents and teachers is evident at every turn, as
parents help to paint the walls (at Saint Teresa's) or redecorate the
teachers' lounge (at Sturgis). Sturgis parents are members of the board
of trustees, and Saint Teresa's pupils may not be expelled without the
consent of the parent advisory board. Such parent representation in
formal governance arrangements are outward signs of the trust teachers
and staff feel parents have placed in them. They act with an easy
confidence that parents have faith in them and in the goals they are
trying to achieve. As the admissions director at Sturgis said, "If we
feel we can't work with the parents, it's no go." However, that trust
also means that parents are not supposed to bargain or negotiate for
their child to obtain preferred teachers in the way that is fairly common
in public schools. As the head of the middle school at Sturgis put it:

"Parents aren't that directly involved in the educational program of their child, but they must be in agreement with us or there is no point in their child coming here. It does no one any good to have tugs of war over a child's program. Parents have to understand what this school is all about and trust that we want good things for their child."

The ethos forms the ground on which all stand in a relation of trust, and as elaborated that ethos constitutes the ends of education. After it has helped to achieve agreement about ends, the role of leadership is to remind others of those ends, to keep them vivid in the life of the school. The critical responsibility of leadership is to ground the daily decisions in an interpretation of that shared ethos— to choose the best means to the agreed-upon ends. The leaders of such schools are chosen because they exemplify those values; they are "the best of us," persons capable of symbolizing the tradition and of drawing others into it. Leaders are supposed to have the wisdom to choose teachers who represent the tradition. They must be able to evoke commitment and to guide others to a fuller realization of the valued goods of the community.

Briefly, then, we have sketched the elements of a strong positive ethos in schools where parents voluntarily join together in a mutual orientation toward valued intellectual and moral virtues. Now we can state a question that has never been far from the surface. Is it possible to create schools with such an ethos where there is less agreement about ends, where a substantial proportion of students and even many teachers did not select the school, and where some may be attending against their will? In such instances must we settle for weakly normed schools tied together by a system of rules and procedures that at best can only ensure that none of the disparate elements within the school gains an edge or a preference over the other? Or is it possible to create diversified public schools with a strong ethos in both intellectual and moral terms?

Objections to Developing a Positive Ethos

Every school, public or private, consists in both an intellectual and a moral order.[18] The intellectual order refers to the skills, concepts, and knowledge that are taught or imparted to students; the moral order, to the impact the school has on their conduct, character, and moral beliefs. All schools touch both the head and the heart of their students, although we have no satisfactory ways to measure their impact on the heart. Further, each of these orders comprises specific means and ends. The books, teaching materials, courses taught, examinations given, and curricula offered constitute the principal formal means of the intellectual order. Some ends will be the same for all students: to read with critical awareness and to communicate effectively. Others may differ: to train cooks or auto mechanics in a vocational program or to prepare students for admission to selective colleges in an advanced placement program. How decisions are made about which students enter which programs also reveals something about the moral order of the school, whether the faculty are aware of it or not.

The ends of the moral order have to do with the shaping of character, ideals, and attitude toward life. As with the intellectual order, the means consist in what the teachers do as much as in what they say. They also include the images and expectations of conduct that are held up before pupils, and the rituals and expressions that bind members of the community to norms all are expected to observe. Both the intellectual and the moral orders are grounded in the complex of authority relations. The private school differs from the public school in that it is less regulated by the policy matrix that restricts public-school officials. The family mix in the private school may also reflect more conscious choice of an alternative form of schooling.

We have said that the ethos depends on agreements about the means and ends of the intellectual and moral orders of the school. But such consent is far from universal, even in private schools. Some parents will pack their children off to a boarding school to be rid of them: others may tolerate a moral order they do not fully accept in order to confer presumed academic benefits on their children, as do some non-Catholic black parents in the inner city who send their children to parochial schools. And private-school novels are filled with portraits of students who may stand out in the classroom but scoff at a moral code they reject. Some pupils, as in public schools, may be alienated from both the intellectual and moral orders of the school. At Hamilton High, especially in the 1970s, it was not difficult for a student to be in school—to hang out there—without participating in any but the most nominal sense. Finally, there are some students in both public and private schools who may agree with the ends of the intellectual order but do not understand the means, who come from disorganized homes and who are unprepared for or bewildered by the process of schooling. We can think of these categories as applying also to the teachers. Some who are asked to teach what they regard as a minutely prescribed curriculum may feel estranged from their task; others may agree with the intellectual aims of the school but feel it is beneath their dignity to attempt to enforce rules against drug use. Hence, it is not only the specific means and ends that a school adopts but the kind of consent that is elicited from parents, students, and teachers that determines whether a school produces a strong positive ethos.

As just illustrated, the enlistment of consent can be problematic for both public and private schools, although the voluntary enrollment characteristic of private schools gives them a decided advantage. Yet some public schools are strongly normed on both intellectual and social dimensions, and like Saint Teresa's and Sturgis exhibit a strong positive ethos. We shall give a detailed account of one such school later in this chapter. But if our interpretation of Coleman's data is correct, the average contemporary American public school is weakly normed on moral and intellectual measures. Why should this be so?

If we inquire first about the moral order, we are confronted with a paradox. For the public schools themselves became a principal means of attempting to impose a new moral order on the country through racial integration programs, in-school services for persons with disabilities, and efforts to combat sexual discrimination.

At Hamilton High we saw that the imposition of this new order resulted in the breakup of the old world based on local traditions and unwritten consensus. The change was initially accompanied by violence, an increase in racism and separatism, and fear about the presence of persons with severe disabilities and emotional disorders. But over twenty years attitudes toward blacks and persons with handicaps changed remarkably; and sports programs for girls approached parity with those traditionally offered to boys. The transformations were reflected nationally as well, although most schools failed to maintain the long-term racial balance that Hamilton achieved. This was particularly true in large cities, where white flight continued and resegregation occurred.[19]

This altered environment was imposed externally through new laws and decisions by the courts; internal attitudes changed slowly with gradual changes of consciousness and apprehensive living through unfamiliar conditions. The law is a teacher. But for the most part the new laws were laid down in public schools in the absence of any internal guiding vision or positive ethos such as we have described at Sturgis and Saint Teresa's. The paradox is that at the same time that a new moral order was being created with respect to large societal goals, the moral order within the school grew weaker in other respects: absenteeism rose, cheating was widespread, drug use became more common, fighting and back talk increased. This, too, was reflected nationwide in poll data as parents repeatedly cited school violence, drug abuse, and poor discipline as their strongest school concerns. The weakening of the internal moral order of the schools in these respects was not a direct result of the external imposition of societal mandates. The problems cited by parents antedated the new laws.

The two phenomena are related in the complex ways we have described in our history of Hamilton High. The social revolutions that swept through Hamilton destroyed the old order and created great doubt and confusion among the faculty and staff about the exercise of the authority on which both the intellectual and moral orders of the school depend. Teachers and school officials themselves were the object of new laws; they were indicted for their failures to create the conditions of equality of opportunity that society now demanded. They were confused, ambivalent, and demoralized. Teachers locked their doors and tried to carry on, hoping that the anger in the halls would dissipate. As in any large-scale egalitarian reform, authority became more centralized and the traditional discretion local school officials had enjoyed was countermanded. Long after the violence had disappeared, the effects of an increasingly bureaucratic and centralized school system were felt at Hamilton High. "I don't make the rules; I enforce them," the principal told students in the 1980s. These were revolutions generated elsewhere, and the principal increasingly felt he was a middleman, a manager who interpreted the rules rather than one who bore a significant responsibility for making a world. [20]

The dominant values of the moral order of the typical public school came to be more legal-bureaucratic, individualistic, and technicist. It was a legal-bureaucratic world in its reliance on written rules within a centralized administrative hierarchy, and in its formalism, impersonality, and emphasis on legal due process. It was individualistic in its accent on freedom of choice in intellectual and moral realms, and its avoidance of imposing any but minimal ideals guiding conduct or character development. It was technicist in its assumption that there were technical solutions to most problems, whether the design of sex education or drug programs, and that these could be pursued without reference to transcendent values or priorities.

There was a paucity of adult-sponsored ceremony in this world, in the same sense that one finds little expressive ritual to move the heart in most bureaucratic settings. Ritual tended to be invented by students and to be expressive of individual freedom, as in wearing crazy clothes or pajamas to school. The ironies attending the civil rights movement are instructive in this regard. This was a movement that began in small churches in the South and as it gained moral power was richly elaborated in song, ritual, and social memory. Yet racial desegregation was carried out in schools in a legal and bureaucratic manner, as a matter of meeting percentages and complying with guidelines. It was seldom seen by school officials as a means of underscoring values about the respect and dignity of all persons. Even if one grants that the social trauma attending racial desegregation was too great and that it would have taken heroic leadership to have achieved such a consciousness, one can still ask why it is that so few schools today celebrate the achievements of racial desegregation with the kind of ceremony that would be appropriate and stirring in a democratic country. Ritual is an indispensable means of binding all members of the school together as a moral community. It is the way we feel the ties that bind us and that connect all—teachers, students and staff—to values all honor and try to live up to.

Bureaucratic legalism was the primary expression of the moral order of the school. The code of conduct held out to students was primarily a legal code. If something was not legally forbidden it was usually assumed to be tolerated, or at least it was possible to make a stiff argument that it was. The presence of police in the halls at Hamilton High said to students that standards here are not different than they are on the street. And the orange handbook that students received at the beginning of the year was written in legalistic prose virtually without reference to any set of ideals or expectations beyond avoiding criminal offenses. At its worst, an adversarial mind-set infected many

schools, and new due-process requirements meant that lengthy litigation and courtroomlike process could be invoked by a student to
stave off even minor disciplinary sanctions such as suspension from
school. Teachers became reluctant to act to impose a standard that
went beyond the legal minimum. Even when laws such as those forbidding drug use were being violated, teachers often engaged in a form
of self-censorship, hesitating to act because they did not feel they had
evidence that would stand up in court, so to speak, or that they could
not afford to get involved in protracted legal proceedings.

Bureaucratic legalism formed the basic substratum of the moral
order, but it was expressed in two other primary ways. The first of
these is what Robert Bellah and his colleagues have called therapeutic
contractualism.[21] The public school, like the modern corporation, has
been infected with therapeutic language and styles of interaction.
Bureaucratic structures have been softened by a therapeutic or "human
relations" management style, and leadership is seen in psychological
terms as motivational training. The therapeutic relationship has in
many ways become the model relationship. Surveys show that the
number of Americans seeing mental-health professionsl has grown
threefold in recent decades.[22] Therapeutic metaphors came to influence the training of schoolteachers. School counselors, psychologists,
and social workers functioned primarily within the mode of therapeutic
contractualism. This is the world typified by the drug counselor at
Hamilton High who queried, "Who are we to say what is right and
wrong?" The therapist does not judge, but helps the individual to
assess the costs and benefits of a course of action. Typically, the
therapeutic approach is a transaction between individuals and seldom
an appeal to values by which all are bound. It is a detached, dyadic
relationship in which "one's growth is a purely private matter," although it may "involve maneuvering within the structure of bureaucratic rules and roles," argues Bellah. "It seeks to find privileged ground
for questioning one's commitments outside the usual frameworks of
action and may actively distrust 'morality.' " Indeed, in *Habits of the
Heart*, the authors write: "The ideal therapeutic relationships seems
to be one in which everything is completely conscious and all parties
know how they feel and what they want. Any intrusion of 'oughts' or
'shoulds' into the relationship is rejected as an intrusion of external
and coercive authoritarianism."[23]

Within the school, this approach may mean that teachers are less likely to say that cheating is wrong than to inquire why this individual is cheating and refer him or her to a counselor. Therapeutic contractualism tends to relieve faculty of the responsibility of encouraging all students to live by worthy standards and to encourage the view that if a student gets in trouble it is a psychological problem to be dealt with in a therapeutic relationship rather than a failure of the community to morally educate. There is a tendency to avoid the public conflict that is often a necessary part of proper socialization and to retreat into private forms of therapeutic management. It diminishes the notion of responsibility for others and reduces it to a contract that can be negotiated on a cost-benefit basis, a contract that substitutes clinical expertise for an absence of a community view of good ends to be striven for by all. From the student's side it may lead to a feeling of being manipulated in a therapeutic situation and to a confusion about what moral matters are public and what are private.

As Philip Rieff has argued in *The Triumph of the Therapeutic*, analytic therapy itself arose in an age of endemic individualism, as a way of enabling persons to "manage the strains of living as communally detached individuals."[24] Usually, no positive community stands behind the analyst or therapist, that is, no agency that seeks to integrate the individual into a community whole. Joseph Veroff and his associates note that the archetype of the therapeutic contract, psychoanalysis, "is the only form of psychic healing that attempts to cure people by detaching people from society and relationships. All other forms—shamanism, faith healing, prayer—bring the community into the healing process, indeed use the interdependence of patient and others as the central mechanism of the healing process."[25] We believe that a school should be such a positive agency, a community in which standards are upheld and in which character is partially formed.

The form of moral education that neatly complemented the world of both bureaucratic legalism and therapeutic contractualism was values clarification. This became the most approved program of moral education among public-school teachers, with a third of all teachers preferring it in a 1975 poll. It was most popular with teachers under age thirty-five, 43 percent of whom favored the values clarification approach.[26] Values clarification was promoted by many but became most associated with Sidney B. Simon, who popularized the method and developed curriculum materials for school use. According to Simon, "the process of values clarification involves knowing what one prizes, choosing those things which one cares for most, and weaving those things into the fabric of daily living." It can be taught by "working on real-life situations." Simon explains: "The values clarification process is at work when you consider what may be a minor decision like your approach to selling a car. It comes into play with heavy issues, too; e.g., will you use drugs? Drug educators across the country increasingly use values clarification techniques."[27]

The values clarification approach is successful in eliciting differences of values among students; many of its exercises are clever games pointed to that end. It assumes that becoming more aware of such differences is an end in itself, that "getting along also requires young people to understand that 'what's important to me is fine for me, but that doesn't make it right for you.' "[28] Teachers stress that values are different, but not that one is better or more adequate than another.[29] Simon is optimistic that "people who go through the process of deciding what they value will in the end reflect the ways one would hope, in any event, that all good [people] would behave."[30] In reality, students may justify cheating or using drugs as a freely chosen activity in accord with their values hierarchy. Under the constraints of values clarification ground rules, the teacher is in a poor position to gainsay the student's conclusion.

Values clarification has come under attack for breeding absolute relativism among students, which it has done: [31] but, as John Stewart has shown, often it also operates in the classroom in such a way as to produce coercive peer pressure to adopt the most popular value choice. For example, one of the strategies used is the "values continuum," which asks students to take positions on an array of value choices. Asked "How do you feel about premarital sex?" students are presented with a continuum that includes Virginal Virginia at one end and Mattress Millie at the other. This "coercion to the mean," Stewart has argued, is a "great factor in many of the values clarification strategies . . . in which the extreme positions are so value-specific and/or emotionally loaded as to preclude them as legitimate alternatives for public affirmation for many people."[32]

All forms of moral education which relegate it to techniques that can be taught in a few classes a week are suspect, particularly if a program like values clarification is seen as an activity in which adults engage only as facilitators. Adults cannot leave their own values at the schoolhouse door and look on as interested bystanders to see what values students invent for themselves. Teachers cannot evade their own responsibility for shaping the moral world in which the practice of education takes place or let values clarification by students become a substitute for the moral reasoning in which they ought to engage as a faculty in order to sustain a good educational community.

In summary, then, we can say that what is troubling about the moral order of the contemporary public school is that it tends to be expressed only in limited ways. Under the bureaucratic-legal aspects, a school tends to be reduced to a set of procedures for guaranteeing individual rights and setting forth what is legally proscribed. At its worst, it is fulfillment of Hannah Arendt's expression of an "infinite system of bureaus in which no one is in charge." Under its therapeutic aspects, it tends toward a contractual relationship in which the individual considers the costs and benefits of a course of action and community is reduced to a series of dyads. Under values clarification, the obligations of a member of the community are always theoretically open to reclarifications that come from nowhere and do not necessarily go anywhere.

Yet the alternative is not the repeal of the modern world. Certainly, individuals must be protected against the abuse of authority, including at times their own parents or teachers. The privileged frame of the therapeutic relationship can be a helpful means of evaluating distortions of traditional moral discourse. And both values clarification and moral reasoning are valuable and necessary activities in the proper context. The alternative is an educational community in which all are bound by some transcendent ideals and common commitments to an articulated sense of the public good for which public education exists. This community would be one in which the responsible adults honor individual rights and procedural guarantees but do not believe these are adequate to express the ideals toward which the community strives; it would be a community in which therapeutic contracts could not override some kinds of common expectations, and in which some values were not endlessly open.

The most serious objection to this view is that many parents and teachers not only believe that the attainment of such an ideal school is impossible, but they want the world they have. Whether reluctantly (because they believe that the moral world of the contemporary public school is the best compromise we are likely to obtain) or willingly (perhaps because they are strong relativists), they embrace a non-judgmental educational world of individual rights and contractual exchange in which impersonal bureaucratic rules guarantee free access to market choices. They are satisfied with or actively prefer a public-school culture based primarily on procedural guarantees and individual choices unbounded by (or at least only minimally connected with) any overarching ideals. They are too keenly aware of the other kinds of reductions that take place when the heavy hand of moralism, bigotry, and class prejudice is laid on public schools in the name of character ideals. Talk of the public good has too often been a screen behind which schools have been made to serve the interests of a privileged few.

No one who has read history can fail to be impressed by the force of this objection. The potential corruptions are legion, although not inevitable. On the other hand, what choice is left to those of us who fear the corruption of education in its contemporary drift toward an impersonal, technicist, rule-bound bureaucratic model? Is private education our only refuge? Must those who wish to pursue the creation of what I have called a strong positive ethos abandon the public sector? I am not ready to conclude that. Nor do I believe that those who sincerely raise strong objections can be overridden or ignored. Hence what I argue here presumes that there will be some real choice among models of schooling *within* the public sector. I do not think it either desirable or practical to attempt to shut down the minimalist bureaucratic model of public schooling. But I hope it will not remain the only model, or even the dominant one. If we do assume that the ground has been cleared for real choice within the public sector (a policy issue to be treated in the concluding chapter) what problems need to be overcome in order to create models of a strong positive ethos? In order to generate such models in ways consistent with a democratic polity, we need a definition of strong positive ethos that is applicable.

A school with a strong positive ethos is one that affirms the ideals and imparts the intellectual and moral virtues proper to the functioning of an educational community in a democracy. It attempts to commit its members to those ideals and virtues in at least a provisional way through the espousal of goals, exemplary actions and practices, ritual celebrations, and observance of norms.

Assume that we have a group of parents and teachers who, although confused and perhaps doubtful of the outcome, are united in their wish to move beyond the minimalist bureaucratic model. Faced with the aim of creating a strong positive ethos, at least four problems are likely to be raised by the skeptics among them. The first of these is fundamentally the problem of separation of church and state, and the belief of many teachers that they are prevented by law from talking about morals or virtue, which they equate with religious teaching. The vigorous action of the courts in striking down school prayer, religious symbolism, and school dress codes has convinced many teach- ers that morality is solely an individual matter (hence the popularity of values clarification courses) or a matter of law. Or, if the teachers are not convinced, they are confused about how to talk about morals and do not know what language is appropriate. The case needs to be made anew that morality is independent of religion and that religion is neither a necessary nor a sufficient justification for the most basic, universal, ethical principles. Even from within, so to speak, new moral standards are often raised in criticism of specifically religious practice, as is the case among some Roman Catholics today who are critical of their church's treatment of women. Ernest Wallwork has drawn the distinction between religion and morality that needs underlining here:

> Obligations are religious in character if they follow from a historically particularistic *way of life* (beliefs, attitudes, practices) based on a concept of sacred authority . . . Obligations are moral if they are "universaliz- able" (in the sense of applying to any similar person in similar circum- stances and to the same agent in all relevantly similar situations), and if they consider the fundamental interests of persons.[33]

Specifically religious beliefs or practices, then, whether expressed in prayers, dietary laws, or Christmas rituals, are ruled out of the public school; but virtues in the sense of morality are not. By virtues we mean those dispositions and qualities of moral excellence that are honored in a community.

Those who agree that this distinction is valid may nonetheless raise a second objection, namely that it simply is not possible to reach agreement today on the most fundamental virtues or ethical guidelines. With the composition of public schools so extraordinarily diverse, how can we expect teachers and parents to reach agreement in the face of deep divisions on moral questions in the society at large? What is "universalizable," when some parents believe that abortion is justified and others are violently opposed to it: when some approve capital punishment and others do not; or (as we saw at Hamilton High) when some parents smoke marijuana with their children while others would like to have those parents arrested? The flaw in this line of reasoning is that it assumes that because it is hopeless to attempt to reach agreement on all moral questions, it is therefore impossible to reach agreement on any. Yet it *is* possible to reach consensus on some moral questions. The issue then becomes, which? We do not have to agree on many questions with persons we happen to sit beside at a crowded motion picture theater: we have little mutual responsibility in that relationship and we are not really doing anything together. If we agree not to disturb one another, that is usually enough. But in an educational community, we do have responsibility for others and there is a great deal that we are doing together and that we cannot in fact accomplish unless we come to some agreements. We need to reach consensus, first, on the necessary moral underpinnings of any community engaged in educational activities; and second, on those virtues and ideals that are proper to the functioning of an educational community in a democracy. In the first category fall such things as providing a safe and secure environment, and assuring the basic order of the community so that education can take place. Five people cannot talk at the same time. Persons must not be abused physically or psychologically; nor must individuals be allowed to abuse themselves with alcohol or drugs, because educational activity will be severely impaired under such conditions. Honesty and truthfulness are included, for educational discourse cannot proceed if one party is dissembling, and science has no meaning if one has no compunction about misrepresenting the evidence.

In the second category are both those virtues characteristic of democratic education and the ideals toward which we strive. Among such democratic virtues would be fairness to all in attempting to assure educational benefits, respect for all persons so that we do not exclude some from the dialogue or take a prejudiced view of how much they are likely to contribute or benefit from it, and a sense of justice with respect to rewards given or withheld. Good schools honor moral excellence that approaches the ideal, although it cannot be a universal expectation. We do not reward students for not cheating but we esteem those persons who are scrupulous about the intellectual debts they owe to others, or who have the courage to acknowledge their own feelings or experience on a particular point even when it may go against an argument they are trying to make. Personal effort and hard work beyond the absolute minimum required are virtues in the pursuit of learning and truth, as are compassion and empathy for others. We cannot mandate these traits, nor can we deny their value in enlarging our understanding. Altruism is in some sense one of the basic virtues of any educational community, for one cannot truly be an educator without a sense of selflessness and concern for others. It is nearly impossible to "work to rule" as a teacher; one has in some sense to give without any expectation of proportionate personal return. Great teachers summon great resources and work late into the night in behalf of students who may only dimly understand or at times even resent those efforts. Not that we should look only to teachers as sources of altruism. In good schools one finds students in peer tutoring and peer counseling roles and sees them undertake a variety of volunteer tasks. Given the needs of many students who are now enrolled in public schools, student help is necessary if all students are going to be enabled to become full participants in the educational community. Without such help the individualized educational plan prescribed by law for each disabled student is likely to be little more than a slogan. But of course it is not only disabled students who need help; many students who enter school from disadvantaged circumstances need tutoring and other kinds of assistance if they are going to experience success in school. As when we give blood or come to the aid of a person in distress, most actions labeled altruistic have mixed into them some element of what Tocqueville called self-interest rightly understood. We know that we may need to draw on the blood bank ourselves someday, and we hope in going to the rescue of a drowning child that someone will come to our aid in similar circumstances. So with most of the tasks suggested here. Studies show, in fact, that tutors benefit as much as tutees in most in-school experiments; tutors learn more in order to teach well. But self-interest rightly understood is not all that motivates such action, and it ought not be the only grounds of our appeal to students.[34]

At this point a third objection may be raised: the fear that this emphasis on virtues will lead to indoctrination. In many school systems, as in Median, school boards have adopted policies forbidding teachers to impose their personal values on students.[35] School board lawyers are inclined to cite the language of the Supreme Court in striking down the compulsory pledge of allegiance to the flag: "If there is any fixed star in our constellation," Justice Jackson wrote in behalf of the majority, "it is that no official, high or petty, can prescribe what shall be orthodox in politics, nationalism, religion, or other matters of opinion or force citizens to confess by word or act their faith therein."[36] But the Court in this case was arguing for freedom of religion, freedom for children of Jehovah's Witnesses not to be compelled to make a pledge of loyalty to an earthly government that they felt violated the tenets of their faith. The Court has also ruled that schools may not restrict the free-speech rights of students even when they may wish to oppose government policy, as when it upheld the right of students in Des Moines public schools to protest the Vietnam War.[37]

But protection of free exercise of religion and of freedom to criticize one's government or one's school should not be interpreted to mean that all moral practices are a matter of personal opinion. As I have attempted to show, it is possible to define the moral practices that are the necessary underpinnings of educational activity in such a way as to respect differences of opinion on other moral questions such as abortion or gambling. These then become not personal values but the justifiable practices and virtues of an educational community.

Yet the skeptic may press: "Doesn't this involve the imposition of some values on the young? You are telling students what to think and feel about certain basic moral matters. Educators should aim at developing critical intellect and personal autonomy. What is being suggested here would shortcircuit true inquiry and amount to a form of indoctrination." The skeptic has a point; it is true that educators must impose some standards even before children have reached an age to reason about them. After all, even a small child might strike a hammer blow at the temple of a sleeping adult. But we are also suggesting that in high schools, when students *can* think for themselves in good measure, adults will, by example and conviction growing out of their responsibilities as educators, be teaching students to uphold certain moral standards and ideals.

What can save this activity from indoctrination is the manner in which these standards and ideals are taught. If adults teach them in an authoritarian manner as a fixed and unvarying code that must be stamped into the consciousness of children, then they can be charged with indoctrination. They will be saved from such an indictment if they give the reasons for the standards, based on universalizable principles undergirding the educational endeavor, and present them as provisional. By provisional I do not mean that they are so tentative as to be made up anew each week, but that teachers convey the understanding that moral standards are always in some sense in the process of development. As R. S. Peters has written, it means that teachers initiate students to such beliefs in a nonbehavioristic way, not fixing a particular moral content for life, but showing students that as adults they will have the responsibility and freedom to reevaluate those beliefs.[38] This means, for example, that while teachers will uphold the ideal of equality, they will also take pains to show how the ideal of equality of educational opportunity was felt to be satisfied in the nineteenth century by providing common schools open to all, whereas today it embodies the concept that compensatory or additional educational services must be provided to some in order to meet everyone's needs. Further, it means that teachers, while insisting on respect for the dignity of others within the classroom, will also show that respect is partly a cultural concept subject to change and revision. They may note, for example, that while the Supreme Court ruled in favor of the Jehovah's Witnesses in 1943, it had earlier supported the school board's contention that "the act of saluting the flag is only one of many ways that a citizen may evidence his *respect* for the government" and thus "did not violate any constitutional rights."[39]

These examples can only illustrate the responsibility that teachers have of conveying the organic nature of ideals without surrendering to a meaningless relativism. It is not possible to go beyond examples, to be exhaustive, for each faculty will have to come to its own understanding of these questions. The state cannot perform this task for them, for that would amount to inert reception of a fixed code. There will be abundant overlap in the kinds of ideals and virtues that schools affirm, but there will also be differences in their breadth and emphasis from school to school, depending upon local traditions and the state of moral development of the faculty itself. The adults primarily responsible for a given educational community should be continually in the process of reflecting upon and renewing their world. It is not a responsibility that they can abdictate, for education, as Hannah Arendt has written,

> is the point at which we decide whether we love the world enough to assume responsibility for it and by the same token save it from that ruin which, except for renewal, except for the coming of the new and young, would be inevitable. And education, too, is where we decide whether we love our children enough not to expel them from our world and leave them to their own devices, nor to strike from their hands their chance of undertaking something new, something unforeseen by us, but to prepare them in advance for the task of renewing a common world.[40]

Finally, a fourth demurral. Parents and teachers may agree that schools have a responsibility for shaping a moral world, and see that it is possible to reach a "provisional" consensus on the moral and intellectual virtues that are proper to the functioning of a school in a democracy. But the task may strike some as utopian. How can we expect public schools to transmit what many adults in our society no longer believe or practice? Personal effort and hard work, honesty and altruism are fine sentiments, but schools do not exist in a vacuum. Americans are increasingly hedonistic and narcissistic; presidents lie, corporations fix prices, and many cheat on their income tax returns. Daniel Yankelovich believes his surveys show that contemporary Americans are beginning to live by some "new rules," not altogether admirable. For example, parents appear to be less altruistic, with 60 percent feeling that "they should be free to live their own lives even if it means spending less time with their children," and 63 percent saying they have a right to live well now "even if it means leaving less to the children." And only a minority (43 percent) now believe "hard work always pays off," whereas 58 percent endorsed that view in 1969. However, 57 percent agree it is important to "demand a lot" from children and presumably believe the schools should teach students that they have to "do their best to get ahead."[41]

Attitudes of first-year college students measured in surveys over a period of twenty years show similar trends. The data show "rising materialistic and power values" and "declining altruism and social concern," according to Alexander Astin, the psychologist who directed the surveys at the University of California at Los Angeles. From 1967 to 1985 the share of students who believe "it is essential or very important to develop a meaningful philosophy of life" fell from 83 percent to 43 percent. In the same period those who felt it was "very important to be very well off financially" rose from 44 percent to 71 percent.[42]

The final outcome is unknown. These trends may prove to be irreversible. Perhaps in the long run, the minimalist bureaucratic model will prove to be the only model that such a "new rules" culture can sustain. American reformers have tended to overestimate what schools alone can do to cure the ills that afflict us, and my own hopes for schools with a strong positive ethos may be similarly skewed. On the other hand, schools are rightfully in the center of most cultural and symbolic battles. Much of what we become as a nation is shaped in the schoolyard and the classroom. If we believe that history is open, then the renewal of the moral order of public schools is one place to make an effort to counter some of the depressing trends revealed by the data of Yankelovich and Astin. Let us turn to one school where such an effort was made.

The Transformation of a Public School

The principal of Robert W. Cook High School, Joseph Conan, had been an outstanding biology teacher to whom the students had at one time dedicated their yearbook. He left his teaching post at the end of the sixties to accept a position as assistant principal at a high school in a nearby district. Cook High and the town in which it was located were changing before Conan left. The school never experienced the traumas of racial desegregation that Hamilton High had undergone— by 1980 there were only twenty blacks among the fifteen hundred students enrolled at Cook. But the school felt the stresses of growth and increased social class diversity as suburban development reached its borders in the sixties and seventies. Cook High had served a farming and working-class community that encompassed a significant proportion of rural poor; in the 1970 census 25 percent of the town's population was below the poverty line.

In the decade of the seventies two major new industrial plants were built near the town, and new freeways shortened the commuting distance to the city. Condominium developments and expensive suburban housing tracts sprang up overnight. The traditions of a fairly tight-knit community underwent rapid change as the children of farmers and small-town merchants began to mix with the more affluent and cosmopolitan offspring of the new executive and middle-management class. When Conan was called back to the school as principal in 1976, he found that vandalism was high, thefts from school lockers were averaging $350 a week, teacher morale was low, drug use was widespread, and absenteeism had increased. Teachers described a world not that different from the "Let the Students Decide" era at Hamilton High in the 1970s. Students had become vocal in demanding their rights, and the expanded teaching staff was divided and factionalized. Some remembered that a teacher who had grabbed a student in the act of pulling a false fire alarm was made to apologize to the student before the day was out. One teacher spoke of the verbal abuse that had become part of life at Cook High: "We had to put up with stuff that kids couldn't get away with anywhere else in society. It's intolerable that teachers have to take such abuse and that other kids have to be subjected to it too."[43] Although they did not lock their doors as teachers at Hamilton had, the faculty at Cook were similarly confused about what had happened, how their world had shifted beneath their feet in little more than a decade. Without talking about it or openly acknowledging it, they began to withdraw and to avoid confronting students over moral or intellectual expectations they had once taken for granted.

Joseph Conan's return as principal was greeted favorably by virtually all of the teachers who knew him. This was no mere law-and-order principal, although the staff soon learned he would not hesitate to use the law and police powers when necessary to reestablish order. Conan was respected intellectually for his excellence as a teacher and morally for his compassion, courage, and spirit of service to others. He rejected the language of modern management techniques. Conan was unashamed to talk to the faculty about "love of mankind" or to ask, "If we are not here to serve people, what else is there in life?"

He visited students in the hospital and took school-work to the homes of those who had been suspended to show that discipline was not born of hatred. He had the capacity to engage the students, faculty, and parents in dialogue about the issues that really mattered.

Conan plunged the faculty into deliberations over what had happened and what troubled them about the school. He began student dialogue groups. He invited parents of students who were floundering to meet with him and the teachers to talk about remedies. Out of these and other discussions came guidelines known as community rules. Unlike the student handbook at Hamilton and other schools, these rules were not written in legalistic language nor were they aimed sorely at students. The community rules were a statement of expectations that all in the school community would be bound by. They spoke of trustworthiness, honesty, fairness, competency, mutual respect, and the responsibilities of members of a caring community. In talks with teachers, parents, and students, Conan was fond of summing up the school's philosophy as the five Rs and the five As. The five Rs were "reading, 'riting, and 'rithmetic plus respect and responsibility; the five As were attendance, attention, attitude, and academic excellence in a caring atmosphere. Buttons were imprinted with the message "We Care" superimposed on a triangle linking students, faculty, and staff.

Buttons and five-point slogans may raise suspicions that public relations outweighed substantive change. Yet declarations of community ideals are characteristic of good schools. Underscoring of revered values, a certain "making public" of central beliefs, is necessary. Declarations alone are not sufficient, of course. Speech acts to remind us of ideals and to symbolically bind the community but it only has substantive meaning if it finds expression in face-to-face interactions and is reflected in interpersonal conduct. Leadership consists in attempting to close the distance between ideals and behavior by reminding all members of the community of what is at stake in the attainment of ideals and by suggesting practical actions that can be taken to help realize those ideals. Leaders must first have a vision and then make it live in the imagination of all members of the community. Convincing others of the distance to be traveled and of the road to be taken often requires courage.

The new principal saw that the drug problem had increased alarmingly. Teachers, like many parents, were afraid or reluctant to confront their students. Some preferred to dispute the existence of a problem. "Some of the parents in this community would deny that they had a child with a drug problem unless that student came home in the middle of a dinner party and puked on the floor," Conan recalled. Yet he knew that most teachers and parents would take responsibility if a way could be found to clearly identify those students who needed help. He felt that neither the therapeutic contractualism model, through usual counseling methods, nor the values clarifications approach had been effective. With the financial help of a wealthy parent and the cooperation of the local police chief, Conan arranged for an under- cover agent to enter the school as a transfer student. After several months' work, three students were indicted by a grand jury for sub- stantial drug trafficking, and sixty others were identified as heavy users. The undercover agent had gathered considerable detail about amounts and types of drug use by these students. Conan invited each of the parents of the sixty heavy users to meet with him and the police chief. Nearly all came. No further arrests were made, but the information about drug use was shared. "We said, 'Look, here's the information, here's what we saw on more than one occasion.' The effect was that even the parents who [formerly] would say 'My kid wouldn't do that' were appreciative. The kid was confronted. It gave them a basis to do some talking." Out of these conversations came also a realization on the part of parents of how urgently their children needed reasonable boundaries, and an awareness on the part of the school of how lonely and isolated many of these drug users were and how reluctant they were to approach official guidance personnel or drug counselors. The revelations galvanized the community also. Conan found ministers, priests, rabbis, and parents willing to come to the school to be available for counseling with students. Parents also volunteered to help teachers police the drug problem in the school and to take duty turns on the smokers' patch.

In response to violation of some community rules, such as littering, vandalism, and smoking in the lavatories, Conan convinced teacher and school janitors to cooperate in supervising a work detail. Students guilty of such infractions repaired windows, cleaned lavatories, picked up trash, and swept floors. Vandalism dropped from an average of fifty-five windows broken per year to almost zero. Trashing of the cafeteria and school grounds also declined markedly.

On other kinds of violations of community rules—disrespect and verbal abuse, lying, cheating, repeated failure to complete assignments, habitual tardiness—it was more difficult to achieve consensus. Teachers were inconsistent about what infractions merited a trip to the "office." Vice principals, especially if they were burdened with a crisis or attempting to counsel another pupil, would send students back to class with varying mixtures of a pat on the back and a slap on the wrist. The problem of how to achieve consistency and fairness in upholding the ideals of respect and responsibility in a caring community was perplexing. Conan kept the faculty working at it for several years.

The solution that evolved was part homegrown and part an adaptation of William Glasser's theories of reality therapy.[44] Instead of being sent to the office, students violating the kinds of community rules noted above were sent to what became known as the "planning room." This was a form of in-school suspension, and the room was manned by teachers on rotation throughout the day in lieu of study hall or other duties. Once in the room, it was the student's responsibility to develop a plan for readmittance to the class that included giving an account of the infraction that both student and teacher found acceptable. This sometimes involved a "cooling-off" period of a day or two—although students were responsible for making up work missed in other classes while working out their plan. The teachers staffing the room talked over the problem with the student and helped in development of a plan—often acting as go-betweens with the teacher who had originally disciplined the student.

The plan at Cook led both teachers and students to reflect on value hierarchies. The difference from values clarification approaches is that these were not fluid but reflected values by which the community as a whole agreed it should be bound as part of its definition as an educational enterprise. Although the student developed a sort of contract, it was embedded in these understandings and extended beyond the private dyadic relationship of therapeutic contractualism. It was a process that required the faculty as a whole to reflect on the values they held and to talk to one another about consistent applications of them. Different faculty members, in taking their turns in the planning room and in acting as mediators between students and other faculty, were developing consistent applications of the norms governing the moral life of the community. Finally, although it allowed for some appeal and negotiation on the part of students, it gave recognition to the primary authority of the teacher and did not reduce discipline to the application of courtroomlike legal procedure. In the beginning, as many as one hundred eighty-five students a month were sent to the planning room. Both the number of students disciplined and the amount of recidivism declined as teachers gained experience with the process. Frequent repeaters were singled out for special help, which might involve extensive counseling or adjustment to their academic program.

Conan also moved in a variety of ways to make good on the school's commitment to academic excellence. He sought to hire fine teachers and spent considerable time in classrooms helping teachers identify their weaknesses. When students who met with him in his weekly dialogue groups complained about boring classes or ineffective teachers, he followed up. He developed an extensive network of community internships to offer students new ways to test their vocational interests. He increased the number of enrichment and advanced placement courses to challenge able students. But he was concerned too with students who were performing below par. One of his early efforts was the GREAT (Graduation Requires Effort And Time) Kids program. This was designed for students whose test scores indicated in freshman year that they were headed for academic trouble even though they were fully capable of doing satisfactory work. Conan brought parents and teachers of more than twenty of these students together and asked them to commit themselves to monthly meetings for the remainder of the year. The aim was to learn how to help these students experience more academic success. Out of it came agreements by teachers to call the parents once a week with progress reports and promises by parents to do more to supervise homework, limit television watching, and show greater interest in their children's schoolwork. In a number of cases, parents were enabled to talk about their fears and anxieties concerning their children, a number of whom were isolates with few friends. Teachers shared some of their frustrations in the classroom. Conan himself attended each of these sessions and brought in other staff to join teachers and parents in talking about problems of motivation or discipline. A parent who had a child in the school before Conan had arrived four years earlier spoke up at one meeting to say, "The school is radically different today. This is due to Mr. Conan being able to stand up in front of a group of parents like this and engage them in this kind of communication."

Nonetheless, the principal encountered opposition from some. Students picketed and distributed leaflets on school buses after Conan brought police into the school, accusing him of operating a "police state." (Conan invited them to one of his dialogue groups.) A few parents and some teachers were opposed to his use of an undercover agent. Two teachers criticized Conan for overemphasizing "health and welfare issues" at the expense of academic concerns. But the majority of teachers believed that the intellectual and the moral climate of the school had improved markedly during Conan's tenure. Faculty felt that he had a vision but that he had not merely imposed it on them. Rather, he had joined them in dialogue about ways to shape and actualize that vision. They admired his courage, the fact that he had confronted them on some difficult issues as well as challenging students and parents. In interviews, though, the words we heard again and again spoke less of his firmness than of his humanity and compassion. Conan had the wisdom not to try to define all moral issues. Nor was he an advocate of school prayer. Yet he understood that a public school did have a moral warrant and a responsibility to affirm certain virtues and ideals.

CHAPTER EIGHT

Two Essential Reforms

The effort of a single teacher is the ultimate resort of
excellence in education.

—*Eva Brann,* Paradoxes of Education in a Republic

T he answer to the question of who will reform the schools is that
teachers and principals will. Others—legislators, parents, school
board members, and teacher trainers—have enabling roles. But the most
meaningful work must be done within individual schools by teachers
and principals. Without it there will be little real improvement in
schools no matter how often organization charts are reshuffled or how
many new requirements are imposed. Two essential reforms are required in order to create the conditions under which teachers and
principals can do the real work of improving schools. First, authentic
local control—local in the sense of the school itself, not the district
or the city—must be provided, to enable teachers and principals to
create schools with a strong positive ethos. Second, the teaching
profession must be reformed so that teachers can assume genuine
responsibility for their practice.

Before we look at these proposals in detail, let us explore whether
the research on which our analysis is based is atypical. Is Hamilton
High a unique case, or have our findings been corroborated by other
research?

Research Findings

The recent wave of reports on educational reform are based largely
on research completed in the 1970s and early 1980s. That work cor-
responds most closely to the portrait of Hamilton High given in Chap-

ter 3, and to some degree in Chapter 4. Although the research shows wide variation in both the conditions within the schools and the quality of education offered, the kind of deconstruction of the old world that we described at Hamilton did occur elsewhere. There were at least four common trends that affected many schools as they did Hamilton High.

(1) *Disorder, misbehavior, and drug use rose and then declined.* Other studies confirm our findings at Hamilton High that teachers and administrators in the period following major desegregation were often confused about their authority, overreacted to legal mandates, and were inconsistent in their disciplinary policies. In a study of three urban high schools in the period following desegregation, Philip Cusick documented the kind of animosity and tension that also characterized Hamilton High in the early seventies. School administrators spent "almost all of their time and energy 'keeping the lid' on these schools," Cusick concluded, yet they were often "idiosyncratic" in the way they handled disciplinary issues. "What happened to a student sent to the administrator's office depended on the particular administrator."[1] In a three-year study of school discipline, Henry Luffler confirmed the change in teachers' consciousness resulting from new legal mandates in the era of student civil rights: "Courts have increased the insecurity of teachers as they deal with the average discipline problems that take place within the school—As we surveyed the teachers we found a great deal of misunderstanding about what the courts have said, and an overwhelming pattern of overestimating the extent to which courts have told teachers what they can and can't do within the classroom."[2]

Physical violence was not a major problem in most schools. A 1977 survey by the National Institute of Education found that fewer than one school in ten was characterized by serious crime, violence, or disruption. About 16 percent of secondary students in the country, however, said they avoided at least three places in school, from fear of being attacked.[3] An analysis of census data by the Children's Defense Fund five years later showed that personal claims of violence in schools had dropped from 6 percent in 1977 to 4 percent in 1982.[4] This matches the kind of settling down described at Hamilton High. Nevertheless, the 1981 survey of public and private high schools by the National Opinion Research Center (NORC) provided "evidence that disorder is still a major problem for American high schools." More than a fourth of public-school sophomores said students in their school often talked back to teachers, and 23 percent perceived their school as one where students often got into fights. Less than 4 percent said students often attacked or threatened to attack teachers.[5] Although drug use peaked nationally in the late 1970s, it continued at high levels into the current decade. More than 40 percent of all school principals in the 1981 NORC sample considered drug and alcohol use to be a serious or moderate problem. Two-thirds of all seniors in a 1980 poll said they had tried an illicit drug while 36 percent had used marijuana in the past month—a figure that declined to 25 percent by 1985.[6]

(2) *Academic demands were reduced as students negotiated their own curriculum.* As a result of policies of social promotion in the lower grades (by which students were passed whether they had learned to read or not), intensified pressures by society to serve and retain all students, and teachers who could not cope with the radical new diversity within the schools, schools everywhere reduced requirements and let students pick their way through the curriculum. The old-core curricula, among the few external props sustaining the curricular authority of the school, were demolished in many high schools, as they had been a generation earlier in the colleges and universities. The fragmentation of the curriculum and the proliferation of often trivial electives were highlighted in numerous reports and studies.[7] Within the classroom of the many-optioned curriculum, demands were often reduced still further and students found they could choose to do very little and still be passed from one grade to the next. Teachers lowered demands in order to keep the peace and avoid confrontations. After reviewing many studies, Michael Sedlak and his colleagues concluded:

> Teachers often cope by making the acquisition of knowledge "easier," less painful, and therefore less threatening, through unchallenging instructional methods: lecturing, assigning more seatwork, reducing complex conceptual problems to factual lists, diluting or omitting essential content knowledge, refusing to challenge students seriously, requiring little reading, minimizing writing assignments, changing instructional and classroom goals on the spot by attending to personal matters, or conversing with students. Together these accommodating strategies . . . help to keep the peace and appearance of tranquility but often at the expense of academic learning.[8]

Sedlak's review also confirms the pattern of student negotiation we described at Hamilton High. The content of what was to be learned was open to cajolery, challenge, and negotiation as students felt empowered to minimize requirements and frustrate teacher assignments. "Students do not hesitate to challenge the legitimacy of anything that is expected of them. 'Why do we have to learn this?' " they ask again and again. 'What difference does it make if we do this?' "[9] Under such conditions students often elected the soft options or in some cases planned "their own educational demise."[10]

(3) *Tardiness, absenteeism, employment, and dropout rates increased.* Administrators put tardiness and absenteeism at the top of their list of school difficulties. In the NORC survey more than half the principals said it was a problem; 38 percent of public-school sophomores surveyed said students were often absent, and 47 percent said their peers frequently cut classes.[11] As concerned as administrators became, teachers indicated that the problem was still worse. In the mid-eighties Detroit public schools reported an absence rate of 20 percent, but teacher attendance figures showed that nearly 30 percent of their pupils were absent from class on an average day. As at Hamilton High, a significant proportion of students who were legally present in school might not stay for more than a period or two, or spend more time in the cafeteria and "talking study halls" than in class.[12] Studies show that absenteeism rose sharply in the late 1960s, then remained at fairly high levels.[13]

If we assume that students were present and in class, the amount of time they spent under actual instruction was markedly determined by the ethos of the school. John Goodlad's clock-hour portrait of life in thirteen high schools revealed that some spent 84 percent of the time in actual instruction, whereas in others—because of socializing, behavior problems, and management routines—teachers taught only 68 percent of the time.[14] One review of the research on time spent in instruction concluded that when average absences, classes canceled for nonacademic events, and percentages of class time not devoted to teaching are added together, at best 612 of the scheduled total of 1,080 class hours per year are spent in learning. At worst, about 310 hours per year, less than 2 hours per day, are devoted to learning.[15] Comparisons with the Japanese (about 210 school days per year, contrasted with 180 in the United States) have heightened American consciousness of time spent in learning.

Less noticed are the sharp differences in teenage employment, which is virtually forbidden by Japanese mothers, who are reluctant to ask children even to do chores at home that would deter them from their studies. In the United States, employment of high school students increased steadily from about one-third with jobs in 1965 to nearly half in 1980, a year when academic demands grew more slack. Many American high schools began to empty out at noon, as students with short schedules went off to jobs in fast-food restaurants or shopping malls. In 1980, 42 percent of all sophomores and 63 percent of seniors had after-school jobs.[16] The trends followed the recommendations of several prestigious national commissions, which in the 1970s urged that high school students have more exposure to work to facilitate their transition to adulthood.[17]

A decade later a new generation of studies, no doubt influenced by the Japanese competition, questioned that wisdom. In their review of the psychological and social costs of adolescent employment, Ellen Greenberger and Laurence Steinberg noted that teenage workers are most often affluent, not poor (twice as many sophomores who work come from families earning more than $16,000 per year than come from families earning less than that). Most do not work out of financial need or to help their families but to finance an adolescent life-style that includes heavy expenditures on cars, stereos, clothes, records, and drugs. The authors argue that intensive involvement in work may cause students to disengage from school, extracurricular activities, and family life. They doubt the value of skills learned in many teenage jobs and recommend that teenagers not work more than fifteen hours a week. In the 1980 NORC survey, nearly two-fifths of the employed sophomores and three-fifths of the seniors worked more than that. Other researchers also questioned the tradeoff of work for study time, noting that holding a job while in school results in lower employment rates for teenagers who do not subsequently go to college.[18] The NORC survey showed that American high school students spend less than an hour a night doing homework, and that those who do not work do significantly more homework than those who are employed more than twenty-two hours a week. Even with these low levels of homework, we heard at Hamilton High the rationalization reported in other research, namely that teachers justify giving less homework because students are burdened with jobs. In Gallup polls, nearly half the students say they are not being asked to work hard enough either at school or in homework assignments. One assumes these are different students than those reported as prone to negotiate with teachers to reduce demands; in fact, higher proportions of higher-achieving students say work is too easy, but many in the middle range do also.[19] Some analysts have speculated that reduced demands and softer curricula intended to help retain students may have had the opposite effect; that is, students left school in greater numbers because there was not enough challenge or engagement in learning. Other analysts have argued that the onset of minimum-competency tests in the last decade may have led students to drop out to avoid the embarrassment of failure. In any event, at a time when Japanese high school graduation rates reached and held steady at nearly 90 percent, the proportion of students who completed high school in four years in the United States fell from 77 percent in 1972 to 72 percent in 1982.[20]

(4) *Student achievement declined for nearly two decades, with signs of slight improvement in the 1980s.* The mean Scholastic Aptitude Test score (1,600 is perfect on combined mathematical and verbal aptitudes) declined from a high of 975 in the mid-sixties to a low of 890 in 1980 and rose slightly to 906 by the mid-eighties. As we have seen, Hamilton High followed this pattern, falling somewhat deeper (to a low of 874 in 1978) and rebounding somewhat better (to 911 by 1985) than the national averages. The SAT has been criticized as testing only aptitude rather than subject-matter achievement; actually, to some degree it tests both. But subject-matter tests showed similar declines. The National Assessment of Educational Progress (NAEP) began testing samples of seventeen-year-olds in 1969. In science, the national percentage of correct answers was 45.2 in 1969, 48.4 in 1973, and 46.5 in 1977. Half the seventeen-year-olds did not know that a star is most like the sun as compared with a comet, meteor, moon, or planet. Only 54 percent chose the one multiple-choice answer containing the word "heat" when asked what happened when combustion takes place. The percentage correct on the math test fell from 64.0 in 1973 to 60.3 in 1982. In tests of political knowledge, scores on the structure of government fell from 64.4 percent in 1969 to 53.9 percent in 1976. Only about half the students knew that each state

has two senators; 42 percent, that it was not illegal to start a political party. In tests of reading, students showed little change in word recognition skills but registered declines in "inferential comprehension"—the ability to infer the meaning of what they have read. These scores fell from 64.2 percent correct in 1971 to 62.1 in 1980.[21]

The NAEP examinations, given in five-year intervals, were most discouraging with regard to writing abilities. Students were asked to write short essays rather than pick answers from multiple-choice tests. Nearly 48 percent of the high school juniors had writing samples judged adequate or better in 1969, 46 percent in 1974, and slightly under 42 percent in both 1979 and 1984. These overall scores of writing effectiveness were based on averaging student ability in informational, analytical, persuasive, and imaginative writing tasks. Students scored highest in simple reporting or informational writing—65 percent of the 1984 juniors could write an adequate letter describing themselves in a job application and 54 percent could construct a newspaper article about a haunted house if given the facts to be included. But once an analytical component was introduced, scores plummeted. Less than a quarter, given information about life on the American frontier, could write an acceptable essay comparing food eaten then with that of today. Only 7 percent could write a paragraph judged to be an adequate answer to the task of describing a favorite type of music and explaining why it is liked. The essays received one of four grades:

Unsatisfactory—mere phrases or disjointed responses.

Minimal—included some of the elements requested but did not manage them well enough to assure the task would be achieved. For instance, with regard to the music question the response "My favorite kind of music is slow or pop rock" earned a minimal score because it said what the student liked but not why.

Adequate—an example was the following: "My favorite kind of music is soft, easy rock because it is soothing and relaxing. I don't like the hard rock kind, it give [sic] me a headache. Soft rock has a nice beat, but it doesn't annoy you like hard rock. It's easy to sing along with, too, because you can understand what they're saying."

Elaborated—a response that went beyond the essential, provided more details, and reflected a higher level of coherence.

Students were not penalized for misspelling or poor grammar, yet less than 30 percent could adequately respond to analytical or persuasive writing tasks. Only 15 percent of the high school juniors could write an adequate or better essay defending a special request to the school principal; 22 percent could do so in arguing for a change in a school rule. They did a little better with three imaginative writing tasks, averaging 34 percent at the adequate level or higher when asked to invent a story.[22]

In a nation as diverse as the United States, it is hard to say that any school is typical. Yet in comparing our portrait of Hamilton High with this largely factual account of trends in the American high school over the past three decades, we can at least say that Hamilton is not an atypical or highly aberrant case. On the question of what the facts mean and what prescriptions they lead to, there is much more disagreement.

Decline in Perspective

It should not be presumed, as it so often is, that the decline in achievement reported above represents a falling off from a plateau of excellence. The early sixties may have represented an irregular peak of not very exalted achievement at a time when less than two-thirds of eighteen-year-olds completed high school. The decline in the decades that followed was genuine and steep, but it could also be viewed as a return to the plateau that was more characteristic of American schools for most of the century. American high schools may have bottomed out in 1980 at a lower level of achievement than characterized them in the 1940s and 1950s, but the real long-term decline is skewed by using the early 1960s as a base line. It is difficult to speak with any certainty, because we simply do not have valid comparative samples of student achievement in the earlier era—although we have some evidence.

The great debate about the American high school was framed at the turn of the century with the president of Harvard University, Charles W. Eliot, on the one side, and the psychologist G. Stanley Hall, president of Clark University, on the other. At a time when only about 8 percent of all youth were graduating from high school, Eliot and the Committee of Ten of the National Education Association, which he chaired, argued that all high school students should be educated with equal seriousness in the major branches of human knowledge and that occupational decisions should be put off until after graduation. As David Cohen explains in his cogent account of the origins of the American high school, [23] Hall challenged Eliot's view in a 1901 debate. Hall, whose position eventually triumphed in the "Cardinal Principles" report of the National Education Association, argued that the schools should serve the needs and interests of all in a diversified curriculum. [24] The issue was joined: could all students be expected to pursue an intellectually demanding course of study, or should most be given more choice, easier routes to a diploma, and a more practical curriculum?

Hall wanted the high schools to adapt their curricula to "the great majority who begin the high school [and] do not finish, instead of focusing our energies on the few who get to college." Eliot's program, he argued, would lead students to become "disenchanted by difficulty or aridity." To avoid such problems, the curriculum should be based on the "nature and needs" of students, including the immediate needs of those who head directly from high school to a job. Students needed practical skills more than a boring academic preparation for colleges they would probably never attend. Eliot, on the other hand, had been appalled by the enterpreneurial style of the rising cadre of new public-school administrators who were trying to lure out-of-school youth into the high schools with a variety of more useful courses. Public schools had begun to offer bookkeeping and mechanical drawing as well as new academic subjects such as physics and French to replace or augment the older classical emphasis. Eliot and the Committee of Ten wanted to cut back the proliferation of courses—not unlike some current reform proposals—and concentrate on the academic core. Eliot was not against change, however, favoring the admission of modern science and languages (which angered the older constituency that wanted to hold fast to the classical curriculum). He wanted all students to enjoy the same intellectual birthright through secondary school, and he opposed what he saw as a second-class curriculum for some in occupational or practical subjects. [25]

As new immigrants and their children poured into the high schools, enrollments doubled every decade and the debate was soon settled in Hall's favor. By 1930 most high schools had adopted some variant of a three-tiered curriculum. Bolstered by a new faith in intelligence tests and new platoons of educational psychologists, school administrators embraced the idea that high schools should function as sorting and selection agencies. Some students took the kind of program Eliot had recommended and went on to college; others enrolled in drafting or machine work to prepare for jobs, while taking softer versions of the academic program in some basic subjects; and the remainder followed the general curriculum, taking a mix of courses from business arithmetic to home economics.

After a careful review of what had happened prior to World War II, Cohen concludes that an enormous opportunity was lost. The system expanded to encompass nearly all youth by taking a dim view of the potential of most youth. By the nineteen thirties high schools were largely given over to consumer choices in which students could follow their bent. Schools had begun to substitute social studies for history, general math for algebra, and they "did away with the old system of requiring all students to take courses in specific academic subspecialties, like physics or history, that built on each other and led, at least in principle, to deeper command of a subject." As in the more recent era, academic demands on students were eased. "Educators desperately wanted their new students to get by . . . By 1930, when high schools enrolled half of those old enough to attend, they had given up the effort to maintain decent performance for all those attending."[26] In 1933 a federal survey of high school grading practices revealed that most high schools made "strenuous efforts" to avoid failing students. Performance standards were low, and half the schools reported that even when students failed they were still promoted. The practice of social promotion had been invented, although it had not been given a name yet, and course offerings were watered down as student choices expanded.[27]

By 1939 the emphasis on practical subjects had been given a new name and a new twist: "Education for Life Adjustment," a curriculum often advanced in John Dewey's name but never championed by him. "Life adjustment" conceived of practical education as extending far beyond training for jobs (which had become scarce in the depression years) to a "practical curriculum for everyday living." In English classes students would be taught how to carry on polite conversations, in social studies how to behave on dates, and in home economics how to keep house.[28] The life-adjustment curriculum spread rapidly in the 1940s and became the official ideology of the National Education

Association in its 1944 report, *Education for All American Youth*, which described the ideal curriculum, restructured to meet "imperative needs of youth."[29] The kind of thinking typical of the curriculum makers of the day was summed up in a popular book, *A Look at Our Schools*, which argued that the special strength of the "modern school" was to properly fit a child for a useful life: "It is vain and wasteful to take a girl who would make a fine homemaker and try to fit her into the patterns of training which make a lawyer, or to take a boy who would be successful in business and try to fit his training to that which produces doctors."[30]

Although the evidence was scattered, several reports and surveys raised questions about the quality of education not unlike critiques of more recent vintage. August Hollingshead's 1949 study of *Elmtown's Youth* indicated that academic demands on high school students were low and that few had to study more than "an hour or two a week outside of school hours."[31] Regional surveys conducted by Purdue University in the early nineteen fifties found that 40 percent of the high school students questioned believed the earth was the center of the universe; one-fifth of the students in the West picked Lincoln as the author of the Declaration of Independence; and three-fourths thought the circumference of the earth was 125,000 miles.[32] A minority of students took advanced science, mathematics, or foreign languages. Eighty percent of all high school students in 1955 took no foreign language, and 46 percent of all high schools offered none, either modern or classical.[33]

While there had been earlier critics (most damaging perhaps was John Dewey's own questioning of the excesses of progressive and life-adjustment curricula),[34] a counterreformation began in earnest in the 1950s. The most notable of these critics was Arthur Bestor, whose *Educational Wastelands* had wide influence. Himself a graduate of an excellent progressive school, Bestor said he had no quarrel with new methods that resulted in improved teaching of subject matter. He opposed "regressive education" that was hostile to intellect and substituted "life needs" for the basic disciplines: "It is a curiously ostrich-like way of meeting life needs to de-emphasize foreign languages during a period of world war and postwar global tensions, and to deemphasize mathematics at precisely the time when the nation's security has come to depend on Einstein's equation."[35]

Even though the critics grew in number and began to be echoed in the mass media, they did not seriously disturb the schools or change public consciousness. When Hamilton High opened in 1953, the taxpayers in Median, as in most of the country, were satisfied with their schools. Despite the debates among educators and philosophers, the schools were generally seen as successful in expanding to meet the needs of a growing population and providing more educational opportunity than the world had yet seen. The progressive emphasis on meeting the needs of all appealed to the pragmatic American temperament. Most parents were not very bookish themselves and were as concerned about their children's popularity as their intellect. The pride of those whose children were the first in the family to graduate from high school overcame any doubts about the quality of education received. And despite the criticisms, many intelligent parents shared the progressive zeal for teaching methods that would increase awareness of individual differences among children and replace lockstep instruction that relied on rote memorization. They applauded the progressive project method where it drew intelligently on the experiences of children, and supported the moves to make room for health programs and vocational education. The SAT was still in its infancy and there were no national assessments of educational progress to trouble the conscience of either teachers or parents. International comparisons were unheard of.

If it could ever be said that anything truly changed overnight, it could be said about the American consciousness of the need for educational reform after the Russians launched Sputnik on October 4, 1957. The debate among educators was now front-page news, and critics who had argued that the schools were not rigorous enough felt vindicated. As Sputnik orbited overhead—a constant reminder of how political supremacy was tied to technological achievement—Admiral Hyman Rickover was only the most belligerent of the critics who blamed America's schools for threatening American security by allowing the country to fall behind the Russians in science, mathematics, and engineering. Diane Ravitch wrote in her history of the period, "For the first time since the end of World War II, people of all political backgrounds agreed that the national interest depended on improving the schools." Sputnik symbolized the consequences of indifference to high standards. "In popular parlance, Sputnik had happened not because of what the Russians had done but because of what American schools had failed to do."[36] The Rockefeller Brothers Fund 1958 report, *The Pursuit of Excellence*, was one of many urgent calls to the nation to raise its educational aspirations.[37] Harvard President James B. Conant's report, *The American High School Today*, came out a year later and offered a blueprint for improvement. It became an instant bestseller.[38]

By the end of the 1950s high schools were moving more rapidly toward the goal of universal education. The graduation rates had passed the halfway mark in the 1940s and reached 63 percent by 1960. Increasing numbers of the poor and minority groups were attending. Under the stimulus of Sputnik, the great debate between Eliot and Hall was posed again in dramatic form. Did universal education mean differentiated courses and curricula devised according to student ability? Hall and his progressive inheritors had so argued. The curriculum should be shaped to the needs and interests of the students. To do otherwise risked boring or driving out the less able. The critics in Eliot's line asserted that the truly democratic approach would be to teach all students the same basic materials, even if at different rates. Their answer to the problem of bored students was better teaching, not differentiated curricula.

Conant's widely influential report was an attempt at compromising these two positions, though he spoke mostly in the progressive terminology of serving the needs of all. He championed the comprehensive high school with a variety of offerings but opposed rigidly tracking students into precollege or vocational curricula. He favored ability grouping, however, so that students would be challenged at an appropriate level. He urged closing small high schools (defined as those with less than one hundred students in the graduating class) so that an academically talented cohort of students could be formed to take advanced classes in science and mathematics. Conant's recommendations had their strongest impact on consolidation of schools and in concentrating more resources on creating advanced sequences in science and math. The U. S. Office of Education and the National Science Foundation sponsored programs to enlist leading scholars from the universities to develop new curricula in these fields, and Congress passed the National Defense Education Act to recruit teachers to teach them. The impact was phenomenal. A national survey of changes in the high school curriculum between 1949 and 1961 showed that while enrollment had grown by about 50 percent in that period, the number of students enrolled in advanced math, physics, and chemistry courses grew by almost 2,000 percent. Whereas only six states had offered advanced physics in 1948, forty-six did so in 1961.[39] It seems likely that this national push for excellence had some impact on the above-average SAT scores registered in the early sixties.

Hamilton High fit this profile. It, too, had expanded advanced-placement courses. Hamilton at that time was not tracked, but the schools in Median were locked into a feeder system that meant some schools were in effect tracked as predominantly black schools. Nationally, black high school enrollment had tripled from 1940 to 1960, and as the civil rights revolution upset the old feeder system, blacks came pouring into Hamilton High in the mid-sixties. Although the school officially subscribed to Conant's ideal of no tracks, just ability groups, less than 10 percent of the blacks were enrolled in advanced classes, and the low-ability classes that were 90 percent black were referred to by the teachers as the "basic track." Nationally, high school remedial classes in basic English and reading had expanded from 36,000 students in 1949 to 276,000 by the early sixties.[40] Although Conant had made "a good general education for *all* the pupils" his first priority, black parents at Hamilton High did not believe that standard applied to their children.[41]

After riots swept through the halls of Hamilton High in the late sixties, the principal followed the strategy that was adopted or mandated in thousands of schools: eliminate or radically modify classes grouped by ability that enrolled disproportionate numbers of black students, and vastly expand the elective system to in effect let the students track themselves. This was only a slight variant of the formula applied in the earlier prewar period of expansion. There was an important difference, however, in that the schools had then enjoyed the confidence of parents whose faith in education and trust in the system was nearly unbounded. The mandates to achieve desegregated education, often imposed by the courts or high levels of the educational bureaucracy, rose from the bitter legacy of the civil rights revolution. In Median, as in hundreds of other cities, black parents showed by protests and school boycotts that their trust had been broken. I have tried to show in my portrayal of Hamilton High the unprecedented cleavage, deconstruction, and slow efforts at repair and reconstruction that took place. For the civil rights revolution was followed by another almost as significant—the effort to mainstream the disabled. During these two decades achievement levels declined and concern about the performance of the educational system again rose to crisis level.

Neither the schools nor educational policy became a focal point of the 1980 presidential campaign, but a sense of emergency grew out of the fifteen-year downward slope of the SAT scores, low levels of performance revealed in the National Assessment of Educational Progress, reports of drugs and disorder in public schools, and international comparisons of educational achievement. The stunning accomplishment of the Japanese, who in the same period far surpassed the United States in the percentage of youth completing high school, was especially telling. The Japanese so far exceeded U.S. achievement that there was little overlap between the average scores of the best American and Japanese students in mathematics.[42] If the sixties and seventies were in some respect an analogue for the thirties and forties, the eighties became an echo of the fifties with a renewal of calls for excellence, for quality, and for equality. Four major educational commissions and national task forces issued reports in 1983. Each suggested that the schools were a major reason that America was losing ground in the economic competition with Japan. The first and most dramatic report, *A Nation at Risk*, came from the Commission on Educational Excellence appointed by President Ronald Reagan. It resurrected cold-war language to make an explicit connection between the Japanese economic challenge and the Sputnik shock of 1957:

> Our Nation is at risk. Our once unchallenged preeminence in commerce, industry, science, and technological innovation is being overtaken by competitors throughout the world . . .
>
> If an unfriendly foreign power had attempted to impose on America the mediocre educational performance that exists today, we might well have viewed it as an act of war. As it stands, we have allowed this to happen to ourselves. We have even squandered the gains in student achievement made in wake of the Sputnik challenge.[43]

The Business–Higher Education Task Force argued in its report, *America's Competitive Challenge*, that a major reason for falling productivity is that "many American workers lack fundamental skills in mathematics, science, critical thinking and verbal expression"[44] Two other generally conservative reports opened with economic arguments—the Education Commission of the States' *Action for Excellence* and the Twentieth Century Fund's *Making the Grade*.[45] No direct causal relationship is demonstrated in these reports, however, to show that the economy declined because the schools declined or that it would improve if schools improved. In fact, it could be argued that the complex economic problems faced by the United States at the close of the twentieth century have little to do with education. American industry may be in trouble more because of its focus on short-term profit maximization than from sagging performance in the classroom. Popular reports of the fifties blamed Sputnik on the schools, but when America landed its astronauts on the moon in 1969, that was not attributed to school success. In fact, SAT scores were already declining. They were poor arguments for improving the schools in the fifties and they are poor arguments today; yet, economic arguments aside, the schools do need improving to provide the basis of a good life and a good society.

Among the dozen or so reports that followed *A Nation at Risk*, a second group could be called more liberal and less strident. These reports differed from the first group in that they were written by individuals rather than commissions. Although they confirmed many of the earlier findings about a decline in school performance, they did not frame the debate in terms of global competition. In part, both their diagnosis and their proposals for reform overlapped as well, but a major difference was that the national commissions tended to take a top-down, get-tougher stance, seeking to impose such across-the-board reforms as a longer school day and school year, more testing, and stiffer requirements.

The later reports were written by authors who had had more experience in schools and took more of a bottom-up view. This was especially true of *Horace's Compromise: The Dilemma of the American High School*, written by Theodore Sizer, former dean of the Harvard Graduate School of Education and headmaster of Phillips Academy, Andover. He felt that a longer school day might help, but believed that the superficial encounter with learning and incoherence of the American high school was the real root of the problem. Rather than legislate longer hours that might result in more of the same, he suggested "the weaknesses of the high school lie deeper, in how it is organized and in the attitudes of whose who work there."[46] He shared with John Goodlad, former dean of education at UCLA and author of *A Place Called School*, the idea that school problems could not be fixed from the top because they required changes of structure from within, and that students needed deeper and more carefully structured engagement in learning rather than longer doses of what they had been getting. In Sizer's words, "less is more [and] thoroughness counts more than coverage."[47] Ernest Boyer, former U.S. Commissioner of Education and president of the Carnegie Foundation for the Advancement of Teaching, was a third member of this group. In *High School*, Boyer joined them in emphasizing the need for strengthening the capacities of individual schools to shape Eliot's core of serious learning in the basic disciplines for all students.

In one respect, the school reform dialogue of the eighties was different from that of the fifties. Partly as a result of earlier changes, schools of education were no longer staffed primarily by teacher trainers and former school administrators. Sociologists, economists, historians, and other social scientists were drawn to the study of education and to education faculties. Included among them were a number of analysts of neo-Marxist and radical persuasion, who focused attention on the inequalities in the educational system. Neo-Marxists are not appointed to national commissions in the United States, but their writings have had an impact on a new generation of teachers and school administrators. The first work in this line to enter the mainstream dialogue of educational reform was *Schooling in Capitalist America*, by the radical economists Samuel Bowles and Herbert Gintis.[48] They argued that the educational system never had provided equality of opportunity because it mirrored the inherently unequal structure of the capitalist economy. Schools gave lip service to the ideal of equality, but in actuality they were authoritarian and racist institutions that served to perpetuate and even increase inequalities as they treated children on the basis of their social class characteristics rather than in light of their inherent worth.

To some degree, our portrait of Hamilton High confirms the flaws that Bowles and Gintis highlighted. The school boundary lines in Median had been gerrymandered and poor black students were initially funneled into low-track classes where they were not challenged. Yet radical writers overstated the degree of oppression and underestimated the amount of real change that took place in a supposedly determined capitalist social structure. Most of all, they failed to see the ofttimes heroic capacity for change and compassionate response that characterized the majority of the Hamilton faculty—who, like the rest of us, were born into a world of prejudice.

If Bowles and other radical writers overstated the oppression that characterized schools in capitalist economies,[49] the liberal and conservative reports seem to have almost forgotten the social revolutions in which the schools played so central a part. There is no sustained discussion there of the incredible burdens that public-school teachers and administrators were forced to assume as the nation attempted to make the schools the main column of advance against the enemies, racism and wrongful treatment of the disabled. Although they amassed volumes of data about the conditions of contemporary schooling, these reports pick up the threads of the excellence discussion of the 1950s with a near-amnesia about the events that shook the foundations of Hamilton High.

Why is it important to recall those searing events? Because without understanding that history we cannot understand the way in which the authority relationships in the schools came apart. Hamilton High recognized in the early 1960s what James Conant had held out as the model for American high schools; it foundered on the long-dormant issue of race. The civil rights revolution cut across all American institutions but it pounded most insistently on the door of the public schools, and the schools bore the brunt of black anger. As inequities, gerrymanders, and occasional biased practices were revealed, trust was ruptured and civil rights leaders escalated their demands. Although the schools—no matter how successful they were at teaching the three Rs—could not then and cannot now produce the equal outcomes that the most radical critics demanded, the civil rights movement achieved incredible success, and nowhere more so than in the effort to desegregate the public schools.

It achieved that success primarily by appealing for redress to the state and federal governments and to the courts. Both levels of government funded massive new school projects, scores of compensatory programs were tried, and the courts began to supplant local school boards in prescribing not only desegregation plans but the most detailed instructions for school organization, curriculum, and staffing. Mountains of new law and regulation radically altered the policy of schools. The principal of Hamilton High who declared in the midst of racial violence that "there's no book to go by any more" was succeeded a few years later by principals who did nearly everything by the book. In fact, they seldom acted without consulting lawyers or regulations. The children's rights revolution and extension of massive due-process guidelines to high school students in the 1970s further solidified this change of consciousness within the schools. In the last decade, advocates of new rights for the disabled patterned their reform movement on the civil rights revolution and succeeded in creating major new policy for the schools.

The Hamilton High of the fifties was flawed in the ways we have suggested, but it was a place that the faculty felt was their school and where they believed they were essentially responsible for their fate and that of their pupils. The Hamilton High of the mid-eighties became a school in which the faculty perceived themselves as workers in a bureaucratic system. While they had some freedom within the classroom, they felt that theirs was a world made elsewhere. Still, most of them did not want to return to the 1950s. They were proud of the gains in justice and equality that had been achieved. They believed in the new rights that had been won, even though they had sometimes been buffeted by them. But they were also troubled, because they knew with Michael Ignatieff that the language of rights "offers a rich vernacular for the claims an individual may make on or against the collectivity, but it is relatively impoverished as a means of expressing an individual's need *for* the collectivity." And they could see, as he did, that "the administrative good conscience of our time seems to consist in respecting individuals' rights while demeaning them as persons."[50] They had the courage, however, to begin to think about how to reclaim their world. They had begun to grapple with the essential question: how to reconstitute the intellectual and moral authority of the school without either sacrificing the gains in equity and fairness that had been achieved or instituting a miseducative authoritarianism.

Necessary Autonomies

Two essential reforms are central to the task of reconstituting that intellectual and moral authority: first, let the schools shape their own destiny; second, put teachers in charge of their own practice.

Most teachers and principals in public schools do not feel that they control their fate. They have lost a sense of efficacy and, like those at Hamilton High, believe that they are on the receiving end of policies made elsewhere. Principals have become middle managers who process directives issuing from a multilayered bureaucracy. In one school a principal pointed to forty-five pounds of circulars that had emanated from the central office in the previous year; in a single month thirty-seven different topics had been covered. In surveys, a third of the principals questioned said that the proliferation of judicial and legislative mandates has led them to think of quitting.[51] In Median the number of central-office administrators had more than doubled in the period since Hamilton High was built, while the total pupil enrollment declined by a third.

Schools labor under an increasingly massive superstructure. Yet there is nothing *educationally* that necessitates such a framework. Some events—say the invasion of Normandy—do require massive organization. But good schools do not require any superstructure at all. Sturgis School had almost none; Saint Teresa's relatively little; and Cook High School, by virtue of being the only high school in a small town, far less than the average. Large organization can be a blessing when it furnishes needed support and services, creates economies of scale, brings resources and expertise to bear, creates linkages that enrich, and performs useful oversight and review functions. These functions are performed to some degree (though seldom well) by modern educational bureaucracies. But the bureaucrats involved do not see these support tasks as their primary role. They see themselves as in charge in much the same way that the central office of McDonald's fast-food chain sees itself as in charge of its outlets. The central officials tend to do the hiring, develop the curricula, impose the tests, plan the budgets in minute detail, make the rules, interpret them, revise them, publish the guidelines, and require the reports to make sure that all the plans and guidelines are being conformed to. Actually, there is no one central office. There are scores of minifiefdoms each with its legislative mandates, advocates, lobbies, and chains of command, many reaching from Washington through state education agencies to the local districts. Rather than one McDonald's, there is a score of different "chains," often in competition with one another in an attempt to run their own local offices—whether these be special education, drug abuse prevention, the new math curriculum, or sex education. Speaking of only one mandated program, the new super-intendent of Philadelphia schools was not different from most, only more honest, when she said she wanted to attempt to reform a vast administrative maze that few school officials claimed to fully under-stand.[52]

The growth of educational bureaucracy is not of recent invention. It goes back to the beginning of the Progressive reforms at the end of the nineteenth century, when schoolpeople became the most impas-sioned advocates of scientific management. Consolidation and cen-tralization were well under way before World War II. But Hamilton High in the 1950s was still primarily a local school with a great deal of local discretion and strong authority rested in the principal. The egalitarian reforms of the last decades were aimed at dismantling that discretion because local traditional authority was often a reflection of local prejudices. But now that the battle has been won, it is time to recognize that central-office bureaucrats cannot make good schools. Only the teachers and principals in those schools, acting in concert with parents and pupils, can create vibrant educational communities. But they cannot do so without a radical decentralization that restores a large measure of autonomy and initiative to the individual school.

Three paradoxes must be resolved. The first is that the laudable effort to overcome harmful inequalities has led to the presumption that all differences between schools must be extinguished on the grounds that they reflect inequalities. As one of the leading teachers at Ham-ilton High said early in our discussions of possible reforms, "But down-town doesn't want us to be different; they won't let us be different."

Tolstoy was wrong when he wrote that "all happy families are like one another."[53] They are alike in that they are happy, but the kinds and qualities of happiness and the forms and activities through which it is achieved are many. If each slavishly followed a plan for happy families developed by the ministry, they might be more alike but fewer would be happy. So it is with schools. I have visited more than two hundred schools. Many were admirable schools, but they differed sig-nificantly from one another. True, they shared much: safe and orderly environments, agreements about purpose, engagement in learning, fairness and decency, and a sense of shared norms and ownership—the sense that "this is our school and we're responsible for it." But they differed in organization, academic and moral emphasis, local traditions, and forms of teaching. If school faculties are doing their job, they must shape their responses to accomplishing broad goals. They must take account of particular constituencies and pupil intakes, of strengths and weaknesses of their colleagues, of opportunities within their particular communities, of needs of faculty to experiment and try new approaches to old problems. The dialogue and reflection that lead to the development of a strong positive ethos cannot have a predetermined outcome. We have seen that the moral and intellectual worlds of such schools will overlap, but they will also differ in their emphasis.

Such differences should not only be tolerated, they should be encouraged. One of the most hopeful developments in some large school systems has been the expansion of choice among schools through magnet-school programs or other plans that allow parents to select among a variety of schools at any given level. This encourages faculties to develop their purposes more clearly, to articulate their special identities and strengths, and to shape an appealing climate. I visited public schools in the Harlem district of New York City before and after the adoption of such a plan. The change was marked, especially after one high school was closed because so few chose it. The building was later reopened as three smaller schools covering kindergarten through grade twelve. When I visited the high school portion in 1986, the faculty had developed special programs in science, math, and the arts. A dance troupe had been formed and attracted considerable notice. Plans were under way for high school students to tutor those in the grade school. A house plan was also being formulated whereby ninth graders entering the high school would be formed into groups of 150 students; each group would have a sustained and personalized relationship with five or six faculty, who would teach an academic core course together. Choice for teachers is as important as it is for students. Faculty who are so disposed should have the opportunity to affiliate with a school that is engaged in experimentation. The Harlem school in fact was drawing new recruits to its faculty: a woman from IBM who wanted to develop the use of computers in the school's math program, and a former college administrator who became the initiator of the ninth-grade house plan. Policies permitting these kinds of choices definitely enhance the possibility of creating a strong positive ethos—and may be a precondition for it in many school systems suffering from bureaucratic overplanning.

Although differences will develop among schools in districts where such choice plans are tried, they need not result in unacceptable inequalities. In fact, it is the role of central authorities to prevent such inequalities. They should ensure that schools have equal claim on financial and human resources. Choice should not be allowed to result in schools with unequal student intakes. This does not mean that every school must reflect an exact racial or social-class formula. But schools should be closed or reorganized as necessary so that each school has a core of able pupils around whom a strong positive ethos can be formed.

Nor does it mean that every school must have complete freedom over the curriculum, or that every school must have the same curriculum. Central authority must reflect the broader policy in establishing goals and standards that all children will be expected to reach. I stand with Eliot and his contemporary colleagues Sizer, Boyer, and Goodlad in favoring a strong academic core for *all* pupils. All should have a foundation in the natural sciences and mathematics, history and social science, literature and the arts. All should learn the skills of inquiry and expression, of literacy and numeracy. The current movement toward increasing the time spent in these basic subject areas and reducing the spread of electives has been salutary in Median, as elsewhere. Nevertheless, it is misleading to think that educational aims can be adequately expressed as so many hours of this or credits in that. Sizer expresses this best when he says that these skills will reflect the traditional academic disciplines, but

> the program's design should be shaped by the intellectual and imaginative powers and competencies that students need rather than by "subjects" as conventionally defined. That is, students' school experience should not be molded by the existing complex and often dysfunctional system of isolated departments, "credit hours" delivered in packages called English, social studies, science and the rest . . . Curricular decisions should be guided by the aim of student mastery and achievement rather than be effort to "cover content."[54]

Central authorities should both establish general goals in this sense and monitor the school's efforts to bring students to appropriate levels of achievement. However, the schools and their faculties should have considerable discretion about the means to those ends and the way they organize themselves to achieve them. This includes room for the schools to offer electives or a special emphasis outside the core subjects, and some freedom for students to choose among these as well within the context of a primary emphasis on achieving mastery in the skills and content areas of the intellectual core.

The second paradox is that while egalitarian reforms have restored trust with minority parents and other aggrieved groups, the continuous extension of heavy-handed bureaucratic mandates has eroded the trust and often broken the will of teachers in ways we suggested in Chapter 6. This was expressed emphatically by one of the Hamilton High teachers in the midst of the faculty's nearly unanimous rejection of a new mandate that 80 percent of all pupils "will pass" a specified state-level exam. "It doesn't matter what we say; they'll shove it down our throats anyway." The mandate, unaccompanied by any enabling changes, flies in the face of pedagogical and common sense. Like others before it, it breeds cynicism. It is a Pentagon approach to education. And just as Secretary of Defense Robert McNamara was provided with the body counts that "proved" the United States was winning the Vietnam War, the educational hierarchy will be furnished with results to show that whatever number are mandated to pass "will pass." The bureau-cratic form will be maintained and the possibilities of education will diminish. Talented teachers—and there are many of them—will an-guish. The failure to trust teachers is leading many to withdraw, to give far less than their best out of the conviction that their best is not wanted; only what fits the predetermined plan is wanted.

Teachers need to be trusted with making judgments about their own practice, a topic to which we shall turn in a moment. But they also need to be trusted with matters of the organization of the school. For example, to have a voice in deciding, when a vacancy occurs, whether it should be filled by hiring a replacement or developing a plan in which three teachers in a team-teaching arrangement would be better served by hiring four part-time teachers' aides for the same money. This implies, of course, that teachers and principals should be given more discretion over the budget at the school level. Careful studies by the Coalition of Essential Schools at Brown University have shown how teaching loads can be radically reduced without major increases in a typical school budget through five different reorgani-zation plans.[55] Surveys show that teachers are more disenchanted with teaching than they were twenty years ago, and that the source of their disenchantment lies more with the organizational context than with what goes on in their classrooms.[56] They particularly feel that they have little or no influence over such matters as the use of teaching assistants, fiscal management, or the selection of personnel.[57] Good schools are places where principals trust their teachers, and in good school systems central authorities trust their principals, which sadly is too often not the case.

The third paradox is that the inherent tendency of all bureaucracy to reproduce itself leads to replacing leaders who exercise discretion with specialists who interpret rules. Nowhere is this more true than in the conversion of principals into middle-management functionaries. In most large school systems—both urban and suburban—the principalship is now seen as a step in a bureaucratic career—say from counselor to assistant principal to program director to division chief to assistant or deputy superintendent. The requirements increasingly become aptitude for success in the bureaucratic career—mastering the maze and demonstrating the political, managerial, and legal skills required. Being an outstanding teacher or showing the potential for creating a good educational community are not a salient part of the dossier. Schools of education have usually been eager coparticipants in this bureaucratic reproduction process. They provide the certificates and courses—in school law, management, finances, collective bargaining—that the bureaucracy mandates for promotion to the principalship. No research shows that completion of such a credentialing process has any correlation with effectiveness as a principal; it is just as plausible that there is a negative correlation, that the process acts as a moat to discourage genuine leadership.

If schools are going to be given more power to shape their destiny in a decentralized system, the best leadership needs to be attracted to the principalship. The expectation that the position is but one step in a bureaucratic career should be set aside. Principals ought to be the best-paid persons in the system, with the exception of the superintendent and a small handful of deputies. All others should be paid below or no higher than the principal to indicate that they are in a supportive, not a superordinate, relationship in the task of creating good schools. The current credentialing and selection process needs to be revised to reduce requirements in educational administration and to give teachers a significant voice in the selection of principals. The relationships between principal and teachers ought to resemble that between dean and college faculty, and the selection process should rely heavily on recommendations by an elected faculty committee, with final authority for appointment in the hands of the top administrator. In some cases, a dean or principal might be appointed over the objections of a faculty because of need to "clean house" or make major changes, but this should be the exception not the rule. Likewise, the principal should be developing plans with the faculty rather than relaying and reinforcing plans made elsewhere. Principals ought typically to come from the ranks of master teachers (a designation to be discussed more fully in the next section) and to be seen by their peers as persons who have demonstrated the capacity for educational leadership.

Instead of wondering whether their new principal will be another conventional bureaucrat dealt to them in the usual administrative shuffle, teachers will be able to say, "This person represents the best of us. He or she embodies the ideals and exemplifies the virtues to which we aspire as an educational community." Not every principal will be like Joseph Conan at Cook High. Schools need principals with different strengths at different points in their development—a matter that teachers can often best judge. But principals who can lead will share many of Conan's virtues. They will not be passive process servers who simply set up meetings and pass along information. They will have the courage and talent to get the difficult and often unpleasant issues on the table in a way that encourages responsible action, whether these pertain to drug abuse or grade inflation. They will create collegial planning and policymaking processes. They will have a vision of a good educational community and draw others into the task of building and sharing and modifying that vision. They will honor expertise but have the skill to prevent jurisdictional battles among specialists from frustrating the possibilities of developing a strong positive ethos. Such leaders will be able to show all specialists and teachers how their authority is grounded in a common responsibility for creating a moral and intellectual world. They will devise a shared language that defines the common purposes of that world. They will inspire others to share that vision and seek ways to celebrate the intellectual and moral virtues of the community in appropriate rituals. They will have the capacity to communicate and share their vision with parents and to strengthen the central purposes of the school through support drawn from the broader community. They will take a firm role in selecting teachers and professional staff who will contribute to the further development of the community.

These kinds of leaders are least likely to be produced through current selection mechanisms. Their qualities are not those that can be guaranteed by more careful specification in formal requirements; they are virtues that need to be judged by peers as a result of shared experiences. Hence the need for the principle of teacher voice in the selection process. And principals now on the job can learn to grow in these ways by developing more collegial forms of governance within the school and seeking fresh means to initiate a dialogue on the critical issues that in many schools get swept under the rug. Faculty in schools of education, through more collaborative efforts with schools, can do much to help in developing new means. Such coordination will also have a beneficial impact on the preparation given administrators in the university. In the Epilogue I report on the initial outcome of an effort to open a dialogue on difficult issues at Hamilton High.

The foregoing account has not emphasized the currently popular description of the principal as instructional leader. If principals do the things just mentioned, they will have an impact on instruction. But the major responsibility for improving teaching ought to be in the hands of the teachers themselves. In a typical high school having seventy-five to one hundred teachers, principals can rarely give more than a pro forma evaluation of the teaching staff; and it is virtually impossible for them to provide the time needed for careful observation and coaching of teachers in a variety of subject areas. This brings us to the second essential reform: put teachers in charge of their practice.

The support for major reform of the teaching profession in the United States has never been greater. A broad coalition and consensus has begun to develop, and action has been taken in many states to raise salaries and institute measures to attract talented persons to the profession of teaching. The focus on teaching has grown out of the realization that all other reforms depend on the quality of the teaching force, yet we have seen that there was a drop in the quality of those being recruited to teaching at the same time that conditions in the schools were driving out some of the best teachers. It is only a slight oversimplification to say that the real choice is between top-down managerial reforms and those that would give primary responsibility for deciding who is fit to teach to the teachers themselves. The former approach emphasizes increased testing, mandated in-service training, new forms of so-called teacherproof curricula, and merit-pay plans with administrators deciding which teachers should receive higher pay. Teachers' unions increasingly have accepted the idea of well-constructed entry-level exams that could serve a purpose analogous to bar exams or medical exams. They distrust the rest of the managerial package—and in national polls two-thirds oppose merit pay if it is simply a matter of administrator-awarded bonuses.[58] But teachers and union leadership have embraced plans where pay differentials are based on a restructured profession in which teachers have a role in determining promotions. Teachers are better educated today, with more than half holding a master's degree. On the one hand, they increasingly reject bureaucratic supervisory practices that have their origins in the birth of mass educational systems. On the other, prodded by a coalition of reform efforts, they have shown a new willingness to move beyond collective bargaining and to undertake fundamental reforms that could establish the basis of a true profession.[59]

A variety of approaches to restructuring the teaching profession has been urged in the recent reform reports. The most promising and potentially transforming avenue to putting teachers in charge of their practice lies in the concept of a career ladder. Sometimes referred to as the development of "master teachers" or "leading teachers," the key elements combine mentorship of beginners with teacher judgments about tenure and promotion. Experiments with the concept have been launched in several states. The plans usually specify three or four stages of a teaching career. Beginning teachers serve an apprenticeship of one or probably two years, sometimes in combination with earning or completing their master's degree. During this period they teach under the guidance of senior or master teachers, who also have the major responsibility for deciding whether the new teacher should be promoted to professional teacher status at the end of the apprenticeship. Professional teachers go on the usual teacher salary scale; they may remain on it for life, or after a period of years may seek appointment as senior or master teachers themselves. As such, they too will have a primary role in deciding who will become their colleagues. Promotion to these ranks carries significant increments of salary over the regular scale, and these senior teachers spend a third or a half of their time in supervisory and mentorship roles. In the version proposed here, principals and school boards would have final authority to reject recommendations produced by committees of master teachers, but the presumption would be in favor of the teachers' judgment within previously established financial constraints on the total number of appointments to be made. In actuality, the question of who decides (and with what kinds of evaluation criteria) matters of promotion and tenure is the significant political stumbling block standing in the way of development of the concept. Let us advance four reasons why the career-ladder concept deserves adoption in the form we have suggested.

First, it would attract new talent to teaching and help to retain the ablest of those already teaching. First-year teachers at Hamilton High today are expected to exercise the same responsibilities as twenty-year veterans. The beginners are rarely ready to assume these obligations, and the flatness of the teaching profession leads to little increased prestige or responsibility for the veteran. Uniform salary scales mean that the best teachers can only expect to double their salaries over twenty years (in Japan they triple), whereas other professionals can expect much higher ratios. Base salary scales for all teachers have recently begun to improve (by about 9 to 15 percent in recent years) and this trend should continue. But the significant increment that would be possible for master and senior teachers (increments provided by state governments under several plans) would establish a top range of remuneration comparable to that of other professionals. The president of New York City's school board, Robert Wagner, has proposed that mentor teachers be paid $60,000 a year, and "lead teachers" in Rochester, New York, who will be eligible for promotion to mentoring roles after ten years' experience, will receive up to $70,000 annually under a contract negotiated in 1987. This sends a new message to talented high school graduates and potential recruits about the status of teaching, and the best teachers will know that they do not have to leave the classroom for an administrative post in order to win a major salary increment. Just as important, the plan provides for the kind of growth, increased responsibility, and mentorship that many senior teachers are eager to assume.

Second, restructuring the profession in this way will provide the means for real improvement of teaching. As a result of estimated retirements and demographic changes, 210,000 new teachers will be hired each year in the 1990s, up from about 170,000 a year in the late eighties.[60] In a typical school district they will be allowed to sink or swim. Many will sink. Within a few years nearly half will leave, and disproportionate numbers of the most capable recruits will go with them.[61] Those who stay, particularly in large schools, will find that by the end of semester few of their colleagues will know their names. Each will struggle to keep up with his or her classes in a cellular structure that isolates teachers and provides little time for collegial interaction. They may have a few in-service days. In Median, these were called superintendent's days. When the first was held in 1979, all the teachers in the city were assembled in a university field house that seats ten thousand persons; they sat on bleachers and listened to a lecture. In the 1980s matters had progressed so that the faculties met in their own schools, but many complained that most of the time was used by administrators to read announcements that could have been easily distributed in newsletters. Typical principal visits to their classrooms, as required under performance review procedures, were often superficial observations that lasted no longer than necessary to complete the required forms. Even when done more sensitively, they were far too infrequent, imposed to meet the schedule of paperwork rather than arranged in response to a teacher's needs.

With the proposed two-year apprenticeships or internships, beginning teachers would teach on reduced schedules while benefiting from the coaching and mentorship of master teachers. There would be time for careful supervision, sustained engagement over issues of practice, mutual reflection on the success of teaching encounters, and lengthy discussion of how to handle specific problems. The best kind of in-service education would result, with senior teachers pooling their knowledge and comparing techniques with one another. It would be possible to reflect on the most important questions for all teachers: What is good teaching? How do we assess it? How do we decide who is fit to teach or who deserves promotion to the rank of master teacher? How do we help young teachers to grow? What does research tell us about improved practice? Surveys show that teachers feel they learn most from their peers, not from principals or supervisors, but that schools are currently structured to frustrate rather than build on this insight.[62]

Genuine learning for novice teachers requires a relationship of trust

and can often be difficult, even painful. Young teachers need con-
structive feedback on their classroom performance, time for observation of superior teaching, and frequent consultations about problems
of practice over an extended period of time. Senior teachers similarly
need time for discourse about these matters, opportunities to invent
new approaches, and visits to other schools to observe the best models
of practice.

Evaluation cannot be a matter of two or three visits a year by an
administrator with a checklist. It requires multiple observations and
ratings in a variety of settings by peers who are qualified to judge one's
subject-matter competence as well as one's pedagogical technique.[63]
Peer evaluation is necessary to assess the quality of judgment exercised
by a practitioner because good teaching cannot be summed up in a
list of rules to be followed. Malpractice must be judged the same way,
and in the long run little progress will be made against malpractice
unless practitioners themselves assume more responsibility for making
judgments about quality.[64]

Some master teachers should have adjunct appointments in schools
of education, where they can have an influence on teacher training.
Similarly, more university faculty should enter collaborative relationships with the schools to help teachers reflect on the quality of practice,
to bring results of useful research into the dialogue, and to develop
innovative research agendas growing out of the questions teachers
raise as they tackle their new responsibilities.

Third, if teachers were given the kind of responsibility suggested
here, the norms and overall climate in the school would be strength-
ened. Hamilton High may have gone through a more wrenching deconstruction than did most American high schools in the last decades,
but its current structure reflects fairly typical patterns of faculty iso-
lation. We have seen that teachers withdrew into their own variously
constructed classroom worlds, struck what bargains they felt they could,
and assumed they could not affect much else anyway. What teachers
suspected through rumor and occasional glimpses of one another's
classrooms, students knew. They knew the extraordinary range of what
was tolerated or could be perpetrated. Student researchers confirmed
this in vivid portraits of the variegated life in the classrooms.

In taking on their new role, master teachers will gain more sympathy for the problems of novices. And as they visit colleagues' classes to make assessments about fitness for promotion and tenure, they will see the need for common policies on homework and for developing consensus about norms that affect honesty, fairness, respect, and quality of life in the school. Inspection of the general conditions of teaching will require teachers to broaden their view. They will transcend their individual concern for their own particular classes, to confront their mutual responsibility for creating the moral conditions in which good teaching and learning can flourish. Teachers will move beyond collective bargaining to reflection on the moral ends of practice and a sense of the collective responsibility on which all true professions are based. A profession, Stanley Hauerwas reminds us, "is inherently a normative concept denoting service to the basic goods which a particular community thinks are essential for its moral identity." The reason many highly skilled specializations still are not professions "is that they are not essential to the community's moral purposes—though they may be to its physical survival."[65]

Teachers will have a knowledge base for formulating changes in the curriculum or in the organization of the school. A teacher's suggested reform is often brushed aside by administrators as idiosyncratic or impractical. In a restructured profession, teachers would have an informed view of practice and forums for reflecting upon and refining their views. They would in fact know more, in a collective sense, than administrators. Good principals have always encouraged the development of such joint policymaking councils and see them as synonymous with the development of the faculty.

The fourth point is that exercise of the responsibilities I have described for master teachers also fosters development of future principals. Master teachers will need to develop the skills of judgment, coordination of the action of others, and initiation of discussion of difficult issues that are at the core of principal leadership. Teachers who observe one another in these tasks are in a responsible position to say who among them is best fitted to lead.

These two essential reforms—enabling schools to shape their destiny and putting teachers in charge of their practice—bring the question of reconstituting the intellectual and moral authority of the school properly into focus. The first speaks to reordering the political or organizational authority of the school; the second, to reformulating the authority of practice. Together they would bring about a balance between the individual and social sources of authority upon which all good teaching depends and provide the basis for creating a strong positive ethos in the schools in which the future of the society will be partly formed.

Voices from Hamilton High

I began teaching the urban anthropology course at Hamilton High in 1984, with a promise to share the data gathered by the students and me. I had two purposes in mind. The first was to elicit a critique of the research and to produce a more truthful book.[1] The second was to initiate a process of reflection among teachers and staff about ways to improve their school. Such a process would also reverse the usual order of school reform, in which instructions come from the top down. As Seymour Sarason has described so well, "The modal process of change in schools is one which insults the intelligence of teachers by expecting them to install programs about which they have not been consulted and which they have had no hand in developing or usually much say in modifying."[2]

Thus, from the beginning, my aim was to test a different order of things, to see what could come of an effort from the ground up. I share with Maxine Greene the idea that what is most lacking in public schools is the space for dialogue, a public forum, "where a web of relationships can be woven and where a common world can be brought into being and continually renewed."[3] Reflection by the teachers on the concrete realities of their own school could be a means of creating that space, of recovering their voice, of developing shared meanings, and of testing the possibilities for recreating and renewing their world. This Epilogue, written in the spring of 1987 after more than a year of dialogue, is an account of that process: their critique of both this book and their world as they attempted to transform it.

The process was first outlined at a meeting of the entire faculty and staff of Hamilton High in March 1986. Of the eighty persons present, seventy-seven endorsed the idea. One of them was the principal, who had said he was willing to test the idea of a bottom-up effort that would be initiated by forming a committee of faculty and staff. Twelve persons were elected to serve on the committee to assess the research and to see what bearing it might have on improvement of the school. Four were males, including a teacher on special assignment as an assistant principal. Among the eight females were a secretary, a counselor, a librarian, and a special-education teacher. Three were members of minority groups, and I knew from my research that the teachers who had been elected were among the best in the school. It was a good cross section of the school with teachers from the mathematics, social studies, English, chemistry, and biology departments. The two union representatives were among those elected, and the teachers tended to be among the most experienced as well as the most able in the school.

The ballot included a short questionnaire asking teachers to cite three things "most in need of improvement at Hamilton High in order to improve the intellectual and moral climate of the school." The largest number of responses spoke of the need for better discipline in the school, noting particularly the failure of the staff to be consistent in enforcing rules on class absence and tardiness, behavior in the halls, smoking, and use of alcohol. There was concern as well with the need to give students more positive reinforcement and recognition, to increase mutual respect, and to be aware that "the staff needs to be less angry and negative." Several teachers echoed the comment that there was "a need to develop a core of beliefs that adults throughout the school accept, practice, and implement." Skeptical voices were raised, voicing doubts that schools can do much more than reflect the climate of the surrounding community, or expressing the view that "we can't expect kids to develop a strong moral posture if society cannot make up its collective mind about what is right and wrong." More than a dozen comments referred to the need to raise academic expectations for both faculty and students, and to "bring academic and intellectual issues to the foreground." One teacher suggested that more attention should be paid to students of average ability and more support given to low-achieving students. There were complaints about the lack of parent involvement, student arrogance, and the poor work ethic exhibited by many students. Seven teachers complained about the poor level of communication throughout the school.

Spirits were high at the first meeting of the new committee—at dinner in a private room of a good restaurant. The teachers felt empowered and legitimated as a result of their election by their peers, and they were hopeful that something worthwhile could come of their efforts. Still, the history of such attempts had not been encouraging. Few responses were made to suggestions that came out of teachers' committees unless the recommendations served the administration's purposes. Committee work often seemed futile and teachers claimed they were infantilized by the administration. Faculty meetings operated in chain-of-command manner, with suggestions being passed up through department heads. This had been true of previous principals as well as the incumbent. The teachers were not too harsh on the principals, however, perceiving them as subject to the dictates of the central administration.

This was the first sounding of what became a strong theme in subsequent meetings. Teachers felt that "downtown" allowed the school and its teachers little autonomy. Central-office personnel issued directives and were condescending to teachers, who were "treated like children" and "expected to follow the schedules given to you." "You have made so many requests and been turned down so much that you just give up or do your own thing." The teachers did not blame all the blockage in communication on the administrative hierarchy, however; they deplored the lack of collegial engagement on matters of substance. Heads nodded around the table as senior teachers considered how few conversations they had had with their peers about either ideas or teaching. One of the teachers, reflecting that her own daughter would enter Hamilton High in a few years, raised the question of whether she would encounter many faculty "who are positively indicating to her how much pleasure there is in simply knowing something . . . I want her exposed in a positive way to learning that she enjoys, that is challenging to her, that isn't always going to be pleasant but that she thinks is something that is worthwhile to her." The librarian commented that Hamilton served the most disadvantaged students as well as the most able, but "I'm worried about the middle-of-the-road kid who is there every day, who does his homework, and who gets no extra attention."

A tone of candid exchange was established early on, with teachers challenging one another and expressing a variety of points of view. After a discussion of the problem of widespread littering and of so many students hanging out in the halls, a math teacher expressed concern that Hamilton not follow the lead of other high schools in the city where tough policies had led to higher dropout rates. A chemistry teacher responded firmly, "I don't really buy that bull because I think there are other ways to keep kids out of the hall without leading to high dropout rates, and you don't have to have garbage in the hall either."

At my suggestion and with the principal's concurrence, the group had been set up as a teachers' committee. The amount and degree of the principal's participation was left open. Some suggested that the principal ought to join the group soon, while others opined that the teachers ought to make their own way for a while. They reached a consensus that it might be appropriate for the principal to join the group from time to time, or perhaps permanently at a later date. Initially, they decided to elect an executive committee of three to meet with him and keep him informed. The principal said the next day that he had no problem with that decision. A week later, however, the superintendent called the principal and questioned the whole project. He wanted to know who had approved it. It was pointed out that he had signed the proposal for foundation funding of the project. He said everything was on hold until he spoke to both the principal and me. The upshot of that meeting was that the superintendent did not want the group to meet without the principal and felt the principal should chair the group. In later discussion the principal accepted my suggestion that he not force his way into the next meeting but give the teachers an opportunity to discuss the matter. He also agreed to consider the possibility of not chairing the group if and when he came into it.

It evolved at the next meeting that most teachers were not opposed to the principal's participation, having raised that possibility themselves in the first meeting. What angered them was the coercion implicit in the superintendent's instructions. They interpreted the superintendent's stance as part of the usual attempt to maintain hierarchical control: "It really insults your intelligence [to be treated this way] . . . What does the superintendent think we're about? What are we going to do that he's afraid of? We only want what's best for the school." At the end of a sometimes-heated discussion, the teachers decided to invite the principal to the next meeting.

The principal opened that meeting by expressing concern about the way his participation had been imposed after the committee had been set up with his approval. He said the superintendent had pointed out that each school already had an official school improvement committee and that this new ad hoc committee might set a different direction for the school. A counselor, expressing the sentiments of several members, responded, "We should have several committees. We work better in small groups. What if we had six [school improvement] groups and at the end of the year we came up with recommendations and listened to each other?" The teachers were united in their distaste for the oppressive uniformity that they felt the central school bureaucracy was imposing on all high schools. Their sense now was that all schools "had to be absolutely the same," when the real problem was how to achieve a unique spirit in each school. The principal shared their assessment, saying that his present embarrassment was symptomatic, because "every time I make a decision, I turn around and get my hand slapped for not communicating with the central office." He also felt that pressures for uniformity were too tightly linked with pressures to achieve equality, because those in the central office "don't want one school to lord it over another, fearing if we're unique we're better or different."

The teachers compared his disillusionment with their own, saying the top-down style he complained of was typical of their own relationships at Hamilton High. Faculty meetings were characterized more by dissemination than by discussion. As a math teacher put it, the meetings were "lists of points A,B,C,D" when the issue ought to be "are we going to make decisions together as a faculty?" The principal initially defended his form of communication as more efficient, but faculty argued that one-way communication could be handled most effectively by a memo in their mailboxes. One of the teachers who had brought in copies of a recent Carnegie Foundation report noted how closely their discussion paralleled that in the report, a main theme of which was that "teachers are not treated as professionals and not listened to as professionals and a lot of teachers resent this." A colleague assented, adding that change in schools was unlikely unless "teachers play a considerably more active role in running schools."

The principal granted that the school was too bureaucratized and admitted he was discouraged to the point of having considered resigning. He felt that teachers did not trust administrators and he was not sure what to do about it. While teachers talked about wanting change in the school, he felt too many "did not give a damn" and most were individuals pursuing their "personal agendas." They might give lip service to the idea of school improvement, but their bodies were not there in the hall confronting students who would not go to class. "Everybody operates as an individual . . . It's very difficult to get a faculty this size to sit together and say we're going to come up with some commonalities and say we're all going to get behind this."

A teacher who felt it *was* possible to reach some commonalities (the same teacher who had expressed the hope that Hamilton High could offer a more positive vision to her daughter) replied that teachers would have to believe in those commonalities for them to make a difference. "Maybe some no longer believe what they do in the hall or inside their classrooms makes any difference. Maybe they're as disillusioned as you are. We need to do something with those people, too."

Two themes were interwoven throughout this quite remarkable exchange. The first was that there had to be space for a genuine dialogue. It had to be "a place where teachers feel comfortable and secure expressing their concerns without feeling that someone is passing judgment on them." Secondly, genuine dialogue implied some changes in the structure of the school. It meant that teachers would participate in decision-making and in creating their world "because there's no sense to continually brainstorming ideas and using your energy in a bureaucracy in which you're going to have to do exactly what you've done before."

By the end of two hours, the principal said he was "going to hang his hat on the future of this committee," adding that he wanted to be a coparticipant, not the chairperson. He knew there had been some changes in the school but they had been "nickel-and-dime stuff." Real change had to come out of the faculty. The librarian cautioned the group that it was not going to happen easily. "There's a lot of self-defense. We can blame others for our problems. Arriving at consensus is a very arduous process. It takes a long time." The group agreed that it would be useful to attempt to reach agreement on what might be done by examining the history of the school and seeing whether they could come to some agreement about what was at the root of the weaknesses that needed remedy. For the next several meetings they examined draft chapters of this book. I chaired the group during this review, after which they elected their own chair, one of the math teachers.

The discussion of Chapter 1, Hamilton High in the Eisenhower and Kennedy years, had the character of reminiscences at a class reunion. Almost without exception the teachers, including three who had taught at Hamilton in the sixties and one who had been a student then, felt the chapter captured the world they knew. Those who had attended high school elsewhere felt it summoned those worlds as well. Hamilton High was not so different. The former student—now an English teacher—criticized the chapter for understating the "perversely smothering sameness—there was no tolerance for anyone who was different from the norm in dress, looks, or intellect." She revealed that she was the student who had written the editorials quoted in Chapter 1 that were critical of the sorority-fraternity system, and as a result she had been treated as an outcast.

The most extended discussion touched on the theme of changing the ethos of the school. It was occasioned by the passage stating that the principal "had few doubts about what most parents expected of him: that he would enforce middle-class standards of courtesy and respect, emphasize a college preparatory curriculum and put winning teams on the Hamilton field." Since Hamilton was no longer a middle-class school nor so uniformly college prep, was it possible today to have common values or standards?

The discussion turned to whether standards were tied to the social composition of a school. While the teachers agreed that social class influenced a school, they also felt that standards could transcend social class. They cited respect for all persons and common expectations for achievement as examples. But most in the group did not believe that the contemporary Hamilton High was characterized by common ex-

pectations, rather that the expectations "were different in every classroom." Another wondered whether "we expect more of kids than we
give them." Recalling the former student's comments, a teacher warned
of the danger of rules that smother; "on the other hand, there should
be some basic human beliefs and values that everyone can agree upon
as members of a human community, that are not very difficult, that
promote and remind people of respecting each other." Several teachers
reflected on the lack of respect shown by the way students trashed the
school, and the school secretary pointed out that the faculty did
the same thing in the teachers' lounge. The librarian felt that change
would have to come from some effort that involved the entire school
community, but the point was made that teachers might have to take
a stand, to assert some standards in order to begin a dialogue with
parents and others.

While no one wanted to resurrect the Hamilton High of the 1950s
or the inequalities it embodied, the school counselor suggested that
some aspects of that world were worth reviving. She reported a small
advance with her advisees in the past year after insisting that they
recognize her in the halls. "I greet them by name and I wanted them
to greet me—just that little bit of courtesy. And they picked up on
it." In support, a teacher suggested they had a vested interest in
change. "Why should we work in an ugly and degenerative environment? It's depressing." The meeting ended without any resolution of
these issues, but all knew that a significant step had been taken in
their common acknowledgment of dissatisfaction with the current
climate in the school.

Chapter 2, with its description of the violence that accompanied
the racial desegregation of the school, was the topic of the next
meeting. In writing that chapter I had tried to control the material,
to keep it from slipping into melodrama or raising suspicions that the
trauma was being overplayed. Half the teachers in the group had lived
through the events described and I feared they might have such qualms.
Some of the white male teachers in the group felt, to the contrary,
that the chapter erred in the other direction. "There was more tension
in the building than there is this document . . . I don't know how
you can write the tension but at the end of the day you were just
exhausted . . . You'd just go home and go to bed . . . Teachers gave

up trying to control what went on in the halls . . . There was no backup . . . It was like gasoline being poured on a fire and it just kept on going."

Two of the minority teachers in the group were largely silent during these mutually reinforcing exchanges among the white males. Then both spoke of that era as the most exciting and fulfilling period in their teaching careers. They had developed new courses, became spokespersons to some degree for minority students, and felt energized as never before. One of them was the first black faculty member at Hamilton High, a highly regarded teacher with a doctorate in chemistry. She doubted that many other minority teachers would have been hired if it had not been for the protests. "But when kids started demanding and tearing down things, they decided to hire more black teachers to control the black students." The contrast between white teachers who were once again the spent objects of the racial revolution and the black teachers who were sympathetic to it and energized by it could not have been more stark. The black chemistry teacher, who as a girl had gone to school in Mississippi, asserted that the black students had no other release for their frustrations: "It was like those of us in Mississippi—we had no outlet, we had to do it. And they had to do it, there was no other way, because nobody listened, criminal or not criminal." One of the white males who had spoken earlier was the social studies teacher who had been struck in the back of the neck with a microphone in one of the first riots. He had the reputation of being a concerned teacher who made efforts to reach students, who invited them to his home near the school for barbecues. He interrupted her and the room fell silent:

First teacher (white): I don't buy that, I . . .

Second teacher (black): I knew you wouldn't.

First: I don't buy that for a minute. Because I talked to too many people in too many homes, and there were outlets. I can no more explain . . .

Second: Really though, what were the outlets? Because I couldn't find them. I wanted to. I didn't see them.

First: I don't believe that wanton violence, that tearing through the place is the answer. If you say, "This is the only outlet they have," it's a copout. You're rationalizing. You're saying, "Hey, it's OK, tear the place apart, we understand."

Second: That's how we got our freedom from the British.

First: I don't think that comparison is valid.

Second: What else could be done? To get attention that I'm hurting, that you're discriminating against me, that I'm not a worthy person, you're not teaching me, you have no expectations for me . . .

First: That's true, I understand that . . .

Second: That I'm in a foreign land. How do I get you to listen to me?

The tension, the gulf between blacks and whites in different worlds two decades earlier, had been recreated in the room. The librarian, who came to Hamilton in the mid-seventies after service in the Peace Corps, had said earlier in the discussion that reading the chapter had frightened her, made her glad she had not been at Hamilton during those years. Now she turned to the black teacher, speaking slowly: "You've got the vocabulary. You say, 'I'm hurting, you're not teaching me.' The kids didn't have the words. Often the adults don't have the words." Would it have been any different if they had been more prepared for the changes that swept over them, she asked—if they had had the math workshops and supportive services that were now provided. A math teacher recalled the painful truth: "We had absolutely no training, virtually no skills, it was a situation that we were not able to deal with in any effective way. The kinds of things that we tried in the beginning to get things jelling the right way just did not work." Yet who would have given the "training" for a revolution? I was moved by the whole exchange and voiced my admiration for them. They had put their lives on the line; they had helped hold the society together; they had shown great courage. "But wouldn't it have been much better if we had had the courage twenty years ago to meet like this and talk?" the black chemistry teacher asked. "Yes, if it had been possible," I replied. It certainly took courage to persevere and to engage in the way they had just done.

The discussion of Chapter 3, "Let the Students Decide," opened with a comment on the shift that took place in about 1970. The speaker recalled that the activism of black students was soon augmented by whites who, following the developments on college campuses, began to demand a voice in a wide range of decisions. "And the teachers all of a sudden got bypassed. The principal went from being the sole person in charge to the principal basically saying, 'What the heck should I do, kid?' " For the better part of an hour teachers told stories adumbrating and affirming the rise of student power and the emergence in that decade of a more radically individualistic world. The faculty had split into a variety of camps, lines of authority had been thrown into confusion, no one had known who was in charge of aides hired under the new programs. The teachers agreed that the school had become a social service center as programs multiplied. The special-education teacher convulsed the group by remembering the day two dogs were loose in the school and the faculty-room comedian said, "Watch it, if three more dogs get in we'll have to establish a program."

While they regretted certain aspects of the reign of student choice, most of the teachers did not know what else could have been done at the time to cope with the pressures for accommodation. "You had to do something. There comes a point when you know what you're doing isn't good but you had to do something. It was sticking your finger in the dike." Another teacher cautioned that things could have been much worse. She felt that the principal, Cunneen, took a bad rap in the chapter: "As for his revision of the curriculum, he was just being true to the enlightened philosophy propounded by schools of education in good universities throughout the nation. All the books, all the experts were saying the same things."

It was not only from students that the demand for more choice came. This was an era of huge increase in parent demands, the principal argued. Negotiating for your child's program or for specific teachers became accepted procedure. Even parents who disagreed with that philosophy began to feel that they were failing to be good parents if they did not become advocates for their children. The practice continued into the eighties: "I couldn't believe the pressure that was constantly coming at me from parents who would just come in with their own agenda and felt they'd get to pick and choose what they want."

Some of those present were distressed about the loss of moral consensus in the school, but a member said she had once taught in a school that was too morally rigid "and I couldn't stand it. At Hamilton you could be an individual. I liked that. I can only work someplace where I can do that . . . I am willing to negotiate but I am an individualist." She at first denied that there were any negative consequences of the individualism that characterized the school. When someone asked about students who were cutting classes or coming to class half-stoned, she granted that such concerns were "a moral responsibility of the entire school and something that an individual teacher cannot solve alone." Others agreed that "an environment which encouraged good teachers to do their own thing was a strong point at Hamilton then and still is." They saw the freedom for students in the seventies as freeing teachers from prescribed curricula, too. But as a social studies teacher put it, they also felt that "sometimes you may be so hung up on your own thing that you don't care about the other things." They were all aware of students for whom "doing their own thing meant not doing anything." They struggled with how to preserve a sense of initiative and healthy individualism while defining core values and expectations by which all would be bound.

The discussion of Chapter 4, "The Second Transformation," was often heated, especially at the start in response to a memo from the principal. He felt he had been quoted out of context at one point and that the chapter presented too negative an image of him and of the school. Some faculty believed that both the amount of drug use (especially the references to "partying in the halls") and the degree of cheating in the school were overestimated. They believed drug use had declined (although alcohol abuse had increased) and that cheating was not widely tolerated. Other faculty did not feel the chapter overestimated either, pointing out that in the early eighties a drug counselor smoked marijuana with students. One teacher criticized the chapter because it blamed most of the ills on students and underestimated the amount of immoral behavior on the part of faculty, some of whom cheated, lied, and shirked their responsibilities. A former student wrote from Brown University that "the paragraph about dishonesty is very true! Isn't it amazing how easily dishonesty remains a norm at Ham?" She also felt that the school's lax attitude about drugs was a factor affecting drug use—although teachers criticized the chapter for implying that the faculty tolerated drug use. A teacher who gave the chapter a careful reading said she could not quarrel with the bad news, but the chapter did not capture the whole truth, in its failure to bring to life the wonderful students who populated the school. "I don't have much in the way of evidence that I could put in a book—no taped interviews, surveys, statistics, outside participant observers' dissertations, just memories . . . but God, they were beautiful."

A few of the white teachers in the group questioned whether the chapter presented too optimistic a view of the improved race relations at the school. But the minority faculty and most of the whites agreed that while racism had not been eradicated in either the school or the society, the dramatic improvement portrayed was on the mark. And the former student felt the chapter "could stress more how each race now accepts the differences of the other." On the other hand, the teachers agreed that the school had not done enough in matters of race relations, or to establish rituals, or to celebrate those who exemplified the ideals that the school hoped to instill in pupils.

The chapter's treatment of the "second transformation" brought about by the entrance of Asian students and the advent of mainstreaming was said to be underplayed, if anything. The teachers reported that these problems were still very much with them, especially in regard to mainstreaming. Teachers still felt underprepared for the students assigned to them. Turning to a special-education teacher in the group, a social studies teacher said: "I don't understand your program. I don't understand the learning disabled. I don't understand what's going on with them, yet I have to teach them." She was given support by the biologist, who said one day a guidance counselor came in to give her a pamphlet on Tourette's syndrome and the next day the child was in her class. "I really didn't feel I had enough information to handle it. Here's the pamphlet, here's the kid . . . We need more in-servicing or something." The alumna now at Brown spoke of the way the lack of positive ethos in the school affected the treatment of disabled children:

> It is important to make clear that though many students have become tolerant of the mainstreamed students, very few have an understanding of the nature of the problems of the mentally disturbed, autistic, and physically handicapped. Even now, years after the program was begun, the special education kids are still taunted and made fun of by other students. Whether or not students vocalize their feelings of unease and even disgust towards the special education students, many find them repulsive and tend to keep their distance. Students were not at all prepared for their new, very different classmates. And teachers have not been instrumental in helping the normal students adjust and accept special education students, perhaps because the teachers themselves were not prepared for handling the effects of mainstreaming. A key point about the effects of mainstreaming is that few students, if any, volunteered to work with special education students and thus never got to know or understand them or realize the rewards of helping them learn.

Aside from directly tormenting the special education students, Hamilton students fully distanced themselves emotionally and physically. These patterns make one question how beneficial mainstreaming really is.

Through the winter and spring of 1986–87, the committee continued to assess the research and to consider ways of improving the school. The process of change that the teachers had initiated was so at odds with usual attempts at school reform that it is worth treating at length. An analysis of the meeting transcripts from the perspective of the change process reveals that the dialogue unfolded in five stages. These did not follow a strict chronological order, for there was a great deal of overlap in the actual conversation. But the process developed roughly in these phases: (1) testing of the need for change, (2) doubt and resistance, (3) emergence of belief that common action was possible, (4) development of shared meaning about desirable policies and practices, and (5) proposal of a strategy for school-wide change.

The first two stages have been illustrated in the discussion thus far. They were often intertwined, as the process of testing the data presented in the first four chapters was accompanied by doubts that anything could be done to change the situation. Although the teachers rejected or modified aspects of the information as given, they developed their own definition of the situation and reached consensus on the strengths and weaknesses of the school. The process encouraged a mutual interrogation and search for confirming or disconfirming evidence. Without any prompting from me, some teachers began to develop questionnaires or interview students about matters discussed at our meetings. They compared perceptions about rude behavior in school assemblies and noticed what kind of models the teachers themselves presented to the students. In the discussion about assemblies, for example, one teacher said that since the principal had specifically requested faculty to be present at the assembly that week, she had counted those who stood talking along the back wall or had ducked out to the teacher's room—forty-six in all. A social studies teacher brought in the results of a questionnaire completed by 750 students, showing that the longer students had been at Hamilton the less they liked it.[4]

Reasoning and comparing evidence in this way was in marked contrast to the usual imposition of new policies, often announced with no teacher input and little justification. In the past, teachers had often been expected to follow prescriptions without any participation in the diagnosis or any opportunity to acknowledge their complaint. This stage of the process led to a sense that common action would be needed to improve the situation.

As just noted, there was pessimism about the possibility of achieving such common resolve, and doubt about whether it could be effective even if realized. But the second stage of the discussion was not all negative; while it could be cast in psychological terms of resistance, it was also a search for understanding of the causes of their predicament. The discussion was an elaboration of the internal and external constraints on change that in good part paralleled the schema of authority relations outlined in Chapter 5. With regard to internal constraints, the principal hammered away at the individualism of the faculty, suggesting at one point that there were too many "prima donnas" and concluding, "I'm going to be really surprised if there is *any* issue this faculty comes together on." He criticized the faculty for their failure to "confront kids" and questioned their desire for more interactive meetings when so many of them "are beating the kids out the front door." Some of the faculty criticized the principal for poor leadership, for failing to inspire loyalty, and for perpetuating a bureaucratic style. The teachers acknowledged that the lack of cohesiveness of the faculty was a long-standing problem and they feared that the number of uncaring faculty and students was growing. They were hard on themselves, disparaging faculty who did not respect students and those who were poor role models. They spoke again of the impotence they felt, a history of believing that few policies or programs made much real difference in the life of the school. A strong theme throughout this phase of the discussion was the concern that any effort to raise standards or establish a more positive ethos might cause less able or disadvantaged students to drop out.

With regard to external constraints or causes, the principal spoke for many teachers as well as himself when he argued that the students' rights revolution meant that "these kids are at an age where I have lost control." The special-education teacher who had been active in working with Students Against Drunk Driving, said students would not come to the dances she helped organize. "We asked students, 'What more can we give you? The music's good, the food's good, everything's good.' But they'd rather party. You know, there wasn't anything missing except the booze." Faculty talked about parents who didn't care. When parents were called about students who had gone to a beer party on senior skip day, some parents were ready to make excuses or cover up for their children. With regard to a significant number of students, said the principal, "it's an uphill climb. We are constantly up against what happens when kids go home." In discussing the possibility of establishing a dress code or a no-smoking policy, a faculty member warned it would never work: "See how fast the liberalized parents will come forth and say 'I challenge that legally,' and we lose." Even if the parents did not, the central school office would not allow them to establish such policies, the teachers feared. "We'd have to take it downtown." Others saw their own teachers' union as a potential obstacle. "We can come up with good ideas but ultimately we have to deal with what contractually can be done. That's the bottom line. That's going to be it."

The emergence of belief that change was possible and that common action could be effective did not arise in a dramatic or sudden way. The teachers knew they were not autonomous, that the objections just raised were serious obstacles. But over a period of months faith in the possibility of change grew. A union leader in the group pointed out that the contract allowed for experimentation in individual schools. Another faculty member argued that they did not have to take everything to the board downtown. And even if some things needed approval from the board, the teachers ought not to assume defeat. In discussing the parents' reaction to the beer party on skip day, some teachers cautioned against overinterpreting the negative responses of a few parents. The principal, acting on their suggestion, appealed for parent cooperation in the next newsletter and found that eighty parents volunteered to help curb alcohol and drug abuse. A social studies teacher said they ought to try to do more to raise the expectations of students, both academically and socially. The school needed more student volunteers and peer tutors, she said. "So what are we saying— that we as adults are so helpless that we can't ask anything of them?" One of the most skeptical teachers in the group said after five months of meetings that she thought if they could get the students and other faculty involved, change could occur. "I found a change myself by attending those meetings. I really do believe now that we can make a change. I might get bashed in a year but I believe it so I am willing to invest." The principal also influenced these beliefs by his own willingness to open up, share his frustrations, and invite new directions. At one point he confessed, "You know, I'm managing the school, but I don't really know what I'm managing because we don't have any philosophy of what we're doing as a school."

The move from pessimism to hope was a prelude to the fourth stage of developing shared meaning about proposed changes. This seemingly commonsense but actually quite complex process is best illustrated by examining a simple proposal to deal with tardiness. The principal initially took the view that it was a straightforward issue of faculty failure to enforce policy. Teachers should be out in the hall "getting their butts in the classroom." Moreover, if teachers were in the hall between bells, "bad things wouldn't happen." Failure to enforce the policy was tantamount to insubordination and disloyalty. Some teachers agreed. One who disagreed said she didn't think that was her job; teaching was her job, taking care of hall traffic was a job for corridor aides. Another said she saw the principal's point, but felt that standing out in the hall and screaming at kids to get them in the classroom was destructive of the kind of personal relationship she wanted to have with students inside the classroom. A teacher who recalled an earlier discussion about all the "legitimate" reasons students could be excused from class asked whether anyone could believe that it was really important to get students to class on time if they could be back out in the halls two minutes later on their way to all kinds of nonacademic functions. Over the course of several meetings, teachers discussed why the faculty might not feel loyalty to the principal on this issue, whether the authority of the corridor aides could be expected to substitute for faculty authority in essential matters, and how to resist the erosion of class time by what should be after-school activities. They did develop consensus about the need to reduce tardiness. It involved admitting and hearing their real differences, developing a policy that all could support (although not everyone had to do exactly the same thing), and recognizing that genuine commitment of the faculty required specific policies that made sense in terms of the overall philosophy of the school.

If a seemingly straightforward matter like tardiness required such an effort, we can better appreciate what is needed to get at issues of raising academic achievement. The necessity for this kind of "working through" has been thoughtfully expressed by Peter Marris:

> No one can resolve the crisis of reintegration on behalf of another. Every attempt to pre-empt conflict, argument, protest by rational planning, can only be abortive: however reasonable the proposed changes, the process of implementing them must still allow the impulse of rejection to play itself out. When those who have power to manipulate changes act as if they have only to explain, and when their explanations are not at once accepted, shrug off opposition as ignorance or prejudice, they express a profound contempt for the meaning of lives other than their own. For the reformers have already assimilated these changes to their purposes, and worked out a reformulation which makes sense to them, perhaps through months or years of analysis and debate. If they deny others the chance to do the same, they treat them as puppets dangling by the threads of their own conceptions.[5]

It was a tribute to Hamilton's principal that he did not shrug off opposition and was himself a coparticipant in the process of reformulation. A questionnaire completed by the group at the end of the year showed that most members felt their relationship with the principal had been transformed. He was perceived as "more willing to listen to, work with, and respect views of faculty"; his whole "modus operandi for dealing with the faculty has changed as a direct result of this group."

Finally, the group proposed a strategy for school-wide change. The crucial insight at this stage—which came midway in the academic year—was the realization that the members could not simply pass their conclusions to the faculty for ratification. If true commitment were to be developed, the faculty as a whole would have to have the opportunity to develop shared meanings and to undergo a process similar to that which the group had undergone. As the English teacher in the group put it, "How about devising a forum for everyone?" They convinced the principal to abandon the usual format for faculty meetings and workshop days. A new participative decision-making structure was developed and put in place that spring. The first two issues on which the faculty reached consensus had to do with tardiness and trash. Not long after the trash policy began to take effect, the fire department cited the school for failing to put airtight covers on the new trash barrels it had distributed throughout the hallways. Most teachers laughed, although some believed that the episode symbolized how heavily the bureaucratic odds were against them. The faculty began to accept responsibility for weightier school-improvement issues. Among them were creating a more caring environment for incoming ninth graders through development of a house plan, thinking through the school's philosophy of education, and rewriting the student hand-book to move beyond rules and legalisms to an expression of the positive aims of the school.

A simple exercise revealed that the members shared more in the way of a common philosophy than they at first suspected. They wrote a list of "the good things you would like to see encouraged, developed, and reinforced among students, faculty, and staff of Hamilton High. Include the impact you hope the school could have on habits, dis-positions, attitudes, behaviors, and actions." In comparing their lists they saw that they had formed the basis for a new charter for the school. They agreed that they wanted the school to emphasize dignity and respect for all persons, to place a premium on academic excellence and seek to motivate all students, to underscore the intrinsic value of learning, to develop a strong community spirit and encourage everyone to do his or her best, and to value the basic virtues of honesty and integrity. Finally, they saw need for a school that was a learning community for faculty as well as students, one that provided for the growth of faculty both intellectually and socially.

Although teachers universally complain about meetings, even through the dark winter months the teachers involved in these group meetings often arrived fifteen minutes early. Absences were rare. The only member who dropped out did so because of hospitalization for a back injury. Their questionnaire responses showed them to be unanimous in feeling that they had personally benefited from participating in the group, and all saw evidence of significant effects on the life of the school at the end of the first year. Although they were paid a stipend, nine of the eleven remaining in the group said they would continue without one. The opportunity for what one teacher called "honest dialogue about the real problems," and the development of more participative forms of decision-making were cited as the major accom-plishments of that first year. Teachers knew that parents had to be mobilized and they estimated it would take two to five years to bring about major changes in the school as a whole. But they felt they had made a good beginning. Nearly all of those who stood for reelection to the committee at the end of the year were reelected by the faculty as a whole.

What can we learn from these experiences? Given the analysis of Hamilton High presented at the end of Chapter 4, the teachers had three choices, similar to those faced by all parents and citizens. The first was to withdraw from the effort to create good public schools—to quit teaching or to put their hopes in private schools, as some parents have done. A second option would have been to allow the minimalist bureaucratic model of public schooling to run to its individualistic limits—to let the public schools operate as contract learning systems and acknowledge that coexistence is all we can legitimately hope for. The third option was the one these teachers chose, that of regenerating a dialogue about the intellectual and moral aims of a public school in a democratic society. In order to accomplish this, they were obliged to rediscover their history, reflect candidly on their present dissatisfactions, struggle with their hopes and their fears, define common purposes, and forge new bonds in recreating their world. Perhaps it is only in this way that the foundations of community life can be restored.

Notes

Wherever necessary in order to maintain the anonymity of "Hamilton High," titles of articles using the real name of the high school have been changed, as have the names of actual newspapers in the school and in the city of "Median." Student work has been cited by initials only. All quotations in the text that are not referenced derive from interviews or observations.

Introduction

1. Michael Walzer, *Spheres of Justice: A Defense of Pluralism and Equality* (New York: Basic Books, 1983), p. 197.

2. See R. S. Peters' thoughtful discussion in his chapter, "The Education of the Emotions," in R. F. Dearden et al., eds., *Education and the Development of Reason* (London: Routledge and Kegan Paul, 1972).

3. Aristotle, *The Politics*, trans. T. A. Sinclair (Baltimore: Penguin Books, 1974), p. 300.

4. Stanley M. Elam, ed., *A Decade of Gallup Polls of Attitudes toward Education, 1969–1978* (Bloomington, Ind.: Phi Delta Kappa Press, 1978), p. 2.

5. Both reports were to the National Institute of Education. The first was a xeroxed volume edited by me: *What Makes a Good School: Five Case Studies*, Syracuse University, 1981; the second was *Education, Character, and American Schools: Are Effective Schools Good Enough?* Syracuse University, 1982. Among my essays were "The Character of Education and the Education of Character," *Daedalus* 110 (Summer 1981), 135–50; "Children's Rights and Adult Confusions," *Public Interest* 69 (Fall 1982), 83–99; and "The Teacher's Predicament," *Teachers College Record* 84 (Spring 1983), 593–609.

6. I regret being unable to give the name of the teacher, but doing so would violate the promises of confidentiality with which I began this work. My colleague in sociology, Robert Bogdan, is the author of several works on research methods, including (with Sari Knopp Biklen) *Qualitative Research for Education* (Boston: Allyn and Bacon, 1982).

7. Peter L. Clark, "Student Group Perspectives on a Secondary School," Ph.D. diss., Syracuse University, 1977.

1. An Elite Public School

1. "Kinney Will Lead Council," *Record*, February 1, 1954.

2. "Strengthen Spirit," *Record*, November 24, 1953.

3. Editorial, "You and Your Conscience," *Record*, December 20, 1957.

4. "Sam Visits Cafeteria," *Record*, January 29, 1958, and "Be Neat," ibid., September 15, 1953.

5. "Under God," *Record*, September 13, 1954; "Boys Favor UMT", ibid., March 1, 1954; " 'Freedom Shrine' Presented to School," ibid., November 1, 1954.

6. James Coleman, *The Adolescent Society: The Social Life of the Teenager and Its Impact on Education* (New York: Free Press, 1961).

7. *Record*, December 20, 1955.

8. Coleman, *The Adolescent Society*, p. 217.

9. "Are We Snobs?" *Record*, May 11, 1955.

10. "Equality for Everyone," *Record*, April 11, 1956.

11. "Hamilton Captures 23 of 60 State Scholarships," *Record*, June 14, 1956.

12. *Median Herald*, November 23, 1960.

13. "Study Aids, Steps in Textbook Study," *Record*, June 14, 1956, offered students five steps to follow in studying and reviewing a homework assignment. A typical "College Corner" article appeared September 15, 1961, contrasting the advantages of attending "Large College or Small?" The essays, often based on a student's visit to a campus, exhibited the enterprising journalism characteristics of Hamilton student efforts.

14. U.S. Commission on Civil Rights, *Process of Change: The Story of School Desegregation in Median* (Washington, D.C.: Government Printing Office, 1968), p. 3.

15. Ibid.

16. Ibid., p. 4.

17. Ibid., p. 5.

18. "Strom One of Top 40," *Record*, December 15, 1965.

19. Letter to the editor, *Record*, April 15, 1965.

2. Deconstruction of the Old World

1. U.S. Commission on Civil Rights, *Process of Change: The Story of School Desegregation in Median* (Washington, D.C.: Government Printing Office, 1968), p. 6.

2. The quotations that follow are from ibid., pp. 6–10.

3. Philip Cusick, *The Egalitarian Ideal and the American High School* (New York: Longmans, 1983). See, for example, the discussion on pp. 50–51.

4. Commission on Civil Rights, *Process of Change*, p. 4.

5. Ibid., p. 12.

6. Ibid., p. 26.

7. Memorandum from Median Public School Research Office dated April 15, 1985.

8. Peter L. Clark, "Student Group Perspectives on a Secondary School," Ph.D. diss., Syracuse University, 1977, p. 111; based on classroom observations in 1971–72.

9. Thomas Green et al., *Predicting the Behavior of the Educational System* (Syracuse: Syracuse University Press, 1980), p. 108.

10. "Hamilton Students Talk Out Grievances," *Median Herald*, May 17, 1968.

11. Letter to the editor, *Median Herald*, July 16, 1968.

12. "Massucco—A Change for the Better," *Picayune Papers*, October 1968, p. 4.

13. Ibid., p. 2; emphasis in original.

14. Ibid., p. 1.

15. "Election Stumps Hamilton Students," *Picayune Papers*, December 1968, p. 2.

16. "City Gets Tough with Hoodlums," *Median Herald*, October 30, 1968.

17. "Hamilton Incident Sparked at School Dance?" *Median Herald*, October 29, 1968.

18. "Operation Understanding," *Picayune Papers*, December 1968, p. 1.

19. "Students Air Racial Problems," *Median Herald*, November 5, 1968.

20. See Janet Ward Schofield and H. Andrew Sagar, "The Social Context of Learning in an Interracial School," in *Desegregated Schools: Appraisals of an American Experiment*, ed. Ray Rist (New York: Academic Press, 1979), pp. 155–200.

21. Hobson v. Hansen, 269 F. Supp. 401 (1967).

22. *Median Herald*, January 31, 1970.

23. Clark, "Student Group Perspectives," p. 253.

24. Ibid., p. 308.

25. This figure was obtained by comparing the faculty listed in the 1966 yearbook with those who returned in fall of 1971. In the preceding five-year period, from 1961–1966, nearly 50 percent had transferred or resigned. If a 10 percent per year loss is normal, it appears that at least a quarter of the faculty left Hamilton for reasons related to the stress caused by desegregation of the school.

3. Let the Students Decide

1. Peter L. Clark, "Student Group Perspectives on a Secondary School," Ph.D. diss., Syracuse University, 1977, p. 2. (Emphasis in original.) This chapter draws heavily on Clark's work, and most direct quotations of students are taken from his dissertation. In addition to his year of observation in 1971–72, Clark visited the school intermittently throughout the early 1970s, conducting some interviews as late as 1975.

2. I have treated these changes at greater length in Gerald Grant, "Children's

Rights and Adult Confusions," *Public Interest* 69 (Fall 1982), 83–99, and in Gerald Grant with John Briggs, "Today's Children Are Different," *Educational Leadership* 40 (March 1983), 4–9; reprinted in Kevin Ryan and James M. Cooper, eds., *Kaleidoscope: Readings in Education* (Boston: Houghton Mifflin, 1984).

3. American Civil Liberties Union, *Academic Freedom in the Secondary Schools* (New York: ACLU, 1968), pp. 9–20; reprinted in Robert H. Bremner, ed., *Children and Youth in America: A Documentary History*, vol. 3 (Cambridge, Mass.: Harvard University Press, 1974), pp. 244–245.

4. Median school board regulations, adopted spring 1972.

5. David Tyack et al., *Law and the Shaping of Public Education* (Madison: University of Wisconsin Press, 1987).

6. Anne C. Lewis, "A Guide for Parents Who Take on the School System," *New York Times*, November 16, 1980, special Education section, p. 3.

7. Albert Solnit, "Too Much Intervention, Too Little Service," in *Child Abuse Reconsidered: An Analysis and Agenda for Action*, ed. G. Gerbner, C. Ross, and E. Zigler (New York: Oxford University Press, 1982).

8. See E. Van Dyke, "Child Abuse," *New York Teacher* 21 (May 18, 1980), 1.

9. Andrew Albert, "The Parent's View," *Median Herald*, July 27, 1980.

10. James Coleman, Thomas Hoffer, and Sally Kilgore, *Public and Private Schools* (Chicago: National Opinion Research Center, 1981), pp 119–21. On fairness of discipline, 52 percent of those in Catholic schools, but only 39 percent of the public school sophomores, rated it as excellent. It is possible, of course, that students in public schools were more sensitized to issues of fairness as a result of the new due-process requirements and hence had higher standards of what constituted fairness than students in Catholic schools.

11. Clark, "Student Group Perspectives," p. 164. The quotations in the following five pages are also drawn from Clark.

12. This quotation and the material that follows are drawn from field notes written by my research assistant Urmila Acharya, during a period of observation that began in April 1979 and ended in June 1980.

13. Clark, "Student Group Perspectives," p. 376.

14. The split on issues of confidentiality is revealed in a survey of 569 school counselors in Pennsylvania and New York. Asked if they would "break confidentiality" to inform a parent that a child was in possession of drugs, 32 percent said they would, 38 percent would not, and "a whopping 29 percent did not answer." Even when the minor is involved in the sale of drugs rather than possession, 29 percent would not inform parents. See C. A. Wagner, "Confidentiality and the School Counselor," *Personnel and Guidance Journal* (January 1981), 305–310.

15. Clark, "Student Group Perspectives," p. 382.

16. The following classroom excerpts are drawn from observations by Urmila Acharya in 1979.

17. "Hamilton's Future Issue before Board," *Median Herald*, December 19, 1977.

18. Median school district records.

4. The Second Transformation

1. Helen Featherstone, *A Difference in the Family: Living with a Disabled Child* (New York: Penguin Books, 1981).

2. "Autistic Children Attend Regular Classes at Hamilton High School," *Median Herald*, December 5, 1981.

3. Philip Ferguson, "If Mainstreaming Is the Answer, What Is the Question?: The Puzzle of Integrating a High School Class of Autistic Students," unpublished, Syracuse University, 1982, p. 18.

4. Ibid., p. 19.

5. LLK, student notes, 1984.

6. This and the following seven quotations are from Robert Bogdan, "Walk across That Stage: A Case Study of a Program for Neurologically Impaired and Learning Disabled Students at Hamilton High," unpublished, Syracuse University, 1982. (The teacher's name has been changed from the original text.)

7. Ferguson, "If Mainstreaming Is the Answer," p. 16.

8. Bogdan, "Walk across That Stage," p. 42.

9. DW, "Autism at Hamilton High," student paper, 1984, p. 5.

10. Ferguson, "If Mainstreaming Is the Answer," pp.7–8.

11. Bogdan, "Walk across That Stage," p. 10.

12. Ferguson, "If Mainstreaming Is the Answer," p. 27.

13. SP, "The World of Foreign Students at Hamilton High," student paper, 1985, p. 25.

14. RKW, "Pressures That ESL Students Experience at Hamilton High," student paper, 1984, p. 4.

15. AG, "Research Project: Mainstreamed ESL Students," student paper, 1984, p. 17.

16. RKW, "Pressures That ESL Students Experience," p. 10.

17. SP, "The World of Foreign Students," pp. 14–15.

18. Ibid., p. 23.

19. Herbert Blumer, *Symbolic Interactionism: Perspective and Method* (Englewood Cliffs, N.J.: Prentice-Hall, 1969), p. 11.

20. Except where otherwise indicated, the quotations in the section on the drug world are from Barry Glassner and Julia Loughlin, *Drugs in Adolescent Worlds: Burnouts to Straights* (London: Macmillan, forthcoming).

21. L. Johnson, "Drug Use Down," Institute for Social Research Newsletter (Ann Arbor: University of Michigan, 1985), pp. 4–5.

22. KB, "Later That Day," student paper, 1985, pp. 5–6.

23. Ibid., p. 6.

24. EK, "Who Sits with Whom in the Cafeteria and Why," student paper, 1984.

25. John Maddaus, "Families, Neighborhoods and Schools: Parent Perceptions and Actions Regarding Choice in School Enrollment," Ph.D. diss., Syracuse University, 1987.

26. The difficulty of assessing the impact of any given policy is illustrated by the comments of the athletic coaches, who feared that the effect would be to encourage students to take less demanding courses. An athlete "could be passing five rinky-dink

courses but failing two core courses" needed for graduation, said one basketball coach. Of course, coaches may not be the most objective judges of the policy. "That Kid Can Play, But He Can't Graduate," *Median Herald,* January 9, 1986.

27. Arthur Powell, Eleanor Farrar, and David K. Cohen, *The Shopping Mall High School: Winners and Losers in the Educational Marketplace* (Boston: Houghton Mifflin, 1985).

28. PW, "Expectations of Teachers and Students," student paper, 1984, pp. 1, 18.

29. Teachers broke a long silence to counter what some felt amounted to media hysteria with respect to charges of sexual abuse. In a three-year period 100 of Median's 1,632 teachers had been accused of sexual abuse, with some teachers tried and convicted in the media and others the victims of innuendo and gossip because child-abuse investigations were carried out without informing the teacher of the charges. Allegations were sustained against only two of the hundred teachers, both of whom resigned. "Teachers Trying to Curb Phony Accusations," *Median Herald,* May 4, 1985; and "Teachers Worry Sex-Abuse Probes Veiled in Secrecy," ibid., May 13, 1987.

30. BW, "Attributes of a Good Teacher," student paper, 1985, p. 3.

31. KC, "The Cafeteria," student paper, 1985, p. 10.

32. JR, "Norms of Moral Behavior at Hamilton," student paper, 1984, p. 8.

33. Sara Lawrence Lightfoot, *The Good High School: Portraits of Character and Culture* (New York: Basic Books, 1983), chap. 5.

34. The quotations in this section are drawn from fourteen essays written by students in the Hamilton High urban anthropology class during the 1984–85 academic year: JW, PG, BW, LLK, ZK, JW, KC, DB, BN, KB, TS, SP, DW, and MC.

35. Lightfoot, *The Good High School,* p. 231.

5. Why Schools Differ

1. Joan Erikson and Erik Erikson, "Generativity and Identity," *Harvard Educational Review* 51 (May 1981), 268.

2. This section is adapted from an earlier essay of mine, "The Character of Education and the Education of Character," *Daedalus* 110 (Summer 1981), 135–150.

3. See Harriet Wilson, "Parents Can Cut the Crime Rate," *New Society* 54 (December 4, 1980), 456–458; Richard Barth, "Home-Based Reinforcement of School Behavior: A Review and Analysis," *Review of Educational Research* 49 (Summer 1979), 436–458; and Reginald M. Clark, *Family Life and School Achievement: Why Poor Black Children Succeed or Fail* (Chicago: University of Chicago Press, 1983).

4. James S. Coleman et al., *Equality of Educational Opportunity* (Washington, D.C.: Government Printing Office, 1966).

5. Michael Rutter et al., *Fifteen Thousand Hours: Secondary Schools and Their Effects on Children* (Cambridge, Mass.: Harvard University Press, 1979).

6. John P. Diggins and Mark E. Kann, eds., *The Problem of Authority in America* (Philadelphia: Temple University Press, 1981), p. 91.

7. Hannah Arendt, *Between Past and Future* (New York: Penguin Books, reprint ed., 1977; first published 1968), p. 119.

8. Christopher Hurn, "Changes in School Authority, 1960–1980," paper de-

livered at the 1984 meeting of the American Sociological Association, pp. 15–16, 18.

9. Arendt, *Between Past and Future*, p. 106.

10. Yves R. Simon, *Nature and Functions of Authority* (Milwaukee: Marquette University Press, 1948), pp. 15–16.

11. Max Weber, *Economy and Society*, ed. Guenther Roth and Claus Wittich, Vol. 1 (Berkeley: University of California Press, 1978), p. 215.

12. For a thoughtful treatment of the effects of the new policy-making agents, see David Cohen, "Reforming School Politics," *Harvard Educational Review* 48 (November 1978), 429–447.

13. David Tyack and Elisabeth Hansot, *Managers of Virtue* (New York: Basic Books, 1982), pp. 239–240.

14. Sarane Spencer Boocock, *An Introduction to the Sociology of Learning* (New York: Houghton Mifflin, 1972), pp. 75–76.

15. Coleman et al., *Equality of Educational Opportunity*, chap. 3.

16. Clark, *Family Life and School Achievement*, pp. 111, 114, 122.

17. J. A. Kahl, "Educational and Occupational Aspirations of 'Common Man' Boys," *Harvard Educational Review* 23 (Summer 1953), 186–203; and R. H. Dave, "The Identification and Measurement of Environmental Process Variables That Are Related to Educational Achievement," Ph.D. diss., University of Chicago, 1963; cited in Boocock, *Sociology of Learning*, pp. 60–66.

18. Rutter et al., *Fifteen Thousand Hours*, p. 159.

19. Arthur Trace, *What Ivan Knows That Johnny Doesn't* (New York: Random House, 1961); and Urie Bronfenbrenner, *Two Worlds of Childhood: U.S. and U.S.S.R.* (New York: Basic Books, 1970).

20. Torsten Husen, ed., *International Study of Achievement in Mathematics*, vols. 1 and 2 (New York: Wiley, 1967), and idem, "Are Standards in U.S. Schools Really Lagging behind Those in Other Countries?" *Phi Delta Kappan* 64 (March 1983), 455–461.

21. National Academy of Education, "Preliminary Reports on Two Cross-Cultural Studies of Early Childhood and Schooling in Japan," *Academy Notes* 13 (Winter 1983), 3–10. See also Harold Stevenson, Hiroshi Azuma, and Kenji Hakuta, eds., *Child Development and Education in Japan* (New York: W. H. Freeman, 1986).

22. Chie Nakane, *Japanese Society* (New York: Penguin Books, 1973), p. 3.

23. See, for example, James R. Lincoln and Arne L. Kalleberg, "Work Organization and Workforce Commitment: A Study of Plants and Employees in the U.S. and Japan," *American Sociological Review* 50 (1985), 738–760.

24. Jack Easley and Elizabeth Easley, *Math Can Be Natural: Kitameno Priorities Introduced to American Teachers* (Urbana: University of Illinois Committee on Culture and Cognition, 1982); reported in Howard Gardner, *Frames of Mind* (New York: Basic Books, 1985), p. 180.

25. Cynthia Hearn Dorfman, ed., *Japanese Education Today* (Washington, D.C.: Government Printing Office, 1987), pp. 15, 20.

6. The Teacher's Predicament

1. The 1979 survey was conducted by the National Education Association; the 1982 poll was reported by Edward B. Fiske, "Survey of Teachers Reveals Morale Problems," *New York Times*, September 1982.

2. Joyce Purnick, "Rise in Crime against Teachers Is Termed a Chilling Fact of Life," *New York Times*, December 15, 1980. Purnick notes that school crime, including crime against students, had increased 150 percent between 1975 and 1980, and that 3,395 incidents of robbery and violence were recorded against New York City teachers in 1979.

3. For an eloquent essay on this theme see Richard A. Hawley, "Teaching as Failing," *Phi Delta Kappan* 60 (April 1979), 597–600. "There is only one thing to do about the inevitability of failure in teaching," says Hawley. "Acknowledge it."

4. These quotations are excerpted from Myron C. Tuman, "Prometheus Bound: The Brief Teaching Careers of Great Writers," *Phi Delta Kappan* 62 (December 1980), 258–261.

5. Dan C. Lortie, *School Teacher: A Sociological Study* (Chicago: University of Chicago Press, 1975), esp. chap. 6. See also Gertrude H. McPherson, *Small Town Teacher* (Cambridge, Mass.: Harvard University Press, 1972).

6. Seymour B. Sarason, *The Culture of the School and the Problem of Change* (Boston: Allyn and Bacon, 1971), esp. chap. 10.

7. See W. Timothy Weaver, "In Search of Quality: The Need for Talent in Teaching," *Phi Delta Kappan* 61 (September 1979), 29–46; J. Myron Atkin, "Who Will Teach in High School?" *Daedalus* 110, (Summer 1981), 91–104; and Lee S. Shulman, "Those Who Understand: A Conception of Teacher Knowledge," *American Educator* 10 (Spring 1986), 8–15, 43. For a thoughtful review of the knowledge base that ought to underlie preparation for teaching, see Lee S. Shulman, "Knowledge and Teaching: Foundations of the New Reform," *Harvard Educational Review* 57 (February 1987), 1–22.

8. This paragraph draws upon (and at two points paraphrases) J. Glenn Gray's essay, "Authority in Teacher and Taught," in *Radical School Reform: Critique and Alternatives*, ed. Cornelius J. Troost (Boston: Little, Brown, 1973).

9. In 1980 the estimated average salary of an elementary-school teacher was $15,691 and the average yearly wage of a plumber was $19,700; a government clerk's pay was approximately $15,500. Salaries for beginning teachers in 1978 were lower than those in all other occupations, with the exception of social and recreational workers. Even when adjusted for twelve months, teachers' salaries were below the average for all occupations. U.S. Census Bureau and National Center for Education Statistics, *The Conditions of Education* (Washington, D.C.: Government Printing Office, 1979 edition, p. 87; 1980 edition, p. 77).

10. Charles Silberman, *Crisis in the Classroom: The Remaking of American Education* (New York: Random House, 1970), p. 81.

11. Emile J. Haller and Sharon A. Davis, "Teacher's Perceptions, Parental Social Status and Grouping for Reading Instruction," *Sociology of Education* 54 (July 1981), 162–74; Ray H. Thompson, Karl R. White, and Daniel P. Morgan, "Teacher-Student Interaction Patterns in Classrooms with Mainstreamed Mildly Handicapped Students," *American Educational Research Journal* 19, no. 2 (1982), 220–236; Jean

V. Carew and Sara Lawrence Lightfoot, *Beyond Bias: Perspectives on Classrooms* (Cambridge, Mass.: Harvard University Press, 1979).

12. Willard Waller, *A Sociology of Teaching* (New York: John Wiley, 1932), p. 40.

13. Basil Bernstein, *Class, Codes and Control*, vol. 3 (London: Routledge and Kegan Paul, 1975), p. 60.

14. W. C. Bagley, *Classroom Management* (New York: Macmillan, n.d.), pp. 95–96.

15. Michael Rutter et al., *Fifteen Thousand Hours: Secondary Schools and Their Effects on Children* (Cambridge, Mass.: Harvard University Press, 1979).

16. See Donald Bersoff, "APA Enters Case of Fired Psychologist," *APA Monitor* 11 (November 1980), 6.

17. Joyce G. Carmen, "Forrest vs. Ambach: The Evolution of Educational Policy," unpublished, School of Education, Syracuse University, April 1982.

18. Emile Durkheim, *The Division of Labor in Society* (New York: Free Press–Macmillan, 1933).

19. Raymond Callahan, *Education and the Cult of Efficiency* (Chicago: University of Chicago Press, 1962); David B. Tyack, *The One Best System: A History of American Urban Education* (Cambridge, Mass.: Harvard University Press, 1974).

20. Tyack, *The One Best System*, pp. 28–29.

21. Ellwood P. Cubberly, *The Portland Survey* (Yonkers-on-Hudson: World Book, 1916); quoted in Tyack, *The One Best System*, p. 192.

22. Philip H. Coombs, *The World Educational Crisis* (New York: Oxford University Press, 1968), p. 126.

23. Frederick Ignatovich, Philip A. Cusick, and James E. Ray, "Value/Belief Patterns of Teachers and Those Administrators Engaged in Attempts to Influence Teaching," working paper, Institute for Research on Teaching, Michigan State University, 1979.

24. Dan Lortie, *Schoolteacher: A Sociological Study* (Chicago: University of Chicago Press, 1975), p. 133.

25. Ignatovich et al., "Value/Belief Patterns," pp. 4–6.

26. Miles Myers, "When Research Does Not Help Teaching," *American Educator* 10(Summer 1986), 18–23, 46.

27. Manfred Stanley, *The Technological Conscience: Survival and Dignity in an Age of Expertise* (New York: Free Press, 1978). See also Arthur E. Wise, *Legislated Learning: The Bureaucratization of the American Classroom* (Berkeley: University of California Press, 1979).

28. James Feron, "Distar May Be Tough, But Mt. Vernon Likes It That Way," *New York Times*, November 17, 1980.

29. The 1980 National Assessment of Educational Progress tests show that nine-year-olds have better word-recognition skills than they did in 1970 but the thirteen-year-olds and seventeen-year-olds register declines in inferential comprehension.

30. James W. Peterson, "What's It Like in a Private School?" *Phi Delta Kappan* 61(September 1979), p. 23.

31. "The Metropolitan Life Survey of Former Teachers in America," *American Educator* 10 (Summer 1986), 36.

32. For a more detailed discussion of these issues see Gerald Grant, "Children's

Rights and Adult Confusions," *Public Interest* 69 (Fall 1982), 83–99; and Gerald Grant with John Briggs, "Are Today's Children Different?" *Educational Leadership* (March 1983), 4–9.

33. Gray, "Authority in Teacher and Taught," p. 170.

34. In 1981 an unhappy sixteen-year-old Connecticut boy was able to divorce ("to separate and disunite") his father and mother under a new state law (*New York Times*, March 1, 1981). A girl the same age in West Virginia was able to divorce her parents and gain the legal right to live with an adult neighbor, arguing she was subjected to "psychological abuse" ("Child Divorce Upheld," *Syracuse Post-Standard*, September 17, 1980). The Sixth U.S. Circuit Court in Cincinnati overturned a lower-court ruling that declared unconstitutional the practice of distributing contraceptives to minors over their parents' objections. The Ukrainian case mentioned in the text was reported by Fred Barbash, "A Boy's 'No' to Life with Parents," *Boston Globe*, August 17, 1980.

35. Katherine K. Newman, "Middle-Aged and Experienced Teachers' Perceptions of Their Career Development," paper delivered at the April 1979 meeting of the American Educational Research Association, San Francisco.

36. John Holt, *Freedom and Beyond* (New York: Dell, 1972), p. 75. Although their solutions are different, other radical critics sound similar themes as they expressed their second thoughts. Compare Jonathan Kozol's *Death at an Early Age*, published in 1967, with his later *Free Schools* (Boston: Houghton Mifflin, 1972); or Neil Postman's *Teaching as a Conserving Activity* (New York: Delacorte Press, 1979) with his earlier *Teaching as a Subversive Activity*, written with Charles Weingartner (New York: Delacorte Press, 1969). Allen Graubard also discusses the widespread concern with issues of authority in his survey *Free the Children: Radical Reform in the Free School Movement* (New York: Random House, 1972).

37. Ann Swidler, *Organization without Authority: Dilemmas of Social Control in Free Schools* (Cambridge, Mass.: Harvard University Press, 1979), p. 80.

38. Merrilee K. Finley also shows how teachers maintain tracking through their competition for preferred students. See her "Teachers and Tracking in a Comprehensive High School," *Sociology of Education* 57 (October 1984), 233–243.

7. Creating a Strong Positive Ethos

Part of this chapter was published in an earlier version as "Schools That Make an Imprint" in John Bunzel, ed., *Challenge to American Schools* (New York: Oxford University Press, 1985).

1. Frances Taliaferro, "Blackboard Art," *Harper's* 263 (October 1981), 89–92.

2. Thomas Hughes, *Tom Brown's School Days* (London: J. M. Dent & Sons, 1957), p. 65.

3. Evelyn Waugh, *Decline and Fall* (Boston: Little, Brown, 1977), p. 8.

4. David Tyack and Elisabeth Hansot, *Managers of Virtue: Public School Leadership in America, 1820–1980* (New York: Basic Books, 1982), p. 23.

5. Robert S. Lynd and Helen Merrell Lynd, *Middletown: A Study in Modern American Culture* (New York: Harcourt, Brace and World, 1929), p. 203.

6. Lester F. Ward, *Dynamic Sociology* (New York, 1883); excerpted in Robert

H. Bremner, ed., *Children and Youth in America: A Documentary History* (Cambridge, Mass.: Harvard University Press, 1971), vol. 2, p. 1104.

7. E. Digby Baltzell, *Philadelphia Gentlemen: The Making of a National Upper Class* (Glencoe, Ill.: Free Press, 1958), p. 10. For a later work in the same tradition, see Peter W. Cookson, Jr., and Caroline Hodges Persell, *Preparing for Power: America's Elite Boarding Schools* (New York: Basic Books, 1985).

8. Survey by the National Catholic Education Association, reported in *Education Week* (May 2, 1984), 18.

9. James Coleman, Thomas Hoffer, and Sally Kilgore, *Public and Private Schools* (Washington, D.C.: National Center for Education Statistics, 1981).

10. See the symposium on Coleman's report by Richard J. Murnane and others in *Harvard Educational Review* 51 (November 1981), 483–564; and Karl L. Alexander, "How Schools Differ: A Review of the Evidence Comparing Public and Private School Effectiveness," report to the National Institute of Education, February 1984. Preliminary results from a sample of one thousand Catholic high school seniors reportedly show that the Catholic high school promotes important values in students but "isn't as good [as the public school] at preventing adolescent behavior we want to prevent," according to Peter L. Benson, director of the study. See Kirsten Goldberg, "Catholic Educators Surprised by Data on Student Values," *Education Week* (April 29, 1987), 1.

11. Burton Clark, *The Distinctive College: Antioch, Reed and Swarthmore* (Chicago: Aldine, 1970).

12. Judith Smilg Kleinfeld, *Eskimo School on the Andreafsky: A Study of Effective Bicultural Education* (New York: Praeger, 1979), esp. chap. 4.

13. Phillips Academy, Andover, Mass., catalog for 1979–80, p. 12.

14. David R. Satterthwaite, "Thanks for the Memories, Palmer," *Georgian* 55 (April 1984). 1. In response to an earlier version of this chapter, Thomas F. Green reminded me that the rhetoric with which stories are told is also vital: "Part of the central power of the Biblical stories is that virtually all the heroes there are 'flawed' persons. The name 'Jacob' after all means 'cheat,' which is why he was renamed. Think of David and Bathsheba. These are very different stories about very different kinds of persons compared to the Russian heroes who always seem to dominate huge, even cosmic, landscapes."

15. Thomas F. Green, "The Formation of Conscience in an Age of Technology," *John Dewey Lecture, 1984* (Syracuse University Printing Services), p. 4.

16. A survey by John Chubb found that "principals at private schools had four to five more years of teaching experience than public-school principals and that they usually did not view their jobs as steppingstones to higher administrative posts." See "Brookings Study Gauges Public, Private Schools," *Education Week* 6 (November 19, 1986), 3. The portraits of Sturgis and Saint Teresa's are drawn from the field notes of Wendy Kohli and Sharon Franz.

17. Carol Gilligan, *In a Different Voice: Psychological Theory and Women's Development* (Cambridge, Mass.: Harvard University Press, 1982). For a portrait of Boyden, see John McPhee, *The Headmaster* (New York: Farrar, Straus and Giroux, 1979); for Peabody, consult James McLachlan, *American Boarding Schools: A Historical Study* (New York: Charles Scribner's Sons, 1970), pp. 242–298.

18. The discussion here and in the paragraphs that follow is strongly influenced

by Basil Bernstein's distinction between instrumental orders and expressive orders. See his *Class, Codes and Control: Towards a Theory of Educational Transmissions*, vol. 3 (Boston: Routledge and Kegan Paul, 1975), esp. chap. 1. To simplify the analysis, we engage in a fraudulent shorthand, treating the moral and intellectual orders as distinct when in reality they are always intermingled.

19. The middecade census reports showed that in the years 1970 to 1985 minority populations in the large cities increased substantially and out-migration of non-Hispanic whites continued. See John Herbers, "New Jobs in Cities Little Aid to Poor," and "Cities' Growing Minority Populations," *New York Times*, October 22, 1986. In terms of total students in desegregated schools, however, the proportion of blacks attending racially isolated schools remained fairly constant in the period 1972–1984, although segregation of Hispanic children increased somewhat. See William Snider, "Black Segregation Remaining Stable, New Study Finds," *Education Week* 6 (November 26, 1986), 1.

20. See, for example, Gordon L. McAndrew, "The High School Principal: Man in the Middle," *Daedalus* 110 (Summer 1981), 105–118.

21. Robert Bellah et al., *Habits of the Heart: Individualism and Commitment in American Life* (Berkeley: University of California Press, 1985), pp. 12–41.

22. See Joseph Veroff, Richard A. Kulka, and Elizabeth Douvan, *Mental Health in America: Patterns of Help-Seeking from 1957 to 1976* (New York: Basic Books, 1981), pp. 166–67: cited in Bellah et al., *Habits of the Heart*, p. 121.

23. Bellah et al., *Habits of the Heart*, pp. 127, 139.

24. Philip Rieff, *The Triumph of the Therapeutic: Uses of Faith after Freud* (New York: Harper and Row, 1968), p. 74.

25. Veroff, Kulka, and Douvan, *Mental Health in America*, p. 6.

26. The poll showed that most teachers felt the schools should play a role in moral education, but they were widely divided in their beliefs about which approach should be used. While 33 percent favored the values clarification approach, 22 percent recommended "a program of services and experiences in which the child is helped to behave in a moral way"; 19 percent chose "a program to make the school an exemplary just and moral community"; 14 percent, "helping children gain ability to think about moral issues," and 12 percent, a "good solid liberal education." See Kevin Ryan and Michael G. Thompson, "Moral Education's Muddled Mandate: Comments on a Survey of Phi Delta Kappans," *Phi Delta Kappan* 56 (June 1975), 663–666.

27. Sidney B. Simon and Polly deSherbinin, "Values Clarification: It Can Start Gently and Grow Deep," *Phi Delta Kappan* 56 (June 1975), 679.

28. Ibid., p. 681.

29. For elaboration of this point see Lawrence Kohlberg, "The Cognitive-Developmental Approach to Moral Education," *Phi Delta Kappan* 56 (June 1975), 673.

30. Simon and deSherbinin, "Values Clarification," p. 682.

31. For a thoughtful case study of developments in one school district see Martin Eger, "The Conflict in Moral Education: An Informal Case Study," *Public Interest* 63 (Spring 1981), 62–80.

32. John S. Stewart, "Clarifying Values Clarification: A Critique," *Phi Delta Kappan* 56 (June 1975), 685. Note also the sex-biased language: it is Virginia and Millie, seldom Virginal Victor and Mattress Mike.

33. Ernest Wallwork, "Morality, Religion and Kohlberg's Theory," in *Moral Development, Moral Education and Kohlberg: Basic Issues in Philosophy, Psychology, Religion and Education,* ed. Brenda Munsey (Birmingham, Ala.: Religious Education Press, 1980), p. 289. (Emphasis in original.) The distinction between morality and religion is itself part of the liberal consensus that some conservatives have recently attacked as a form of secular humanism. Nor would all moral theorists subscribe to such a distinction. My colleague Emily Robertson, in commenting on this chapter, noted: "If one adopts some form of relativism, the distinction between obligations grounded in an historically particularistic way of life and moral obligations themselves would be regarded as having arisen in that way and to be binding only on those who share the relevant history." Yet there is a significant difference between those who, while recognizing that they are a part of history, argue that sexual discrimination against women is immoral, and those who assert the dominance of men on the grounds of particularistic practices in a religious tradition.

34. Mickey Kaus, in "Up from Altruism," *New Republic* 195 (December 15, 1986), 17–18, makes a good argument against the politics of compassion, asserting that the aim of government "should be not to increase the incidence of compassion but to reduce the opportunity for it." I agree with Kaus that we should avoid appeals to compassion on the basis of pity, but not where the aim is to instill feelings of sharing the sufferings of others in the inclination to give aid or support. Even where an adequate safety net is provided by the liberal state for the poor and the afflicted, there will still be misfortunes—families will still break up, fellow workers will become alcoholics, pupils will suffer cruelties and disabling conditions. Without compassion, we have only individuals receiving their entitlements. Without compassion, life in any group is bleak and heartless.

35. See Jonathan Friendly, "Public Schools Avoid Teaching Right and Wrong," *New York Times,* December 2, 1985.

36. West Virginia v. Barnette, 319 U.S. 624 (1943).

37. Tinker v. Des Moines, 393 U.S. 503 (1969).

38. See R. S. Peters, *Authority, Responsibility and Education* (London: Allen and Unwin, 1973), esp. pp. 140–156. In *Quandaries and Virtues: Against Reductivism in Ethics* (Lawrence: University Press of Kansas, 1986), Edmund L. Pincoffs makes the point that some moral positions are so basic that, for instance, "it is hard to imagine what a debate would be like on the 'doctrine' that dishonesty is a bad thing" (p. 143). In Pincoffs' view, which I find persuasive, "no one is a moral indoctrinator, then, because he inculcates in his pupils a distaste for dishonesty, a revulsion against cruelty, or a sense of outrage at injustice. In teaching his pupil in such a way as to encourage these *qualities of character,* he is not closing his pupil's mind, stunting his growth, or making it impossible for him to think for himself. He is, rather, giving him the *kind of character* without which he would be unable to carry on a moral discussion" (p. 147). (Emphasis in original.) Yet Pincoffs would agree with Peters that we do not want to educate a child in such a way as to prevent the adult from thinking for herself or himself. With respect to issues of dishonesty, this would involve thinking more maturely about occasions when a lie is justified. I am grateful to Emily Robertson for bringing Pincoffs' work to my attention.

39. Minersville v. Gobitis, 310 U.S. 586 (1940). (Emphasis added.) The vote

upholding the compulsory flag salute was eight to one. In 1943, in West Virginia v. Barnette, with two new justices hearing the case, the Court reversed itself six to three.

40. Hannah Arendt, *Between Past and Future* (New York: Penguin Books, reprint ed., 1977; first published, 1968), p. 196.

41. Daniel Yankelovich, "New Rules in American Life," *Psychology Today* 15 (April 1981), 35–91. Yankelovich did not separate responses from men and from women in reply to the question about parents feeling free to live their own lives, but the data were no doubt influenced by responses from women who feel liberated from traditional homemaking careers. Nearly as many women as men (about 80 percent) now say they would go on working for pay even if they didn't have to, whereas in 1957 only 55 percent of women felt that way. Thus it is probably women who are now claiming a traditional male prerogative to spend less time with their children. Although men are more likely than in 1957 to say they want to do more around the home, including spending time with their children, patterns of behavior have been slow to change.

42. Alexander Astin, quoted in *Chronicle of Higher Education* 33 (November 5, 1986), 32. Also see idem, *The American Freshman: Twenty Year Trends, 1966–1985* (Los Angeles: Higher Education Research Institute, UCLA, 1986).

43. This account of Cook High and the quotations in this section are drawn from field notes of Richard Hawkins, who spent a year of participant observation at the school in 1979–80. See also his "Cook High," in *What Makes a Good School: Five Case Studies*, ed. Gerald Grant, chap. 2 of a report to the National Institute of Education, Washington, D.C., 1981.

44. William Glasser, *Schools without Failure* (New York: Harper and Row, 1969), esp. pp. 186–192. Although he is a physician and clinical psychologist who has had wide experience in schools, Glasser is no advocate of therapeutic contractualism.

8. Two Essential Reforms

1. Philip A. Cusick, *The Egalitarian Ideal and the American High School: Studies of Three Schools* (New York: Longman, 1983), pp. 31, 41.

2. Quoted in Cindy Currence, "Discipline Codes Must Foster Balance of Order, Autonomy," *Education Week* 3 (January 18, 1984), 8, 18.

3. National Institute of Education, *Violent Schools—Safe Schools: The Safe School Study Report to the Congress*, vol. 1 (Washington, D.C.: Government Printing Office, 1977).

4. The census analysis by Paul Smith of the Children's Defense Fund is reported in Michael W. Sedlak et al., *Selling Students Short: Classroom Bargains and Academic Reform in the American High School* (New York: Teachers College Press, 1986), pp. 85–86. The discussion in this section is indebted at several points to the review of the literature conducted by Sedlak and his colleagues.

5. Thomas A. DiPrete, with Chandra Muller, *Discipline and Order in American High Schools* (Chicago: National Opinion Research Center, 1981), pp. 22, 111.

6. Ibid., p. 10, and Institute for Social Research newsletters, Summer 1981 and Summer 1986.

7. On the reduction and abandonment of core requirements see John I. Good-

lad, *A Place Called School: Prospects for the Future* (New York: McGraw-Hill, 1984); Ernest L. Boyer, *High School: A Report on Secondary Education in America* (New York: Harper and Row, 1983); and Theodore R. Sizer, *Horace's Compromise: The Dilemma of the American High School* (Boston: Houghton-Mifflin, 1985). For accounts of the proliferation of electives see Diane Ravitch, *The Troubled Crusade: American Education, 1945–1980* (New York: Basic Books, 1983), and Cusick, *The Egalitarian Ideal.*

8. Sedlak et al., *Selling Students Short*, p. 103.

9. Ibid., p. 160. For a classroom view of student negotiation of academic demands, see also Robert G. Wegmann, "Homework and Grades: Where Is the College Student Coming from?" *College Student Journal* 8 (February-March 1974), 13–22.

10. Sedlak et al., *Selling Students Short*, p. 159.

11. DiPrete, *Discipline and Order*, p. 111.

12. The Detroit figures were reported in Sedlak et al., *Selling Students Short*, p. 84.

13. See J. Meyer, C. Chase-Dunn, and J. Inverarity, *The Expansion of the Autonomy of Youth: Responses of the Secondary Schools to the Problem of Order in the 1960s* (Stanford, Calif.: Laboratory for Social Research, Stanford University, 1971); and Beatrice F. Birman and Gary Natriello, "Perspectives on Absenteeism in High School," *Journal of Research and Development in Education* 11 (Summer 1978), 29–38; both cited in Sedlak et al., *Selling Students Short*, p. 84.

14. Goodlad, *A Place Called School*, p. 99.

15. Nancy Karweit, "Time on Task: A Research Review," report to the National Commission on Excellence in Education, 1983.

16. Noah Lewin-Epstein, *Youth Employment during High School* (Chicago: National Opinion Research Center, 1981), p. 8.

17. President's Science Advisory Committee, *Youth: Transition to Adulthood,* a report of the Panel on Youth (Washington, D.C.: Executive Office of the President, 1974); National Panel on High School and Adolescent Education, *The Education of Adolescents* (Washington, D.C.: Government Printing Office, 1976); and Carnegie Council on Policy Studies in Higher Education, *Giving Youth a Better Chance* (San Francisco: Jossey-Bass, 1979).

18. Ellen Greenberger and Laurence Steinberg, *When Teenagers Work: The Psychological and Social Costs of Adolescent Employment* (New York: Basic Books, 1986). The data on hours of work can be found in Lewin-Epstein, *Youth Employment*, p. 48. The findings on postemployment prospects of working teenagers who do not go on to college are from S. P. Stephenson, Jr., "In-School Work and Early Post-School Labor Market Dynamics," working paper, Department of Economics, Pennsylvania State University, 1980; cited in Lewin-Epstein, *Youth Employment*, p. 6.

19. Noah Lewin-Epstein reports on the self-estimates of homework done by reported hours of work per week. For male seniors, those who did not work averaged 4.1 hours of homework per week, whereas those who worked more than 22 hours did 3.0 hours of homework. For sophomores, the figures were 3.9 and 3.3 hours. Females did roughly half an hour more homework per week and the declines with work were less steep. See Lewin-Epstein, *Youth Employment*, p. 55. For an analysis of the tradeoffs between employment and homework see Linda M. McNeil, "Lowering Expectations: The Impact of Student Employment in Classroom Knowledge" (Madison: Wisconsin

Center for Education Research, 1984). The Gallup poll was reported in *Phi Delta Kappan* 61 (September 1979), 74. It showed that 58 percent of teenagers in a national sample felt that students are not asked to work hard enough in elementary schools, and 45 percent said the same about high schools. Black teenagers (61 percent and 48 percent, respectively) felt this more strongly than white teenagers. A poll of two thousand high-achieving students, those listed in *Who's Who among American High School Students*, found that 82 percent felt that the reason some students graduate from high school without basic skills is that they are permitted to choose "easy" courses. Reported in *Education Week* 3 (November 16, 1983), 2.

20. George Madaus argues that competency tests may have increased the dropout rate in "NIE Clarification Hearing: The Negative Team's Case," *Phi Delta Kappan* 63 (October 1981), 92–94. The dropout data may be found in National Center for Education Statistics, U.S. Department of Education, *State Education Statistics* (Washington, D.C.: Government Printing Office, 1984). For Japanese graduation rates see Cynthia Hearn Dorfman, ed., *Japanese Education Today* (Washington, D.C.: Government Printing Office, 1987), p. 7. Chester E. Finn, Jr., citing studies by Andrew Kolstad and Jeffrey Owings, points out that nearly two of five dropouts have returned to school to earn a diploma within two years of their normal graduation date. See Finn, "The High School Dropout Puzzle," *Public Interest* 87 (Spring 1987), 3–23. Analysis of census data that sampled youth from ages fourteen to twenty-four also indicates that, if diplomas awarded by examination or through other programs are taken into account, there may have been an overall decrease in the school completion rate from 1973 to 1983. See James R. Wetzel, "American Youth: A Statistical Snapshot," William T. Grant Foundation report, 1987, pp. 15–17.

21. An international science study showed that U.S. students in 1986 were at or below their level in 1970, when they were near the bottom. In physics, for example, American students with one year of instruction got 34 percent of the twenty-six test items correct and those with two years, 44 percent; the average of twenty-four countries was 62 percent. Students in England got 71 percent correct. See Robert Rothman, "Foreigners Outpace American Students in Science," *Education Week* 6 (April 29, 1987), 7. The other data in this section are drawn from Boyer, *High School*, pp. 22–39; and Fred Hechinger, "About Education," *New York Times*, January 6, 1987.

22. Arthur N. Applebee, Judith A. Langer, and Ina V. S. Mullis, *The Writing Report Card: Writing Achievement in American Schools*, report of the National Assessment of Educational Progress (Princeton, N.J.: Educational Testing Service, 1986); quotations from p. 22. All data reported were collected in 1984.

23. See David K. Cohen, "Origins," in Arthur Powell, Eleanor Farrar, and David K. Cohen, *The Shopping Mall High School: Winners and Losers in the Educational Marketplace* (Boston: Houghton Mifflin, 1985), pp. 233–308.

24. The report, *Cardinal Principles of Education*, was circulated as Bulletin 1918, no. 35, by the Bureau of Education, U.S. Department of the Interior (Washington, D.C.: Government Printing Office, 1918).

25. G. Stanley Hall's argument was published originally as "How Far Is the Present High School and Early College Training Adapted to the Nature and Needs of Adolescents?" *School Review* 9 (November 1901), 649–681, with an untitled response by Charles W. Eliot, quoted in Cohen, "Origins," pp. 239–244.

26. Cohen, "Origins," pp. 251–252.

27. The U.S. Office of Education survey, *National Study of Secondary Education: Provision for Individual Differences*, Bulletin no. 17 (Washington D.C.: Government Printing Office, 1933), is quoted by Cohen, "Origins," p. 267.

28. "Education for Life Adjustment" was the title of a lecture given by Charles Prosser at Harvard in 1939 and developed in his book, *Secondary Education and Life* (Cambridge, Mass.: Harvard University Press, 1939), cited in Cohen, "Origins," p. 274.

29. Educational Policies Commission, *Education for All American Youth* (Washington, D.C.: National Education Commission, 1944), p. 142.

30. Paul R. Mort and William S. Vincent, *A Look at Our Schools: A Book for the Thinking Citizen* (New York: Cattell, 1946), quoted in Ravitch, *The Troubled Crusade*, p. 64.

31. August B. Hollingshead, *Elmtown's Youth* (New York: Wiley, 1949), p. 199.

32. Sedlak et al., *Selling Students Short*, p. 18.

33. The survey of foreign languages was reported in Edward A. Krug, *The Secondary School Curriculum* (New York: Harper and Bros., 1960) pp. 258–259; cited in Ravitch, *The Troubled Crusade*, p. 68.

34. See John Dewey, *Experience and Education* (New York: Collier Books, 1963; originally published, 1938).

35. Arthur Bestor, *Educational Wastelands: The Retreat from Learning in Our Public Schools* (Urbana: University of Illinois Press, 1953), quoted in Ravitch, *The Troubled Crusade*, p. 76.

36. Ravitch, *The Troubled Crusade*, p. 228–229.

37. Rockefeller Brothers Fund, *The Pursuit of Excellence* (New York: Doubleday, 1958).

38. James B. Conant, *The American High School Today* (New York: McGraw-Hill, 1959).

39. Grace Wright, *Subject Offerings and Enrollments in Public Secondary Schools* (Washington, D.C.: Government Printing Office, 1965), pp. 8–9; cited in Cohen, "Origins," p. 286.

40. Wright, *Subject Offerings*, pp. 8, 100; cited in Cohen, "Origins," p. 288.

41. Conant, *The American High School Today*, p. 37.

42. See Torsten Husen, "Are Standards in U.S. Schools Really Lagging Behind Those in Other Countries?" *Phi Delta Kappan* 64 (March 1983), 455–461; and Edward Fiske, "U.S. Pupils Lag in Mathematics Ability, 3 Studies Find," *New York Times*, January 11, 1987.

43. National Commission on Excellence in Education, *A Nation at Risk: The Imperative for Educational Reform* (Washington, D.C.: Government Printing Office, 1983), p. 5.

44. Business–Higher Education Task Force, *America's Competitive Challenge: The Need for a National Response* (Washington, D.C.: Business–Higher Education Forum, 1983), p. 22.

45. Education Commission of the States' Task Force on Education for Economic Growth, *Action for Excellence: A Comprehensive Plan to Improve Our Nation's Schools* (Washington, D.C.: Education Commission of the States, 1983); Twentieth Century Fund Task Force on Federal Elementary and Education Policy, *Making the Grade* (New York: Twentieth Century Fund, 1983).

46. Sizer, *Horace's Compromise*, p. 223.

47. Ibid.

48. Samuel Bowles and Herbert Gintis, *Schooling in Capitalist America: Educational Reform and the Contradictions of Economic Life* (New York: Basic Books, 1976).

49. For other works in this tradition see Martin Carnoy, *Education as Cultural Imperialism* (New York: McKay, 1974); and Michael Apple, *Cultural and Economic Reproduction in Education* (London: Routledge and Kegan Paul, 1982).

50. Michael Ignatieff, *The Needs of Strangers: An Essay on Privacy, Solidarity and the Politics of Being Human* (New York: Penguin Books, 1986), p. 13. (Emphasis in original.)

51. Boyer, *High School*, pp. 222, 225.

52. Vernon Loeb, "Philadelphia to Study Classification of Learning-Disabled Pupils," *Education Week* 3 (April 25, 1986), p. 1.

53. Leo Tolstoy, *Anna Karenina*, trans. David Magarshack (New York: New American Library, 1961), p. 17.

54. Sizer, *Horace's Compromise*, p. 225–226.

55. Susan Tollett and Theodore R. Sizer, "Budget Projections for Mythos Junior-Senior High School," Coalition of Essential Schools working paper, Brown University, 1986.

56. Dan Lortie, "Teacher Status in Dade County: A Case of Structural Strain," *Phi Delta Kappan* 67 (April 1986), 568–575.

57. See Goodlad, *A Place Called School*, table 6.2, p. 190.

58. Of teachers asked "How do you feel about the idea of merit pay?" 64 percent were opposed. Alec Gallup, "The Gallup Poll of Teachers' Attitudes toward the Public Schools," *Phi Delta Kappan* 66 (October 1984), 103.

59. Albert Shanker, president of the American Federation of Teachers, took the lead in this effort and was an early proponent of rigorous entry-level testing for teachers. He also served on the Carnegie Foundation's Task Force on Teaching as a Profession, which in its 1986 report, "A Nation Prepared: Teachers for the 21st Century," adopted most of his program. For a summary of Shanker's views see Gene Maeroff, "Shanker Urges Teachers Move Past Bargaining: Suggests New Strategies to Enhance Profession," *New York Times*, April 28, 1985.

60. U.S. Labor Department, "Occupational Outlook Quarterly," January 1987, Government Printing Office.

61. See Victor S. Vance and Phillip C. Schlechty, "Recruitment, Selection, and Retention: The Shape of the Teaching Force," *Elementary School Journal* 83, no. 4. (1983), 469–487; and Phillip C. Schlechty and Victor S. Vance, "Do Academically Able Teachers Leave Education? The North Carolina Case," *Phi Delta Kappan* 63 (October 1981), 106–112.

62. In a Florida survey twenty-seven hundred teachers were asked who provided the most help with curriculum development and pedagogical problems. Four percent said it was the principal; 2 percent, central-office supervisors; and 60 percent, other teachers, including resource teachers and teacher heads of their own departments. See Robert B. Kottkamp, Eugene Provenzo, Jr., and Marilyn M. Cohn, "Stability and Change in a Profession: Two Decades of Teacher Attitudes, 1964–84," *Phi Delta Kappan* 67 (April 1986), 563.

63. For an excellent discussion of these issues see Linda Darling-Hammond,

"Valuing Teachers: The Making of a Profession," *Teachers College Record* 87 (Winter 1985), 205–218; and Arthur E. Wise and Linda Darling-Hammond, "Teacher Evaluation and Teacher Professionalism," *Educational Leadership* 42 (December 1984–January 1985), 28–33.

64. One currently hears demands that medical review boards include lay representation precisely on the grounds that peer review among doctors has not been an adequate protection against malpractice. In the career-ladder concept advocated here, teachers would have a major but not an exclusive responsibility for promotion and tenure decisions. With respect to the American medical profession, however, peer control has in general led to the highest standards of practice in the world.

65. Stanley Hauerwas, *Suffering Presence: Theological Reflections on Medicine, the Mentally Handicapped, and the Church* (South Bend, Ind.: Notre Dame Press, 1986), p. 58. I am grateful to Thomas Green for bringing Hauerwas' work to my attention.

Epilogue

1. Chapters 1–4 have been revised to reflect factual inaccuracies discovered in the course of this dialogue. Otherwise the chapters are close to the version that the teachers read, with this Epilogue providing the vehicle for their criticisms and any contrary interpretations of events.

2. Seymour B. Sarason, *The Culture of the School and the Problem of Change* (Boston: Allyn and Bacon, 1971), esp. chap. 4.

3. Maxine Greene, "Excellence: Meanings and Multiplicity," *Teachers College Record* 86 (Winter 1984), 296.

4. Seventy-one percent of the freshmen, but only 49 percent of the seniors, said that most of the time they liked attending Hamilton. Ratings of school spirit fell from 50 to 30 percent. Those who said "I do my very best" dropped from 57 percent to 36 percent in four years, and the percentage of those who felt it was important to be on time to class from 52 to 34. Positive feelings about teachers rose slightly, however, from 50 to 53 percent, and although there was a 10 percent decline by senior year, 59 percent still felt "I'm getting a good education." Taken from "The Hamilton Student Organization Needs Assessment," fall 1986.

5. Peter Marris, *Loss and Change* (New York: Anchor/Doubleday, 1975), p. 166; quoted in Michael Fullan, *The Meaning of Educational Change* (New York: Teachers College Press, 1982), p. 25. The discussion in this section has also benefited from David Gordon, *The Myths of School Self-Renewal* (New York: Teachers College Press, 1984), and Chris Argyris, *Strategy, Change and Defensive Routines* (Boston: Pitman, 1985).

Acknowledgments

Acknowledgments are like footnotes in that they only account for the debts one remembers. I cannot fully express here the appreciation that I ought, partly from my failures of memory but mostly because of my promises of anonymity to the students and faculty of Hamilton High. I owe them so much, especially those students whom I taught in 1984–85 and those teachers with whom I worked in 1986–87. The students provided some of the finest grist from which this book was made, and the teachers granted me a year of extraordinary colleagueship. The cloak of anonymity falls as well over the thirty-three schools my associates and I visited in the initial stages of the project and the four schools where, as at Hamilton High, we spent a year of fieldwork. To those principals, teachers, and students who sat for interviews and let us into their lives and classrooms, I am most grateful.

Initial support came from the National Institute of Education, where I spent eighteen months as a senior research associate in the company of advisers who became friends—especially Tommy Tomlinson, Michael Timpane, Peter Gerber, and Gary Sykes. The Ford Foundation provided support during a year of intensive fieldwork, and in the last stages of the project William Bradley of the Hazen Foundation put me in contact with a donor who wishes to remain anonymous. I am indebted to the Annenberg Center for the Study of the American Experience at the University of Southern California and its director, John Weaver, for providing a semester free of teaching under ideal conditions, which included funds to bring together a wide range of scholars to discuss themes related to my work. Theodore R. Sizer, Larry Cuban, Ann Swidler, Eva Brann, Robert Daly, Peter Elbow, Bennett M. Berger, Laurence R. Veysey, Tommy Tomlinson, and Barbara P. Norfleet gave encouragement and helpful advice at the Annenberg conference.

I was blessed with five exceptional research assistants during the fieldwork phase of the project: Urmila Acharya, Sharon Franz, Richard Hawkins, Wendy Kohli, and Madhu Suri Prakash. Without their unstinting efforts, there would have been no book. I wish also to thank Rachel Janney, Nancy Suchman, and Adele Baruch, who performed ably as assistants in other phases of the work. And I would like to acknowledge Barry Lentz's help in the last year of the research.

I am deeply indebted to Robert Bogdan, Peter Clark, Barry Glassner, and Julia Loughlin for permission to quote from their manuscripts.

The embryo of this book formed as I was producing an article for *Daedalus* in 1981. I benefited greatly from the criticism offered by fellow contributors to that issue, particularly Robert Coles, David Cohen, Joseph Featherstone, Patricia Graham, Elisabeth Hansot, Philip Jackson, Sara Lawrence Lightfoot, Michael Kirst, Barbara Neufeld, David Tyack, Myron Atkin, Gordon McAndrew, Jerome Kagan, and the editor of *Daedalus*, Stephen Graubard. I am especially grateful to those who read and criticized early portions of my manuscript: David Riesman, Emily Robertson, Peter Clark, Thomas Green, Kay Kasberger, Laura Lee Ketcham, Robert Daly, Robert Bogdan, Joan Burstyn, Susan Hoffman, Robert Ashton Grant, Robert J. Grant, Judith Grant, Arthur Blumberg, John Briggs, Wendy Kohli, and Linda Davern. They tried to correct my errors. Where they succeeded, I owe them warm thanks; where they did not, only I am to blame.

Judith Grant's editing improved this manuscript at every turn. How many times would I restore what she cut, only to strike it weeks later when I had gained her distance and her discerning eye. While I was regaining my balance, Florence Knox and Jean Perry never lost theirs. They typed field notes and drafts of the manuscript with light hearts and attentive eyes. And Jane Frost struggled valiantly to decipher the audio tapes on which the Epilogue is based.

I owe my colleagues in Cultural Foundations of Education at Syracuse my deepest thanks for plugging the holes I left in the teaching schedule during the leaves required to do the research, and the additional leaves required to write it up. I am grateful to Syracuse University for permitting those leaves and for providing sabbatical support. I am indebted also to Dean Joan Burstyn for allowing me to resign as chair of the department in order to complete the book, and to Vincent Tinto for assuming my duties without complaint. I cannot find words to express the gratitude I feel to the late Dean Burton Blatt. He inspired me as he inspired virtually all who knew him.

Index

Please remember that this is a library book,
and that it belongs only temporarily to each
person who uses it. Be considerate. Do
not write in this, or any, library book.